An Actor's Guide

YOUR FIRST YEAR IN HOLLYWOOD

Michael Saint Nicholas

ALLWORTH PRESS, NEW YORK

Published by Allworth Press, an imprint of Allworth Communications, Inc.
10 East 23rd Street, New York, NY 10010

Cover design by Douglas Design Associates, New York, NY

Book design by Sharp Designs, Holt, MI

ISBN: 1-880559-34-X

Library of Congress Catalog Card Number: 95-76690

To:

Jerhoam, thank you for sharing your wisdom and inspiring me to write this book;

John Oliver, an amazing source of wisdom, true friendship, and perpetual fun;

and the others who have helped along the way.

TABLE OF CONTENTS

AUTHOR'S ACKNOWLEDGEMENTS

In writing this book, I was fortunate to get assistance from many generous and talented people. Many thanks to:

Earl Hamner, one of the nicest and most talented writers and producers in show business; Mike Fenton, a friendly, knowledgeable, and distinguished casting director; Tony Shepherd, a prominent, insightful, and respected casting executive; Eric Morris, a phenomenal acting coach and a giving human being; Mariette Hartley, a wonderful actress and a great source of wisdom; William McNamara, a brilliant, dedicated, and personable actor; Michael Harris, a fine actor with a great approach to this business; Julian Neal, a guru of acting, teaching, yoga, and life; Michael Levine, a wise public relations expert; Sherry Robb, a literary and talent agent extraordinaire; Buzz Halliday, a smart and caring talent agent; Onley Cahill, a superb personal manager; Diana Carroll, a friendly and warmhearted extras casting whiz; Linda Poindexter, a creative and congenial casting professional; Veanne Cox, a radiant and vivacious actress; Brad Greenquist, an exceptionally talented actor; Jimmy Wlcek, another outstanding actor; Michael Helms, an excellent photographer; Craig Tapscott, a helpful friend who has assisted me in completing this book in many important ways; and Kirk Schroder, an excellent attorney and a caring friend.

INTRODUCTION

So, you want to be an actor? Well, good for you. Probably a few friends, relatives, and co-workers think you are crazy for wanting to pursue such a dream, but I think it's a remarkable choice.

Following through on your creative impulses will bring you some of the most rewarding moments of your life. Whether it's painting, dancing, singing, or acting, you will rediscover yourself and grow as a human being as you develop artistic skills and face the challenges associated with them.

Acting, in particular, will require a tremendous amount of self-reflection and determination because there are often many hurdles to overcome. Plenty of starving artists will attest to that. And that's why this book was written: to help you to leap gracefully over many of those hurdles.

Its purpose is to provide actors like you, who have little or even lots of experience, with useful and practical information for your first year in Hollywood. Packed full of suggestions and strategies, it addresses things like relocation, explains in detail how the entertainment industry functions, and specifically outlines ways to get started as an actor in the City of Angels.

Unfortunately many people arrive each year not knowing where to begin or what to expect. They become victims of con artists or get frivolous advice from people who really just want their cash. In this book, you'll find that the material is concise and, most important, relevant. It will save you time and money, hopefully allowing your adjustment to L.A. and the development of your acting career to flow smoothly, quickly, and prosperously.

In addition to the information in this book, you'll also need several more important things: an excellent attitude, courage, confidence, and unyielding perseverance. Nobody can give you these but yourself.

And don't forget talent. It's a very important element that's sometimes overlooked. Fortunately though, it's something that can be developed and enhanced along the way. (But hopefully you've already got some!)

With all of these things and the right information, the possibilities are unlimited! I wish you the best success. Believe in yourself and you can accomplish anything.

An **Overview** of **Los Angeles**

As an actor, even if you have never visited Los Angeles you probably have already heard a lot about it. Think for a moment. What images pop into your mind? Besides earthquakes and an occasional riot, you are probably conjuring pictures of Hollywood, studios, bright lights, and movie stars. And let's not forget limousines, palm trees, Beverly Hills mansions, and paparazzi. What about movie premieres, Rodeo Drive, Rolls Royces, and the Sunset Strip? Yes, these are all valid images that have come to symbolize one aspect of Los Angeles, also known as the City of Angels, or simply, La La Land.

You'd have to be a hermit to miss them. Every day people around the globe see, hear, and read about life in L.A. Just turn on the news. Chances are, at some point, you will be treated to a small slice of juicy Hollywood gossip. If you're tuned into a tabloid TV show, then you'll probably get a whopping portion! Open a magazine or newspaper. Somewhere inside lurks a tell-all report on your favorite celebrity or the latest rundown of a high-profile court case. Or go to the movies. There's a strong probability that those palm trees, that street corner, or that sandy beach can be found somewhere in Los Angeles.

So whether you realize it or not, you have had more exposure to L.A.

than probably any other city in the world. However, it is important to realize that much of the imagery—the famous people, the beautiful scenery, the extravagant lifestyles, the glamour—while truthful, has been sensationalized to some degree. You will find that, like any other big city, Los Angeles has its own unique personality with both enjoyable and aggravating qualities, and actually many down-to-earth characteristics.

Being an actor, you will quickly notice that the greatest aspect of Los Angeles is that it's the mega-metropolis for work in the arts. It is here that all the major studios and independent production companies are busy churning out thousands of feature films, television programs, commercials, and music videos in Hollywood and its surrounding areas every year. In addition, tremendous opportunities exist in theatre and dance throughout the vicinity. There are over 240 performing arts theatres in Southern California alone! And if that's not enough, you will find a significant presence of the art, music, and modeling industries as well. So grab your paintbrush, string that guitar, and head on down the catwalk! No other place has so much to offer actors, artists, musicians, and models. Hollywood is truly a magnet for artists of all kinds!

You ought to know that "Hollywood" refers to both a general vicinity (although there are no defined boundaries, and it technically doesn't exist) in Los Angeles and to the entertainment industry as a whole. Around 1910, the motion picture business was born in what is now considered Hollywood, and for many decades it served as the center for all show business-related activities. Hence, Hollywood became synonymous with show business. Today studios and entertainment firms can still be found in the Hollywood area, but many have expanded into neighboring areas. Nevertheless, the term "Hollywood" is still used, mostly by the media, to refer to the industry which in reality often has little to do with Hollywood, the area.

Besides Hollywood, there are many other well-known regions that make up Los Angeles, which is actually a county. Some of these include the cities of Beverly Hills, Malibu, Santa Monica, Burbank, and Pasadena—to name a few. In all, there are eighty-eight incorporated cities and over one hundred unincorporated areas linked by more than a dozen freeways within the five districts that comprise L.A. County! It really is an enormous place! And most of its 9.5 million inhabitants find it extremely helpful, almost a necessity, to have an automobile (more on this in chapter 3). This inevitably leads to frequent traffic congestion, which has tested the patience of many. Fortunately for actors, the entertainment industry is somewhat localized in Hollywood, West Hollywood, the Westside, and the Eastern San Fernando Valley, though these areas are still hardly within walking distance of one another.

FIGURE 1 LOS ANGELES

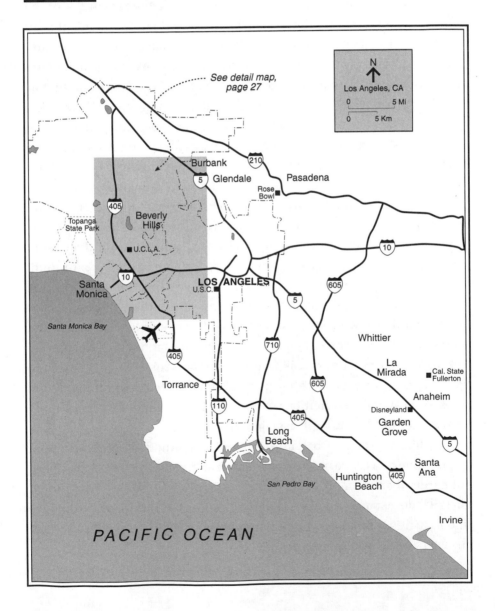

Undoubtedly most would agree that one of the better features of Southern California, or the "Southland," is the superb weather. One can generally anticipate year-round comfortable temperatures. During summer, temperatures usually range between eighty and one hundred degrees, and the air is dry. During winter, temperatures drop to between 50° and 70°. Thus, you will never have to shovel snow off of your driveway in Los Angeles. From late April through October it virtually never rains, and only does so sporadically during the remainder of the year; so expect lots of California sunshine. The only time you might need your heavy-duty galoshes is from late December through March, when rainstorms historically can pummel the region. But be sure to bring your entire wardrobe anyway. You never know what you might need for an audition.

For many people the usually incredible weather outweighs L.A.'s negative attributes, which include smog, crime, fires, winter floods, and earthquakes. Smog is a problem that has slowly been improving, though it is still quite significant. Strict emissions regulations for automobiles were enacted in recent years which have helped curb the problem; however, a majority of regions still succumb to moderate or poor air quality for much of the year. One can literally see a brown cloud hovering in the sky from many locations. To avoid the smog, some seek out the coastal communities, which are bathed by cooler, cleaner ocean air year-round.

As in most major cities, another negative aspect of life in L.A. is crime. For a while, car-jackings were on the rise, although they seem to have diminished ever since such crimes became federal offenses and since companies began selling increasingly popular tracking devices for automobiles. One simply has to use common sense when it comes to safety in L.A. for cars and all aspects of life (i.e., lock your doors, don't walk alone at night, be cautious of strangers). The same safety rules apply in L.A. as would in any other major city.

While any large urban area can expect predictable problems such as pollution and crime, no one can deny that in recent years L.A. has been hit harder than most cities with other difficulties. Terrible riots erupted in 1992, devastating floods and fires struck in 1993, a major earthquake shook in 1994, and even more floods rose in 1995. It seems as though disasters have become commonplace.

On the positive side, these events have brought the people of Los

Angeles together. They have shown that love, compassion, and a willingness to assist rests within the hearts of many. And despite these calamities, many Angelenos still count their blessings. Most are willing to cope with these disturbances in exchange for comfortable weather, close proximity to beaches, exciting city life, and, of course, show business.

In terms of human relations, Angelenos are perceived to have a more relaxed and liberal approach to life. In this transient town, acceptance and tolerance of others is more common than in other parts of the country, though it would be ludicrous to suggest that problems are nonexistent. Here you will find people from every imaginable background pursuing their own unique lifestyles—ethnically, spiritually, sexually, and/or economically. Nothing is too unusual for L.A.

This melting pot of many different people, including considerable Hispanic, Asian, and African-American populations, as well as many other sub-groups, makes for a unique cultural and culinary experience that cannot be duplicated in many other cities. Here you will find more Thai restaurants than McDonald's. Additionally, there is no shortage of Mexican, Japanese, Chinese, Indian, or American cuisine. Whatever your palette desires, the people of L.A. will provide.

Another nice quality of the residents, specifically the actors, is that many are big dreamers. They easily could have pursued careers in their hometowns or in smaller cities, but chose L.A. because they are dreamers. They are a particular breed of people, filled with optimism, spontaneity, and an ability to imagine greatness. They have somehow come to believe that in Los Angeles just about anything is possible. And they're right. If there is one truth about Los Angeles beyond all the hype and the hoopla, it is that anything and everything can happen, and does all the time.

But beware: Big dreamers also tend to have big egos. It has been said that some people in L.A. are plastic, superficial, and narcissistic. This, of course, can be said about people anywhere. But in Hollywood, the quest for fame and fortune can sometimes overtake the individual. For some, the car they drive or the clothes they wear become more important than the people in their lives and life itself! And while there's nothing wrong with driving a fancy car or wearing nice clothes, just be sure that your focus on "making it big" doesn't leave you dazed and confused about what really counts in life.

When you do make a ton of money, and hopefully are still a balanced person, there will be plenty of ways to spend it. By taking a drive around town, you'll notice that a tremendous amount of money is made in the entertainment industry not only by performers, but by agents, directors, writers, and producers as well. Go for a ride in Beverly Hills and Bel-Air. You'll see a multitude of luxury automobiles and elegant homes throughout. The same is true for the Hollywood Hills, Brentwood, Pasadena, and Malibu. Next, take a stroll down Rodeo Drive. All of the top fashion designers have store-fronts with clothing and jewelry worth more than most people's cars. For trendier shopping, head on over to Melrose Avenue. You'll find a hipper crowd and a more eclectic environment. Finally, steer over to Malibu to see sprawling ocean-view estates. You will realize that there is a large pie out there, and a piece of it may as well be yours.

To every newcomer, Los Angeles can seem like an intimidating place. It is easy to get lost in such a large and diverse city, not only physically but emotionally, so it will be important to get your feet on solid ground. Unfortunately many people come to this town with unrealistic plans. They have little money saved, no understanding of how to proceed, and no strategy to survive. Desperation often follows when stardom doesn't happen in a few weeks or months. Many leave disappointed and feeling like a failure, others repeatedly call on friends and relatives to finance their venture, and still others join the homeless population, standing at intersections begging for money. You don't want to do any of those things.

The following chapters will show you the best way to start an acting career in Los Angeles. They will show you how the business works and help you to develop a strategy that will allow you to play the game successfully.

◆

For additional information on L.A.: The L.A. Chamber of Commerce (213/580-7500) sells relocation packages. Included are maps, a renter's guide, an apartment and home buyer's guide, job information, and a community choice book with information on schools, shopping, weather, and cost-of-living. Currently, the package costs $23.

CHAPTER TWO

A Basic Understanding of How Actors Get Work

Before you embark on an acting career in the entertainment industry, you first need to learn the nuts and bolts of the business. This will help you in developing your strategy for survival, by giving you a concise understanding of what to anticipate along the way. There is much information to take in, but for now, a brief summary follows with more detailed information to come later in the book.

Most new actors arrive in Hollywood with little knowledge of how the system operates. They expect that getting cast will be as easy as it was in high school or college, where a handful of people showed up for open auditions, and one of them got the part on the spot. Others buy into the great myth that people are simply "discovered" off the street and made into mega-stars overnight. To these people, I lovingly say "Wake up!" While stories of instant and seemingly easy stardom from the early days have been told many times, it is extremely rare and unrealistic in today's world. Hollywood does not hire actors or create stars that way. Most successful actors in Hollywood have worked long and hard for years trying to establish themselves. Generally they have followed certain steps and have understood how the game is played.

Aside from having friends and relatives who will hire you, which, by the way, happens frequently, as a new actor in town you will typically have to follow a standard cycle to gain professional, or paid, employment:

It All Starts with You, the Actor

Before you get the ball rolling, you'll need to examine your skills, talents, background, and credits. As with any profession you are seeking to enter, it helps to have experience and/or training. Maybe you've got experience from high school, community theatre, or college. Maybe you've been in a commercial in your hometown, you've won a beauty pageant, or you've been a model or dancer. Anything related to the field of acting, or entertainment, will help you.

If you have no credits, it will be a good idea to start with some training right away. This will not only help you develop your craft, but also show you are serious about it. It's true, some of today's stars haven't had one acting lesson in their lives, but the vast majority have. Even working actors study regularly. Therefore, consider studying regardless of your background.

Once you've determined you have some talent, and hopefully some experience, then it's time for professional assistance.

You'll Need an Agent or Manager

While it will be extremely important to pursue acting jobs on your own, you will need to have an agent or manager representing you if you want to have a professional acting career. I can't stress how important this is if you want to be taken seriously in Hollywood.

An agent acts on your behalf to arrange auditions and interviews with casting directors, and he or she then negotiates your contracts when you are hired. Agents do not actually get you the job, you have to do that with your talent. Some actors forget this. Powerful and respected agents can be persuasive and in some instances help to obtain work for their clients, but you realistically can't count on their influence alone, especially if you are a newcomer.

Regardless of how established you are, the standard agent fee is 10 percent of the money you earn from your acting work—a modest fee for all the work they do. Agents and ways to obtain them will be discussed in greater detail in chapter 10.

Managers assist in career planning, development, and strategy. They complement the efforts of an agent by arranging additional auditions and meetings with casting directors and producers. They are typically hired by established actors only, however some newcomers have had luck in securing a manager who believed in them when agents would not. Managers can take anywhere from 10 to 15 percent of your paycheck.

In order to hook up with a legitimate agent or manager, you typically have to be a member of the Screen Actors Guild, most commonly known as SAG. (There are some agents and managers who take non-SAG clients, but the majority won't). SAG is a union that protects actors' rights, looks out for their interests, and guarantees those big wages that everyone hears about. If you are seriously considering a professional acting career, then you will need to become a member, since most paying jobs in this town are union. Unfortunately, getting into SAG is a little tricky. You can't just show up and slap down your initiation fee. You have to become eligible, and to do so is a Catch-22. To qualify, you must work a union job and be paid union wages; however, you are not supposed to work union jobs unless you already are in the union. It's seems rather crazy, but there are ways to sneak in, and they will be discussed later in the book in chapter 6.

Off to Auditions!

After securing representation with an agent or manager, hopefully they will be arranging auditions for you on a regular basis, as you continue to pursue auditions yourself. Some weeks you may have five or more auditions, others you may have none. It varies a lot.

Auditions can take place at any time during the day, though usually they transpire during business hours. They can be located anywhere in L.A, but typically they happen somewhere in Hollywood, the Westside, or the Valley. Usually you'll get a day's notice to prepare for an audition, but on occasion your agent will call and ask you to be ready in just a couple of hours. Therefore, you'll need tremendous flexibility in your schedule. (This is why so many actors historically have worked as waiters late at night).

The Casting Director

Once you've driven across town to your audition, maintaining balance and composure amidst the traffic and heat of L.A., you'll swiftly go inside and wait to be seen by the casting director. Newcomers have all kinds of scary images of casting directors, but in reality, they are surprisingly normal people who are hired by producers to cast, or assemble, a particular project. Their job is to find the best actors for all the roles in the production (though the lead roles are usually pre-cast from lists). To accomplish this task, they do one of two things: they call on a pool of actors whom they already know, or if they have time, they submit their casting needs to the Breakdown Services to get submissions from agents. The Breakdown Services are a daily rundown of what is currently being cast for television, films, commercials, and Equity theatre. Only agents and personal managers can receive them. Everyday they are delivered to agents who in response submit headshots, and videotapes when available, of suitable actors for consideration.

The audition process is an art in itself, one that you will continually practice and improve upon. While many actors, given a few weeks, can give a superb reading of a script, much fewer can do the same when given only twenty-four hours' notice. Therefore, ways to develop a more clear and confident approach to the audition process will be explained in great detail in chapter 12.

Once a casting director has auditioned a group of actors— anywhere from twenty-five to a hundred people, or up to a thousand or more for larger roles in movies—he or she selects the most appropriate and has them come back to read for further evaluation. This situation is termed a "callback." Most times a handful of actors are called back, other times ten or fifteen might be called back. Regardless, they all return and eventually meet the director.

The Director

The director has the job of artistically navigating and conducting the course of the movie, television program, or commercial being made. Directors are considered the men or women with the "vision" for the project. They take a script and turn it into real life, taking responsibility for every shot in the final product. Through thousands of creative choices, they bring their own particular flavor and mark to the film. Once the casting process has reached its final stages, they have a strong influence as to who will be hired, especially if the project is a film.

The Producers

Producers are the people who manage the entire project from start to finish—creatively, logistically, and financially. There are many producers on any given project, with each having specifically defined responsibilities. Of all the producers, executive producers have the most clout because they often have a significant financial interest in the project, representing either a studio, network, or their own independent production company. They ultimately hire everyone—actors as well as the director—and usually have the power to make the final decision on everything, especially in television projects.

Getting the Part

Because you are talented, intelligent, charming, and confident, you will hopefully book a job soon. Some actors "get the part" on their first audition in Hollywood, others go to fifty or one hundred auditions before they finally land something. The key is persistence. Generally, as a new actor you are doing very well if you book one out of every ten auditions you attend. Therefore, be prepared. Such odds make it a very challenging process.

Also, depending on the role, you might be called back four or five times before finally securing it. This can be very grueling, especially if the part ultimately goes to someone else.

But you will know you are on the right track if you are consistently being called back on your auditions.

With each job you land, you try to build on that success and become more and more well-known. As this happens it will become easier to gain entry into casting directors' offices for auditions. They will have seen your work and won't have to be persuaded to meet with you. Some directors or producers may also specifically request you for parts. This process of establishing yourself usually is a lengthy one though, and it may span many years. But don't be discouraged. Some young actors have made great strides during their first year by landing just one impressive role.

Other Ways In

You've just read the conventional way actors obtain work and you might be thinking that there has to be an easier way. A back-door entrance. A way to sneak in and avoid the system. Well, there is. Sort of. While you continue to pursue an acting career by auditioning, which is absolutely essential, there are several ways to increase your chances of success.

Over the years many actors have attracted the attention of agents and casting directors in a variety of unconventional ways, successfully and unsuccessfully. Some have placed ads for work in the trade papers or painted their cars as billboards, others have pretended to be agents or managers and submitted themselves for parts. A few actors have even posed as messengers and driven through security gates of the major studios undetected to make late-night deliveries of their own headshots to the offices of casting directors. Many more have schmoozed their way into the Hollywood elite, attending party after party, networking a chain of high-powered acquaintances.

I can't say that all of these unconventional methods are positively proven to be effective, but schmoozing and networking do seem to have a high success rate in terms of helping to land work. This is based on the simple truth that people tend to hire people they know and like, as opposed to strangers they don't know and might not like. People simply want to help their friends. Therefore, the more of a friend you are to people in the industry, the greater your chances of success. But remember, I said "friend," not a "I'm just being nice to you so that you'll help my career" kind of person. People can spot those types a mile away.

Whatever you do, don't try anything obnoxious, dangerous, threatening, or in poor taste. Those are sure ways not to get hired. Being creative is one thing, but being a jerk is another. A variety of examples of what not-to-do include: bringing a gun to an audition when reading for a villain role, stalking and/or calling casting directors at their home address, or writing frequent, lengthy letters to industry people as if they are your best buddies. In fact, if you're a real pest, you may end up with a bad reputation that could overshadow your good qualities and significantly decrease your chances for auditions in the future.

But if you are a charming and crafty individual, then you might have some luck doing things "your own way." However, it's still strongly recommended that you simultaneously pursue work through the conventional way of auditioning. You have to play all your cards, not just rely on a shot in the dark. It will actually be good for you; auditioning is part of the acting experience and will improve your acting ability. Even if you get lucky and bypass the system once or twice, you will eventually have to back-track and audition for a director or producer in the traditional way. So keep your auditioning skills polished.

Now that you have a basic understanding of how actors get work in Hollywood, you probably can't wait to get started. Your blood is racing, your excitement is overwhelming, and your confidence is sky-high! In order to keep that enthusiasm going, you will need to establish some normalcy in your new life in L.A. This means taking care of one of the basics in life first: finding a place to unpack your bags and call "home."

CHAPTER THREE

Starting Your Life in L.A.

Because Los Angeles is such a gigantic city, finding a place to call "home" can at first seem overwhelming, especially if you don't already have friends or relatives somewhere in town. There are literally hundreds of areas from which to choose, which makes throwing a dart at a map seem like an attractive solution! But don't get frustrated. Being an actor, you probably will want to live somewhere near the action of the entertainment industry. Though it's not essential, it's nice to be around other actors and industry players on a daily basis to keep your interest peaked and focused, and your desire alive. Therefore, this chapter aims to show you where the entertainment industry is located and why you might want to live within its domain. It also covers the basics of renting a space, and discusses the benefits and drawbacks of owning a car in L.A.

Where Is the Entertainment Industry Located?

It's actually difficult to pinpoint exactly where the boundaries of the entertainment industry are. In the old days, Hollywood would have been the decisive answer. But with expansion of the industry, there are actually several major regions where actors and other industry people can be found buzzing around town.

There are basically three areas where the vast majority of studios, talent agencies, and casting directors are located: 1) Hollywood/West Hollywood, 2) the Westside, which includes Beverly Hills, Century City, Westwood, West L.A., Brentwood, Santa Monica, Culver City, Venice, and Marina del Rey, and 3) the East San Fernando Valley, specifically Burbank, Toluca Lake, Universal City, Studio City, Sherman Oaks, North Hollywood, and Van Nuys. While the Valley is clearly defined, the Westside merges with Hollywood and West Hollywood. For the sake of simplicity, I've tried to separate all locations into three basic regions, but understand that the boundaries are not and cannot be precisely defined.

The San Fernando Valley (more commonly known as "The Valley" —remember the movie *Valley Girl*?) is separated from Hollywood and the Westside by the Santa Monica Mountains, which are commonly referred to as the Hollywood Hills, or simply the Hills. This mountainous region is speckled with beautiful homes in many sprawling canyons, including Beachwood Canyon, Laurel Canyon, Coldwater Canyon, Nichols Canyon, Benedict Canyon, and Topanga Canyon, to name a few. If you have the money, then contact a broker and purchase your palace in one of these canyons; otherwise plan to move into one of the other more economically feasible regions for now.

All of the regions have their own unique ambience, some more enticing than others. You ought to drive through each to determine which best suits your lifestyle. Once you find an area you like, be sure to check it out at night too, as some neighborhoods change for the worse at sundown. Also, be aware that even individual neighborhoods vary a lot from street to street. Often a seemingly safe block can border an undesirable one. So make a thorough investigation into locating the safest, nicest, and most affordable housing available to you. A brief description of each of the regions follows.

Hollywood/West Hollywood

Mann's Chinese Theatre! The Hollywood Bowl! The Walk of Fame! Yes, Hollywood is indeed filled with all of these famous landmarks and more, not to mention multitudes of tourists. You've seen or heard about these famous structures often in the media, but rarely do you hear about the real Hollywood. Beyond its glamorous image, Hollywood has more commonly come to be associated with crime, drugs, prostitution, and transients. It's also known for some of the eccentric types you'll find

FIGURE 2 ENTERTAINMENT INDUSTRY VICINITIES

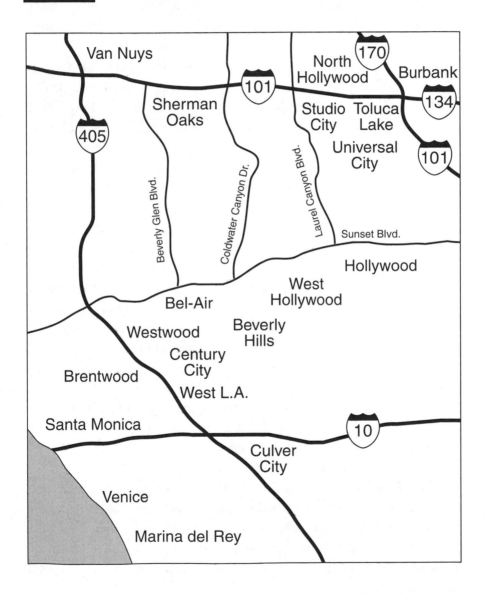

walking the streets in L.A. If you take a drive down Hollywood Boulevard, you could see a real life cast of unusual characters. Hence, some have nicknamed it "Hollyweird."

For a real good peek at Hollywood, rent the movie *Jimmy Hollywood*, starring Joe Peschi and Christian Slater. It gives a real good glimpse into life in Hollywood—the actual place—as much of it was filmed within its confines.

Despite its negative aspects, you will still find many talent agencies, theatres, acting schools, and nightclubs, along with myriad tourist attractions in Hollywood. There is a definite urban feel, though it's still a far stretch from New York City. Probably the best aspect is that the rent is lower on average than in most other locations. Because of it, Hollywood's countless apartments have become home for many, many actors. Studios in the area include Paramount, Sunset-Gower, CBS, and ABC-Prospect.

West Hollywood is filled with many popular nightclubs and fine restaurants, and has a trendy and hip feel to it. It's where the actual "Melrose Place" is located, with many unique clothing stores and artsy hang-outs dispersed along Melrose Avenue. There are also many fine bookstores and antique shops, in addition to the Beverly Center, a huge shopping mall on the corner of Beverly and La Cienega (See-eh-neh-ga). Many entertainment industry people, including casting directors, agents, and public relations folks, have offices scattered throughout the vicinity. There are also many theatres, and of course, many actors to be found. In addition, West Hollywood is known for its gay community.

The Westside

The Westside has an air of wealth, activity, and sophistication. Many of its residents feel that it's the only place in L.A. where "life" happens. Heavily penetrated by the entertainment industry, it's a popular place for actors of all levels. Cities in the Westside include:

Beverly Hills. You'll find Beverly Hills to be one of the nicer areas in Los Angeles. In addition to the rich and famous, many top talent agencies and production companies have established themselves here. Tall office buildings and elegant hotels line Wilshire Boulevard, and just north lie the elegant shops of world-renowned Rodeo Drive. You won't have to look hard to see famous designers' boutiques, Rolls Royces, and even celebrities along Rodeo Drive and its surrounding streets. North of Santa Monica Boulevard are mostly elegant and quiet neighborhoods occupied by many people who have been successful at one time or another in the entertainment industry. Most new actors have a hard time finding affordable apartments in Beverly Hills, though plenty of apartments exist (mostly south of Santa Monica and especially Wilshire Boulevard). As a result, many more established actors and industry players dominate the scene in this posh community.

Century City. West of Beverly Hills, Century City essentially has an urban atmosphere because of a collection of some of the tallest buildings in L.A. (besides downtown L.A.). Located between Century Park East and Century Park West, they are home to a wide range of professional businesses, including numerous production companies and some leading talent agencies. Directly south, you'll find 20th Century Fox studios. Below Fox and to the West, you will find upscale apartments, condos, and houses. Lots of established actors live around here, too.

Westwood. Both a strong "city" ambience and a cozier collegiate atmosphere blend together in Westwood. A long string of luxury high-rise apartments line Wilshire Boulevard in this part of town, with the UCLA campus resting just north. In Westwood Village, you'll find many movie theatres, popular restaurants, and several square blocks of shopping. Obviously, a lot of UCLA students live in the area in many of the apartments, but you'll also find a fairly wealthy mix of retired and industry people living in condos, and, farther north, in the expensive homes of Bel-Air.

West L.A. You'll find a combination of old and new apartment buildings interspersed with businesses, warehouses, and a few high-rises. Bisected by the 405 Freeway, also known as the San Diego Freeway, it's a busy area with both urban stretches and others dominated by single family homes. Many find its greatest asset to be its close proximity to the beaches, freeways, and the entertainment industry. A wide variety of professional people live in this area, along with many actors.

Brentwood. This classy neighborhood, made famous by O. J. Simpson, is home to many celebrities as well as many lesser-known working actors. Located just west of the San Diego Freeway, it's lined with many upscale and trendy restaurants, fine shops, and elegant homes. The southern portion, between San Vicente and Wilshire, is filled with hundreds of higher-end apartments. Though not heavily dominated by entertainment companies, it's within close proximity to all the action, and therefore many actors live throughout the area.

Santa Monica. This beach community has an inviting, friendly atmosphere. Elegant hotels and condominiums line much of Ocean Avenue, which overlooks the Pacific Ocean, and many comfortable, yet expensive, homes lie nearby. Two of its most notable attractions are the Santa Monica Pier and the Third Street Promenade, a lengthy outdoor mall that attracts many talented street performers. You'll also find many, many restaurants and bars here. It's a great place for entertainment and becomes crowded on the weekends.

There are many nice apartment buildings in and around Santa Monica. Being a rent control district, one would think great apartments could be acquired for cheap, cheap, cheap! Unfortunately, that's not the case. Overall, you can expect to pay higher than average rent. (You might be able to find a steal once in while, but such an apartment is usually on the lower-end, in terms of quality and location). Even though it's a little out of the way from the heart of the entertainment industry, many actors prefer the area because of the cooler temperatures, the cleaner air, and the beach.

Culver City. A tremendous array of people, including actors, live together in Culver City, ethnically, spiritually, and economically. You'll find upscale neighborhoods, juxtaposed with average surroundings, and even seedier ones. It's really a tossed salad, but overall the rents are more affordable than in other places. Much work in the entertainment industry transpires here, with Sony Pictures and Culver Studios in the neighborhood.

Venice. A quaint and unusual beach community, it has attracted many actors and artists of all kinds. Densely packed, here you will find a wide range of residents, tourists, street performers, eccentrics, body builders, and rollerbladers on any given day strolling the boardwalk. In recent years, several incidents of gang violence and increased crime have tarnished its image. But for the most part, it still flourishes with a diversified group of mostly artistic people, even though few entertainment firms are situated in the area. In terms of housing, you will find numerous apartment buildings, and, closer to the beach, a concentrated mix of houses, duplexes, and small apartments.

Marina del Rey. Home of the Marina City Towers, a series of luxury high-rise condos built by Howard Hughes that surround L.A.'s largest marina, Marina del Rey is another wealthy part of L.A. You'll find plenty of expensive restaurants and popular nightclubs in this well-kept community. Many of the residents are retired or currently involved in the entertainment industry. You can be sure that most apartments or condos are fairly expensive here.

The San Fernando Valley

As a whole, the Valley is more of a family community and calmer than the Westside. However, it's certainly not dead; parts of it are still bustling with activity. Ventura Boulevard, which runs the southern length of the Valley (about 17 miles), is lined with hundreds of great restaurants, eclectic shops, bookstores, clothing outlets, and just about everything imaginable. The rest of the Valley is composed of thousands of apartment buildings, single family dwellings, small office buildings, and shopping strips. High-rises are virtually non-existent, except for a few lining or nearby Ventura Boulevard. There are many places within the Valley in which actors choose to live, but the most popular ones are listed in detail below.

Burbank. Many of the major entertainment firms (Disney, Warner Bros., NBC, and other smaller ones) can be found in Burbank. Surprisingly, it maintains a suburban feel. A fresh and clean place, it has both many single family dwellings and apartment complexes. Besides the studios, its other major attraction is the Media Center, a large shopping mall just east of the Golden State Freeway, also known as the "5 Freeway." Burbank is filled with many people who work in the entertainment industry in varying capacities.

Toluca Lake/Universal City/Studio City/Sherman Oaks. Another mecca for industry people, this region contains many affordable apartment buildings and homes. In the hills south of Ventura Boulevard, more expensive houses and estates are tucked away. Overall, there is a cozy and charming ambience combined with fairly safe neighborhoods. Many entertainment people live here because it is close to studios and has easy freeway access. You'll find many smaller talent agencies and several important casting offices located here as well.

The major attraction is Universal Studios, which is both an actual studio lot where movies and television programs are taped, and a theme park that attracts thousands of tourists every year. For nighttime entertainment, many flock to Universal City Walk, which offers great restaurants, unique shops, and an enormous movie theatre complex, in a safe, sanitized, and colorful environment.

North Hollywood. Lying just north of Studio City, it is home to many actors because of its very affordable rents. The southern part, which borders Studio City, is the nicest. The farther north you go, the more run-down it gets. In recent years an effort has been made to upgrade it and make it a friendlier place for artists and actors, and it is starting to look better. Its best quality is its close proximity to the major studios, agents, and casting offices in the Valley.

Van Nuys. Many single family homes and apartment buildings make up this rather plain, and sometimes poor-looking area. Located in the middle of the Valley, Van Nuys is sought out by many because of its economical housing. Not much happens in this part of town with regard to the industry, so you'll find all professions of people living here. However, it's close to both the San Diego Freeway (405) and the Holly-wood Freeway (101), which means it's not too far from all the action.

Renting an Apartment or House

Now that you are familiar with the areas often sought out by actors, you'll need to know what to expect when you try renting an apartment or house. Many of the questions newcomers frequently contemplate will be answered on the following pages.

Is it Hard to Find an Apartment in L.A.? No. In fact, most buildings have vacancies. People from New York City find this difficult to compre-hend, since securing an apartment in the Big Apple can be a major undertaking. So don't worry! A buyer's market definitely exists. You literally will have tons of apartments to choose from. Even with the 6.8 earthquake in January 1994, when thousands of people were displaced and had to find temporary residences, there was still an abundance of vacant units.

What about Finding a House? You may have to search harder if you are on a budget and want to live in a house. Most houses, for example a two bedroom and one bath, start at about $1000 and can easily be $1500 or more. In the Hollywood Hills or Malibu where the houses are usually larger, you could easily pay $2,000 to $10,000 a month! Needless to say, most new actors in Hollywood can't afford that.

If you plan to arrive with a few friends or already know some people in L.A, then living together in a house might be affordable. For instance, you could possibly get a four-bedroom house in the Hills for $2400 a month, which equals $600 apiece—a fairly normal rent to pay.

Some people prefer not to live in houses because ground level structures are easier to burglarize. This explains why many house-dwellers have placed bars on the windows, especially in lower- and middle-class neighborhoods. Of course, the most important factor will be the neighborhood. If the house is situated in a good vicinity, say somewhere south of Ventura Boulevard or up in the Hollywood Hills, then it will probably be very, very safe.

Where Should I Stay Before I am Able to Rent a Place? You've got several options. By far, the best thing you can do is stay with friends or relatives, if possible. Of course this will not apply to everyone; so if this isn't you, then skip this paragraph. If this is you, then it can be an ideal situation because you have someone to show you around town and hopefully direct you to specific buildings or homes in his or her neighborhood.

Another option is to stay at a hotel. Many offer special rates if you stay from a week to a month. Several apartment complexes, specifically "Oakwood" in Sherman Oaks and also near Warner Bros., offer affordable monthly rentals in addition to long-term leases. Such places can be extremely beneficial, as it may take you more than a week to determine exactly where you want to live.

To find a hotel before you arrive, you should obtain a copy of the *L.A. Times* Sunday Edition from a major newsstand in your city or at your closest airport. If you cannot find a copy of the *L.A. Times* anywhere, then order a copy directly from them (1-800-LA-TIMES). Inside the Classifieds, you'll find the Residential Rentals section where several hotels usually advertise. You should make a few calls to inquire about rates. Also, you can check with any major hotel in your hometown. They'll have a catalog listing all of their affiliated hotels nationwide. Find one in the L.A. area, preferably in one of the locales mentioned earlier, and then inquire about prices and availabilities.

Finally, some people opt to make a short trip to L.A. one to three weeks before they move here permanently to arrange an apartment lease. They stay at a hotel for a few days and sign a lease that starts at the beginning of the next month. They then return home, finish up their old life, pack up the car, and zoom into town to a new apartment that's ready and waiting!

How Much Will an Apartment Cost and What Can I Expect in Renting?

Compared to other cities in the country, living in L.A. is very expensive! You can expect to pay anywhere from $500 to $900 a month for a nice unfurnished one-bedroom apartment, and from $800 to $1200 dollars for a nice unfurnished two-bedroom apartment (98 percent of all apartments are unfurnished). In places like Beverly Hills or Brentwood, you'll probably have to pay several hundred dollars more.

On top of your first month's rent, you will often have to pay a security deposit (which will be refunded at the end of the lease, unless you decide to have a punching contest with a wall), which usually amounts to one-half or a full month's rent. So expect to pay a total of about one-and-a-half to two months rent (first month plus security) just to move into an apartment.

You will also probably have to pay a non-refundable fifteen to thirty dollars for a credit check. If you have bad credit, then you will have some difficulty renting at many places. You may have to stay away from the bigger or corporate-owned apartment complexes, since their credit departments won't accept people with blemished records. Your best bet will be a smaller, independently owned apartment complex, and you might have to beg.

It is important to note that some of the bigger apartment complexes also require a current pay stub or your previous year's tax returns to verify that your monthly income is approximately two-and-a-half times your monthly rent payment. If your tax forms show little or no income, then you will have to look for independently owned buildings not requiring this. All of this may seem a bit overwhelming, but regardless of your circumstances, you will definitely be able to find a place to live in L.A.

Most buildings in L.A. offer six-month or one-year leases, and only a handful offer terms that are month-to-month. As an enticement, some will offer two weeks free on a six-month lease or one month free on a year's lease. You should always ask about this, even if the apartment manager fails to mention it while showing the apartment.

Also, a majority of apartments do not come with a refrigerator. Therefore, you will have to rent one from the landlord or an outside vendor, buy one, or bring one (which could be a difficult feat, unless you're arriving via U-Haul).

Finally, negotiate everything you can possibly think of, especially the price. Landlords are eager to fill vacancies, so you have an advantage. But before deciding to rent out any given apartment, you should visit at least five different ones. This will help you know whether you are getting a good deal. Many people have the tendency to become overly excited about the first apartment they see, not realizing that there might be better existing values. So don't be too quick to sign on the dotted line. No matter how good a deal sounds, it probably will not disappear overnight.

What If I Have Pets? Most apartments allow small pets like cats, but usually there is an extra security deposit of about two hundred dollars. Most do not allow dogs, so be up-front about this when looking at an apartment. You won't be able to hide your Chihuahua from your landlord, no matter how small it is. You may have to search longer if you're a dog-owner, but there are thousands of buildings and eventually one will accept you and all of your animal companions.

What About Living with a Roommate? Many young actors live with roommates simply because it saves them money. Almost always, the cost of splitting a two-bedroom apartment is much less than living alone in a one-bedroom. Therefore, if you are on a budget, you might consider having a roommate.

If you don't already know someone with whom you would like to share an apartment, there are several roommate placement agencies that can help. Their fees are typically $40 to $60, and they offer you unlimited leads on affordable apartments (you specify the price range) with compatible people (you specify the traits). These agencies can be found in the yellow pages and many advertise in newspaper classifieds—check the *L.A. Times* or *The Recycler*. Also, you can often find individuals seeking roommates who have placed their own ads in the classifieds.

If you end up meeting your new roommate through one of the services or the classifieds, make sure he or she is someone you like. This sounds obvious, but you'd be surprised at the number of people who choose roommates that they come to dread. Use your gut instinct—if the snake crawling around his neck doesn't mix well with your fear of reptiles, then don't move in together.

Should I Search the Newspaper to Find an Apartment? This is not necessary and can actually be rather disappointing. Many times an ad in the paper sounds fabulous, but in reality the apartment is the pits. It's not always the case though, so if you feel inclined, you should try it a couple of times. Maybe you'll get lucky and find your dream apartment.

One of the easiest things to do is drive around a neighborhood that you prefer and investigate buildings that appeal to you. Usually a sign will be posted outside, often with a phone number and specific information about the available unit(s). Many times a manager lives on the premises, so an apartment can be inspected immediately. Even if no sign is apparent, it is still wise to stop and ask because some owners never bother to advertise publicly.

What About the Safety of Buildings? Many apartments offer gated parking, which is an excellent option to have in L.A. because thousands of cars are stolen here. At least a hundred thousand cars are snatched up every year! A gated parking facility helps keep your car safer, though not completely secure, as criminals can get into any parking lot they want to. A gate is just a good deterrent.

In terms of the safety of your apartment, you should ask the manager about any crimes that have occurred in the building or on the premises. If you sense any hesitation or vagueness in the response, ask again and be very specific. If you feel uncomfortable with the answer, it's probably best to look elsewhere.

When choosing an apartment, it's always a plus if it comes with an alarm. If not, you can easily install a magnetic alarm yourself in five minutes to any door or window, and they cost only about five to ten dollars a piece. Such alarms can be found at hardware stores. The nominal price is worth it if you have any concerns about safety.

A Review of Good Questions to Ask Your Potential Landlord:

- What's the rent?
- Is the rent negotiable?
- Is the lease for one year, six months, or month-to-month?
- Is there a month's free rent on a year's lease?
- What, if any, utilities are paid?
- How many parking spots do I get? (in case you have a roommate who also has a car)
- Has there been any crime in the building or parking garage?
- Does a refrigerator come with the unit?
- What about washer/dryer facilities?

What About Earthquake Safety in L.A.? It's wise to choose a building that appears to be newer, because it will probably be more structurally sound. In 1971, and again in the 1980s, stricter earthquake building codes were established; therefore, buildings built after these dates are going to be safer during a major earthquake. Most buildings that suffered structural damage in the January 1994 quake were built before 1971.

Newer buildings are built on rollers, which allow them to rock back and forth during a quake, much like a raft on the ocean. Rollers are supposed to make buildings safer and less prone to structural damage. Thus, you should always inquire about the age of a building and its seismic, or earthquake, safety while an apartment manager is showing you a unit.

An apartment on the top floor might be the safest, not only because it's guarded from prowlers, but because most apartment buildings in the 1994 earthquake suffered the worst damage on the first floor. This is because the building is anchored to the ground level, and that area experiences the most pressure when the building shakes.

Should I Really Be Concerned About Earthquakes? Earthquakes come with the territory in Southern California, as with many other places in the world. It is not suggested that you live in constant fear of them, as most earthquakes are very minor and can barely be felt. The worldwide publicity that is generated about them makes many people believe that the earth is shaking violently in L.A. on a regular basis. It isn't, just once in a while!

For example, an earthquake that measured 6.8 on the Richter scale shook for about one minute on January 17, 1994, causing a major disturbance for the city. Nevertheless, the city recovered quickly, as it always seems to from any disaster, and life is back to normal. Just remember that environmental hazards exist wherever you live—snow and ice in the Northeast, hurricanes in Florida, and tornados in the Midwest. You should have awareness about earthquakes, but don't let a fear of them stop you from pursuing your dream!

By the way, since you'll be living in earthquake country, you ought to know how the Richter scale works: a tremor that measures 4.0 on the scale is ten times stronger than a 3.0 (a 3.0 can barely be felt). A quake that registers 5.0 is ten times stronger than a 4.0. Thus, a 5.0 is one hundred times stronger than a 3.0! You get the idea.

Transportation in L.A.

In addition to addressing your living situation, you will have to face another important aspect of life in L.A.: Getting around town.

The Need for Reliable Transportation. Life in L.A. is much easier if you own some form of reliable transportation (i.e., a car or motorcycle). The reason is that the city is so vastly spread out, and as an actor you will have to be traveling to auditions all over town. One alternative is a bicycle, but unfortunately bikes are not permitted on the freeways or on the key links between Hollywood and the Valley. Another option is the bus system, but be prepared to tack considerable time onto your round trip (at least an hour or more) to compensate for waiting, bus changes, and the ride itself. Therefore, you probably should bring a car with you or buy one soon after your arrival.

Getting Your Hands on a Map. First, you'll need to get a map of L.A., preferably a Thomas Bros. Guide, which covers the entire metropolitan area. This is an absolute necessity and can be found at any bookstore, drugstore, or club warehouse. Nearly every actor in this town keeps one in their automobile because sooner or later they find themselves in a strange place—be it for work, auditions, interviews, or fun. This small investment, about fifteen to twenty dollars, is well worth it.

Insurance and Registration. You should know that insurance rates are extremely high in Southern California. For example, just having the minimum state-required liability insurance for a male under twenty-five years of age starts at about $1700 a year! (They are, however, considered the worst drivers.) But overall, rates are still extremely high for good drivers of both sexes and all ages. If you want theft or comprehensive coverage, your rates skyrocket even higher. This can be quite a shock for people new to Southern California.

To avoid the higher rates, some actors keep their cars registered in their home state, but technically this is a "no-no." California law states that you must register your car here within twenty days of relocating. Therefore, actors who don't register their cars in California are always prepared to explain that they are "only visiting" in the event of an accident or being pulled over by the L.A.P.D.

If you do register your car with the state, there is an additional entrance fee (currently $300) to bring in a vehicle that is not up-to-par with California emissions standards. You won't have to pay for an inspection though, as California does not require vehicle inspections ever. Your only fees will be an emissions test every two years and an annual registration payment. The registration payment is equal to about two percent of the value of your car plus approximately thirty dollars in fees.

Protecting Your Car. It is strongly advised that you purchase a device that locks onto your steering wheel while your car is parked. Such a device is not fool-proof, but it is a powerful deterrent, and the forty-five to sixty-five dollars is well worth your money. It will help keep you from being one of the tens of thousands who lose their automobiles each year to thieves.

Parking. You should pay close attention to parking signs. Abiding by them can be quite a challenge in L.A. It's not that parking spaces are scarce, rather there are just so many signs with so many different restrictions. For example, one post might have as many as four signs with varying restrictions for different times of the day and/or days of the week! If you violate any of the posted restrictions, then usually one of an adept team of parking enforcement officers will happily ticket your vehicle—and they mean business! So please read all signs carefully and keep plenty of quarters, dimes, and nickels in your car to feed all those hungry parking meters.

Getting settled is an important step in beginning your career in Hollywood. You need to have stability in your life with regard to shelter and transportation if you hope to have any time to focus on your career. With these covered, your next task will be finding a way to support yourself financially.

CHAPTER FOUR

Finding Ways to Support Yourself

Supporting yourself financially will be one of the most important aspects of both keeping your acting career alive and maintaining a sense of peace. Simply put, you can't focus on acting if you're worried about paying the rent! To survive in L.A., you will need to have enough money to cover certain necessities, such as food, housing, utilities, and transportation. In addition, as an actor, you'll need money to pay for such essentials as photographer's fees, headshot duplication, resumes, acting classes, postage, and envelopes—to name a few.

If you've already got a bankroll stashed away, then you've got a head start. The more money you have saved, the better. It will give you a cushion, as you adjust to life in L.A. and begin pursuing your career in high gear. But regardless of your situation, you should still devise a plan to keep money flowing into your life, in the event that your well runs dry, whether it be in a month or even a year.

So how are you gonna make some dough? Well, in Los Angeles there are many different ways actors earn survival money. Actors are creative people, and when it comes to making money, we have to be. The reason is that we must keep our daytime hours free for auditions and interviews. This means that most nine-to-five jobs are out of the question. Thus, many actors choose to work for themselves independently, or they work a number of widely varied jobs in the evenings. The common thread that distinguishes most of the jobs is flexibility: flexibility to work odd hours of the day or flexibility to take time off during normal business hours. Many actors even have two or three jobs in the event that one drys up.

Common Jobs Actor Hold to Support Themselves

Following is a list of some of the common positions that actors hold. Keep in mind that these don't have to be considered second careers, rather they are temporary work actors take on during lean times to pay the bills. Some actors get frustrated because they envision doing these jobs for decades! The key is understanding that such jobs simply help to pay the rent until acting does. Remember, many great actors have at one time or another labored at these less-than-glamorous positions:

Bartender/Waiter/Waitress. By far, this is the most common (and most stereotypical) job held by actors. Good nightly cash income combined with flexibility have made this an ideal position. Some actors have even caught the attention of agents and casting directors, by waiting on them in popular restaurants near studios and agencies. This is rare though, so for the most part you'll just be earning some survival money and getting a few free meals.

Office Temp. Temping allows you to earn a livable income while maintaining tremendous flexibility. Though most of these jobs take place during the daytime, actors can usually get out of work when an audition comes up. The key is to be tactful and crafty, by using standard excuses like "I've got a doctor's appointment," "My car is making this strange noise and my mechanic says he can only look at it tomorrow," or "My Aunt Nellie is in the hospital . . . I must see her before it's too late!" (These excuses actually can be used with any job.)

The best strategy for working consistently as a temp is to be signed up with several large agencies. The more agencies you're registered with, the greater your chances of steady employment. If you are unfamiliar with wordprocessing or spreadsheet software, such as WordPerfect or Lotus 1-2-3, which temps frequently need to use, nearly all of the agencies allow you to learn them for free in their offices on their computers. (Whether or not you plan to temp, it's still a good idea to know them.)

If you have absolutely no desire to deal with computers, there are still many unrelated temp jobs, like reception and warehouse positions, which pay less but are just as prevalent.

Chauffeur. Many actors have made good part-time money driving high-powered people all around town. Usually working in the evenings for special events, parties, or dinners, many have found chauffeuring to be a flexible job that potentially can provide important connections with industry people; that is, if the partition in the limousine isn't closed. To be a chauffeur, you need a special license from the D.M.V.

Security Guard. Many private security companies and the major studios often hire young actors to be security guards. A relatively easy job, security patrol can be a regular gig or a temporary "on-call" type of position. You can work any time of the day, as most companies need guards around the clock. Positions vary in pay, depending on whether or not you are licensed to carry a gun.

Some actors find it a nice way to practice monologues or memorize lines while on the job! Sometimes you won't have time for such rehearsal, but just being stationed on a major studio lot is a great opportunity—and that happens frequently. You'll have the chance to learn more about the business and possibly even meet some important people.

Gym Membership Salesperson/Personal Trainer. For those actors who are into health and fitness, earning an income at a gym might not be a bad idea. You can make not only good money selling memberships, but fantastic money in personal training, which happens to be a huge business in L.A.

If you have nutritional, exercise, and body-building knowledge, you're a prime candidate for personal training, working through a gym or independently. Most personal trainers make anywhere from $20 to $50 an hour.

Gyms are also great places to network, as many celebrities and other industry folks work out regularly in facilities near studios. Whether or not you decide to work at a gym, joining one still might be a good idea.

Usher at Tapings of Studio Shows. This is a good way learn about the business and make new friends. You'll learn how television shows are taped, and you might even become buddies with some of the cast, crew, or producers. Tapings are weekly and the wages aren't the greatest, so you might not be able to support yourself entirely with a job like this. However, you could make good connections.

Catering. Many actors have found this to be an excellent way to make money, maintain flexibility, and meet industry people. Most catering companies hire on an as-needed basis for movies, gala events, and parties, so you ought to hook up with a few of them to maintain steady work. Very often, you'll be serving celebrities and industry people, and while there's no guaranteed consistency in the work, you will definitely learn more about etiquette in the business. It's a very popular way for many actors to pay their rent.

Retail. L.A. is home to dozens of huge shopping malls with thousands of retail stores. It's also a mini-mall heaven! Many actors work in these retail shops during the evenings and weekends, selling everything from perfume and cosmetics to veg-o-matics! Because retail sales generally doesn't pay very much, most actors try to sell on a salary-plus-commission basis at the nicer upscale department stores, where they can earn bigger paychecks.

Massage Therapist/Healing Arts Practitioner. There is great flexibility in this field, as one can schedule clients at any time during the week, day or night. To be certified in L.A., you must take a one-hundred-hour course given by one of several county-authorized schools. There also some complicated regulations, which vary from city to city (and there are over eighty incorporated cities in L.A.!), which has caused some practitioners to simply bypass the whole system of certification. However, if you are seriously considering doing this, you should call the county to find out the details and the risks of working as an uncertified practitioner.

If you are talented, then there is potential to make great income, from $40 to $60 an hour and up. You also could develop a client list of industry people with the right marketing, which could be extremely helpful to you in the future.

Aerobics/Yoga Instructor. If you are skilled in aerobics or yoga, you should strongly consider offering some classes. In L.A., there are hundreds of gyms where you could make an arrangement to teach your aerobics/dance classes on an ongoing basis. There are also a number of yoga centers that rent out space, for both classes and private instruction. This type of job offers great flexibility and can be very rewarding with the right advertising and commitment. While certification isn't technically required, most facilities only hire certified instructors.

Tennis/Golf Instructor. If you are talented in one of these sports, not only will you make a lot of money teaching others, but you'll befriend many entertainment industry people while doing it. Many top executives in the industry are always seeking to improve their game, and are willing to pay top dollar for your services. You should check out your options at all the country clubs and community facilities to find out where there's an opening or need. You might even advertise in the industry trade papers for private instruction.

Computer Software Tutor. Some actors, who are also computer whizes, have placed small ads in the industry trade papers or have mailed flyers offering to tutor celebrities and industry people on how to use their computers at their own homes. You'd be surprised how many bigwigs aren't up-to-date with modern technology! If you know the common wordprocessing and spreadsheet software programs, then this might be a way to make good extra income while helping and schmoozing with high-powered people.

Studio Tour Guide. All of the major studios offer guided tours to the public, which flocks from around the world every day by the hundreds to get a closer glimpse at Hollywood. If you are charismatic and would enjoy speaking to groups of tourists, you should inquire at all of the studios. They usually have seasonal interviews and the competition is fierce for the moderately paying jobs, but the reward is learning about the business and making some good contacts.

Landscaping/Lawn Maintenance Personnel. Because the weather is so nice in Southern California, landscaping and lawn maintenance is a year-round business. Frequently hiring illegal immigrants, landscaping companies also hire actors looking for some cash. The work can be tough and dirty though. If you can start your own business, working part-time on weekends or on a couple of weekdays, you might be very satisfied with the results.

Arts & Crafts Maker. Throughout L.A. county, indoor swap meets (flea markets) are held every weekend where entrepreneurs sell everything from luggage and clothing, to homemade arts and crafts. There are even a few stores around town that specialize in handmade crafts. If you've got a special talent for making unique objects or art, you could supplement your income by partaking in these extravaganzas. To understand what I'm talking about, look through the *L.A. Times* on Friday or Saturday, and you'll find advertisements for these weekly swap meets. You'll also see posters attached to telephone poles around the city. Attend a few swap meets and talk to the people. You might get some great ideas for your crafts.

Multi-level Marketer (MLM) or Cooperative Marketer. In the tradition of Amway, many multi-level companies have sprouted in recent years. Sales representatives are always looking to recruit new people to sell products that encompass a wide range, including skin care, nutritional supplements, water filtration, and even gold coins. For those who work hard at these businesses, by building large sales forces beneath them and selling a lot of products or services themselves, there can be tremendous profit potential. Some young people make six figure incomes, recruiting masses of people to sell their products, and taking a percentage of all their sales. For part-timers, the result can be a good monthly supplement to your income. However, you really have to be a go-getter or you risk ending up with a closet full of products.

Telemarketer. One of the most dreaded professions, telemarketing has been a great source of income to some actors who aren't concerned with rejection (as if actors don't get enough of that anyway!). Some have said that it teaches them how to really listen to other people and develop a stronger sense of confidence. If you think you can handle this type of work, selling everything from newspaper subscriptions to adjustable beds, you'll find plenty of opportunities advertised in the newspapers on a daily basis.

Salesperson. Salespeople are the highest paid people in the world. As in any major city, you'll find hundreds of opportunities to sell in L.A. If you're good, you'll make a great income that will easily cover all of your basic necessities. As an actor, the key is finding a job that will allow you to work part-time or on weekends. Check out the *L.A. Times* for a smorgasbord of opportunities.

Construction Worker. Because of the sunny weather in Southern California, construction work happens virtually year-round. There is a lot of competition for a limited number of jobs, but if you should happen to land one, it generally pays very well. It is important to be in contact with as many contractors as possible.

Singing Telegram Performer/Stripper/Dancer. Some actors have supported themselves working only one or two days a week doing singing and/or stripping telegrams. If you've got a good voice and body, and know how to advertise, you might make some great money. Whatever you do, you'll have to be creative. You don't necessarily have to strip: you could be in a gorilla suit! It really doesn't matter as long as it's unique.

These aren't particularly popular with industry folks—many are worried the gorilla might be an out-of-work actor who's just harassing them or trying to get their attention. But there is still a big market throughout L.A. for private parties, birthdays, and events. There are also many clubs that hire exotic dancers and strippers, however working conditions might be degrading and possibly even dangerous.

Operator for Telephone Company or Answering Service. Some actors have made money answering phones because it's relatively easy, and it can be done in the evenings. Also, such a job sometimes allows for personal study or line/scene memorization while you're at work. This is best for those who don't like to be active while at work.

Cleaner. Though hardly a glamorous job, some actors have earned a livelihood by cleaning office buildings, studios, houses, and cars. This work, which usually occurs at night, can be permanent or temporary. Many cleaning people are hooked up with several agencies or companies that can place them on an as-needed basis.

Airline Employee. Airlines offer a variety of round-the-clock jobs. Whether working in reservations, loading, security, or administration, you will find jobs accommodating to your schedule. You'll have your pick of airports, though you probably should stick with Los Angeles International Airport (LAX) and Burbank Airport, since they are the closest to where you'll probably be living.

Manufacturing/Warehouse Worker (Second- or Third-Shift Job). As in any large city, you'll find scores of manufacturing companies that stay open twenty-four hours a day, producing everything from apparel to vitamins. Though usually monotonous and not always the highest paying, such work could provide temporary stability if you have no other skills or income at the moment. Temp agencies can help place you in these types of jobs.

Owner of a Home-Based Business (Other than Acting). Of all the jobs you might pursue, this can be one of the best or worst. When working for oneself, one has to be extremely motivated, especially when the television or refrigerator beckons from the other room. If you are a go-getter, have a good business idea, and hate to work for other people, this might be the best solution for you. If you find you can only produce when a boss is looking over your shoulder, this might not be a wise alternative.

Starting up a business requires a lot of effort and varying degrees of capital. Most actors who start a company begin on a small scale and develop their business if there is reasonable expectation of continued profit. Those who succeed are able not only to cover their basic necessities, but, sometimes, to live very comfortable lifestyles. Examples of home-based businesses include editing/typing/document preparation, mail-order, distributorships, gift baskets, commercial or graphic art, fine art, and sales. The possibilities are endless.

Entertainment Industry Employee. Though not usually flexible in terms of having daytime hours free, some newcomers in Hollywood opt for an industry job for a few months that will help them to understand the business and possibly offer some connections.

Industry-related jobs are advertised everyday in the classifieds of the two industry trade papers, *The Daily Variety* and *The Hollywood Reporter*. (Even if you aren't looking for a job, you ought to read these on a regular basis to find out what's happening in Los Angeles.) Smart seekers also send cover letters and resumes to department heads of studios, talent agencies, casting companies, and production firms, as well as to directors, producers, and celebrities, asking them for jobs.

Many of the positions offered are for assistants, coordinators, receptionists, or production help. The greatest aspect of industry jobs is that you learn how the business works in a relatively short period of time. You also make contacts and connections that may prove to be valuable in the long-run.

You can also search for industry-related jobs by contacting the major studios via job hotlines. They frequently list availabilities in a wide variety of categories: office-related, production, security, reception, kitchen, maintenance, and others. The job hotlines for several studios are as follows:

MCA/Universal City Studios, Universal City	818-777-JOBS
Universal Studios Hollywood, Universal City	818-622-JOBS
Warner Brothers, Burbank	818-954-5400
Sony Pictures Entertainment, Culver City	310-280-4436
Walt Disney, Burbank	818-558-2222
NBC, Burbank	818-840-3172
Paramount Pictures, Hollywood	213-956-5216
20th Century Fox, Century City	310-369-1360

A Flexible and Industry-Related Option: Extra Performer. Finally, another good source of income and education for the brand new actor in town is "Extra Work." The next chapter covers the ins and outs of extra work in great detail.

Whatever you choose to do, remember that having flexibility and enough income to survive should be your greatest concern (unless of course, you've decided to take three months to work an industry job as an assistant on a movie set). Having money to support your higher vision—your acting career—will make your journey much, much easier.

CHAPTER FIVE

Getting Your Feet Wet with "Extra Work"

The best way to learn about any business is through a "hands-on" approach. For new actors in the entertainment industry, that approach is "extra work," a great way to quickly learn more about the world of television and film.

What Is "Extra Work"?

"Extra work" refers to employment as a background performer in scenes for television or film. People who do this, "extras" or "atmosphere," have no speaking lines and are barely ever recognizable; however, they are vitally important in creating realistic depictions of public places. Scenes in restaurants, courtrooms, hallways, and outdoors usually need to be filled with people who are walking, sitting, eating, or chatting. Just take a closer look at television one night. You'll see that there's a tremendous need for extras in Hollywood.

Extra work is not considered to be one of the most glamorous or financially rewarding aspects of show business. For that reason, some aspiring and working actors never even consider it. But before you dismiss it, as a newcomer to Hollywood you should read on to learn about the potential benefits of doing extra work for a short period of time.

There are several fantastic aspects you can look forward to. First, you'll have the opportunity to familiarize yourself with a real television or movie set. If you've never worked professionally before, it will help you immensely for your first principal acting job. Second, working as an extra is one of the ways a non-union person can become eligible to join the Screen Actors Guild (SAG). Becoming a union member is one of the trickiest first hurdles for newcomers, and extra work is a great way to get your foot in the door. Third, while working, you'll be able to share and swap information with other extras about agents, casting directors, and all kinds of show-business related matters. Finally, you might even make a few good friends!

How Does One Become an Extra?

The nice thing about extra work is that you don't need to meet many qualifications or have any skills. You only need a body and an ability to follow directions. Therefore, chances are that you're probably well-qualified. And the types they're looking for? Well, all kinds are desirable. That includes people who are tall, short, fat, skinny, young, old, and from all ethnic backgrounds. In fact, there is really no one who is unsuitable—though you'll probably have more opportunities to work if you're a clean-cut, mainstream type of person.

In L.A. there are many extras casting agencies. Some are legitimate and many are rip-offs. Only a few handle the bulk of the work in town. Some agencies are one or two person operations, others have up to twenty people or more. It really varies a lot from agency to agency.

So that you don't waste your time and money registering with a bunch of agencies that have little or no ability to get you extra work, I've made a list of several agencies that seem to have a consistent stream of work. Some may be casting extras for twenty or more television shows at one time, others may only be handling a few feature films or commercials per month:

- Central Casting (Union)/Cenex Casting (Non-Union)
  1700 West Burbank Blvd., Burbank, CA 91505
  Central (818) 562-5100, Cenex (818) 569-5800
- Bill Dance Casting (Union & Non-Union)
  3518 W. Cahuenga Blvd., Suite 210, Los Angeles, CA 90068

(213) 878-1131

- Rainbow Casting (Union & Non-Union)

  12501 Chandler Ave., Suite 206, N. Hollywood, CA 91607

  (818) 752-2052

- Charlie Messenger & Associates (Union & Non-Union)

  (818) 760-3696

- Cast of Thousands (Union & Non-Union)

  4011 W. Magnolia Blvd., Burbank, CA 91505

  (818) 955-9995

- Axium Casting (Union & Non-Union)

  4001 W. Alameda Ave., Burbank, CA 91505

  (818) 557-2980

To register with any of these agencies, you'll have to go to their offices during designated hours. Be sure to call first before showing up, or they probably won't see you.

Are There Fees When Registering?

If you are non-union, most agencies will charge you a one-time registration fee ranging from five to sixty dollars. (A lot of the illegitimate agencies sometimes want upwards of $300. Stay away from anyone who wants that kind of money!) This registration fee usually includes having your picture taken for their files, in their own format or style. Sometimes if you bring your own three-by-five color snapshot of yourself, your fee will be waived.

In addition, some agencies withhold five percent of a non-union extra's paycheck, as a service fee. If you are non-union, you'll quickly see how non-union people always get the short end of the stick. This service fee is another type of inconvenience you will have to put up with until you're a union member. Chapter 6 will cover how to improve your status to "union."

If you are a union member, you can never be charged a registration fee, as mandated by the Screen Actors Guild. However some agencies avoid the rule by imposing a small "picture fee," which is usually five to fifteen dollars, but no more. Often though, there are no fees for union members.

It is best to call each agency ahead of time to obtain the specific details regarding what you must pay and what you must bring to registration. Usually you'll just need two forms of identification (a driver's license and Social Security Card), and you'll be on your way to working as an extra. But always inquire ahead of time, so as not to waste your time or theirs.

What and How Are Extras Paid?

The pay rate for non-union extras is forty dollars a day, based on eight hours of work—a small pittance for work that can often be exhausting. Paradoxically, the exhaustion is frequently the result of sitting around all day doing nothing. Union "general extra" wages are seventy-two dollars per day, also based on eight hours. (On July 1, 1996, the rate goes up to $79 per day, and on July 1, 1997, it becomes $86 per day). Likewise, this is not a tremendous salary, but keep in mind that many shoots typically run longer than eight hours, usually ten or twelve hours, which will result in overtime. In the event that you go to work and are released after only one or two hours, you'll be pleased to know that you'll still get paid for a minimum of eight hours work! This happens a lot! It surprises some new people, but if you think about it, there would be no justice in scheduling someone for a whole day, and then only paying them for an hour or two of work and sending them home.

Overtime for Extras

Non-union overtime is paid at time-and-a-half for the first two hours after eight hours. After that, you'll receive twice your hourly rate until you've worked sixteen hours in one day. After sixteen hours, known as "golden time," you'll start earning your daily rate every hour. This happens rarely, but when it does you'll feel as if gold coins are falling from the sky.

Union overtime is paid at time-and-a-half for the first four hours of overtime, and twice your hourly rate from twelve to sixteen hours. At "golden time," you'll earn you're daily rate every hour, as do non-union extras. For both union and non-union, overtime is paid in increments of tenths of an hour.

Additionally, there are various pay supplements known as "bumps" that you may receive depending on the requirements of the day. For example, you'll be given additional pay if you wear your own formal clothes, change your own wardrobe several times (if required), use your car in a scene, perform hazardous duties, operate firearms, or wear prosthetics. The amount of these bumps usually varies from five to fifty dollars.

Now That I'm Registered, How Do I Get Work?

Unfortunately, getting work or "getting booked" requires a continual effort on your part. Although you probably will have completed an extensive personal information form at each extras casting agency, most extras casting directors will never look at it. It's simply not worth their time.

Typically, an extras casting director books extras in one of several ways. The most common method is to have a message line, either voice-mail or a continuously repeating loop, which is updated throughout the day with the specific types they are looking for. For example, a typical message might say "we need males, 5'8" to 5'10", ages forty to fifty, with short hair, any race, to play cops." Upon hearing this message, if you fit the description, then you would call the designated number and try to get booked. The extras casting director will either pull your image up on a computer, or pull your picture from a file and check to see if you are, in fact, right for the job. If you are, then you'll most likely get booked.

Another way casting directors fill their needs is by allowing extras to call them directly throughout the day to inquire about work. Some don't prefer unsolicited calls, but many don't mind once they get to know you. A good way to determine how an extras casting director feels about this is to first get booked by responding to a message line, and then ask if you can call them directly in the future for work. If they say it's okay, then be sure to check back with them in a day or two. Don't wait a couple of weeks because they will have forgotten you by then. Extras casting directors deal with hundreds of people every day and have a hard time remembering everyone, especially new people. Also, as a newcomer it's best not to engage these casting directors in long conversations. This is because they are frequently busy and under pressure, with phones ringing off the hook. Over time, progressively develop your relationship and it will become easier to chat and ask about work.

A third way agencies book extras is by having a general work line that actors can call, and if extras are needed, a casting director may pick up. Usually you'll supply three important bits of information: your name, age, and race. They are needed because the requirements for scenes are usually very specific. In no other profession would you be asked such personal questions, but in this line of work such personal data is essential. Think about it. Wouldn't a casting director need a predominance of Chinese people when casting a scene set in Chinatown?

Finally, the last way extras may be booked is through a "calling service." A calling service is a small company, usually one to four people, that has connections with most of the extras casting agencies. They call casting people directly to get you work, and frequently casting people call them to fill work when they are swamped. For instance, a casting director may have to book fifty extras for a show quickly. Rather than put this information on a message line and take calls from countless people who may or may not be right for the job, he or she will contact the calling service and tell them what types are needed. Calling services also usually supply books of their clients to agencies for quick reference. The calling service then does most of the work by gathering up and scheduling a list of people. Essentially, they book the show for the extras casting director. This whole process happens frequently in the world of extras casting.

Thus, calling services are like agents or brokers for extras who want to work regularly. They cannot guarantee employment, but usually can get an extra two to six days of work per week, depending on how much work is available and how good of a calling service they are.

If you are planning on doing extra work on a regular basis, you might consider signing up with a service. The fee is usually about $45 to $55 a month. This may seem expensive, but you might spend this much yourself at pay phones on sets trying to book work during any given month. You should ask the extras casting agencies which calling services they recommend and prefer before picking one.

When You Are Booked

Once you've lined up an extra job, you'll be given a call time, a location address, an assistant director (A.D.) to check in with, and any wardrobe requirements. (Since you won't be getting paid very much, never go and buy clothes specifically for work. You will hardly be noticed working as an extra, and ninety-nine times out of one hundred, the wardrobe you currently own will be suitable.) All you need to concern yourself with is showing up on time, acting professionally, and doing what you're told. Every day will be different. Just have fun!

Getting Booked Is a Part-Time Job Itself

Working regularly as an extra will only come with a lot of effort. If you don't have a calling service, then you will have to do a lot of calling on your own, anywhere from one to one hundred calls a day. Even if you do have one, you'll still need to make some calls, since calling services can't ensure work for every day of the week. At first this process can be frustrating and annoying, but with time, the ritual of searching for work will become second nature to you.

Industry Interview:
Advice from Diana Carroll, Extras Casting Director at Central Casting, on Extra Work

Could you tell me how you go about casting extras? What does your day consist of?

Basically we get calls from assistant directors, A.D.s, and they'll tell us what types they need for tomorrow. Often, we'll cast from people calling us. People call us daily. We ask extras to use call-in lines, and we have personal lines for people that we cast often.

People who are clean-cut, good-looking business types always get cast. They'll be calling in on the lines, and we'll hear their names flying around the room, and we'll pick up. We also go to calling services. They have books of one hundred to two hundred people, depending on the calling service, and we can cast ten people at a time with one phone call. But we do hand-pick each person, and we think about the look that the production company is seeking before we cast somebody.

And it's a pretty busy day?

It's an extremely busy day because phone calls are coming in with orders every hour, and inconsistently too. It could be 12:00 P.M. and I'll get a call, 12:01 P.M. and I'll get another, and at 12:03 another. Or could be that I'm sitting until 4:00 P.M. waiting all day. You never know. Every day is different and everyday is like a roller coaster. Sometimes certain production companies don't need anything the next day, and some days they need tons of people—hundreds of people. However, a typical call is about twenty to fifty people.

So how would you sum up the casting process?

Basically: 1) For something specific I will call a particular person I remember in my head that I've seen before, or 2) I'll go to calling services and handpick people that I think fit the call, or 3) I'll cast from people on the lines—people calling in for work. When I hear their names or when I pick up the phones and they fit something I'm looking for, I'll book them right then.

What are some things that people can do if they want to work regularly as an extra?

There are several things you can do. 1) Get working headshots. Get a picture of yourself, just a generic commercial shot, and maybe some other pictures where you are dressed in different or character ways. Just little snapshots would help, because so often we have to turn in photographs. You'll be open to a lot more possibilities this way—dressed as a homeless person, dressed as a business person, or in a bathing suit (if you're a bathing-suit type of person). Just anything you can think of that we possibly might be casting. If you can show versatile looks with snapshots, it really helps us.

Another way is a calling service. Everyday we call calling services. They're all over L.A. There are about ten or twelve in town and there are a lot of new services cropping up. We probably use about five more often than others. The calling services are a wonderful opportunity for you to get more extra work.

Also, realize the parts that you can play. A lot of people with long hair and trendy looks are wonderful for particular calls, but more often, we have calls for people with short hair to play cops, business types, and clean-cut, conservative types. But I don't encourage anyone with long hair just to cut their hair because of that. I'd just ask them to be a little more patient and understand that work may not happen everyday.

In summary, get headshots that work for you, get a calling service—it does help, and be persistent on the lines. Be very professional about making friends with casting directors. Don't go in to visit when it's not visiting hours. Don't call them twenty times a day on the phone. If they choose to give you their personal line, it's because they think they can work with you. Don't get in their face and say, "I want your personal line!" because that only gets on their nerves.

What words of wisdom would you give someone moving to Los Angeles?
My advice would be to definitely try and do some extra work, and don't listen to stereotypical advice like "Oh my God, you're doing extra work, you'll be pigeon-holed." (Meaning you'll be perceived as an "extra" forever.) If you've never been to this town before, you have no idea what it's like to be on a set. If you actually did get cast as a principal, and you went to a set and lacked that professionalism and the knowledge of how a set runs, you would be in trouble. You'd look like an amateur. So get the experience. Go do that non-union work. Go try and get your SAG card, and get the agent.

If you don't have a lot of experience, perhaps some of the student films or cable TV can help in familiarizing yourself with sets while getting a reel of yourself. I know agents want that too.

Industry Interview:
Advice from Linda Poindexter, Associate Casting Director for "Days of Our Lives," on Soap-Opera Extra Work and Under-Fives

Could you tell me how you go about casting extras and under-fives?
The most important tools I use are pictures and resumes. I need to have eight-by-tens from actors.

The atmosphere parts are filled according to the sets working in each episode. For instance, an upscale restaurant scene requires actors with elegant wardrobes, and the nightclub set calls for actors who are trendy and know how to dance. I look at hundreds of pictures and resumes each day and try to fill the roles with actors that are fitting for each story line and setting. If you are established as a nurse in the hospital, then I won't be calling you to be a cop in the police station.

The under-five roles are cast by having actors do cold readings in my office. A lot of times I know an actor's work from having hired them previously, but if not I have them come to the office and read for me. I try and have general interviews so I can get to know as many actors as possible.

Actors who use beepers tend to work more than those that do not. It's as simple as that. In terms of both atmosphere and under-fives, there isn't a lot of time to wait for people to call back. I have to cast the show for the next day so production can do the preparation and paperwork. We also do contracts on a daily basis for each episode.

We have a call-in line where actors call and leave their availability. My assistant gives me the list of names every morning and I try to hire people on the list because it shows me that those actors are really interested in working.

What should someone do if they want to be hired as an extra or an under-five on a soap?

They should have a professional picture and a resume. That is a necessity. You need to present a professional image, composite, and everything. You can't just take a Polaroid or jot something down on binder paper and send it in.

You need flattering eight-by-ten headshots. However, there's nothing more disconcerting to a casting director when they meet someone and they look nothing like their picture. If you loose or gain a lot of weight, or dye your hair, you should send in new pictures.

Also, most soaps have call-in lines, so call the call-in line. Once a week is fine. A lot of actors send postcards and their effectiveness depends on the casting director. I look at them, and they do jog my memory. We time and date stamp every picture and resume we get. Sometimes someone will send in a picture and I'll call them the next day because I need that type or look. Sometimes people say, "Well I've been sending pictures for a year and haven't heard from you." It's nothing personal, it's just that we get hundreds and hundreds of pictures every week. So if you sent a picture a long time ago and haven't heard anything, I'd send a new picture and just be patient.

*Some people have a misconception that you only need certain types on
soap operas. But you actually cast a wide variety of people, don't you?*

Yes. For instance, tomorrow there are some characters that are
supposed to be in L.A. (Our story takes place in Salem, a fictional town
in the Midwest.) For the L.A. scenes, we need trendy, hip looking people.
And around the holidays we had a homeless story.

There's an image that everyone on soaps has to be beautiful, and to
a point, that's true because a lot of viewers tune in to live this fantasy.
So we can't have really "down" stories. There's a lot of tragedy, but it's
tragedy with beautiful clothes and beautiful people. We try to be as real
as we can. I cast actors from all age and minority groups, and utilize many
different looks.

What should they know and understand as they pursue their career?

People ask me all the time, "If I do extra work, am I ever going to
be considered for a day-player or under-five part?" The answer is it really
depends on the show and on the casting director. On our show, if you
do extra work, it doesn't mean that you'll never be considered for under-
five and day-player parts.

I try to hire people for under-five roles who have done extra work,
for a number of reasons. First, I think it's only fair to give actors a chance
to move up, and if I know the actor and their work, why do I need to go
outside looking for somebody who's never worked in daytime before? It
is also very important because there could be somebody who is a
wonderful actor who's done tons of theatre, but has never been on a
daytime set. We shoot an hour episode every day, so you really can't
afford to hire somebody who doesn't understand how it works—
somebody who doesn't know about blocking or cannot handle the fast-
paced shooting schedule. Though you might be the best stage actor in the
world, you have to really know the genre you're dealing with. So what I
tell people is "No, it will not hurt your career if you do extra work."

Plus, doing extra work in daytime is different than doing extra work
on films. You are treated with a lot of respect, you learn a lot, and
occasionally we upgrade people on the set. If people really have a hang-
up about doing extra work, nobody's going to know anyway. You don't
have to tell people if you think it's beneath you. But I really don't

understand it because extra work pays well in daytime and it's a great experience.

There are several people who started as extras and now have contract parts, or have gone on to work in feature films. If you have a desire to move up, then just make that known. When you get the opportunity, just say you're studying here, or you're studying there, or you're in this showcase, or whatever it is you're doing to promote your acting career.

In terms of how Hollywood works, you hear those vignettes about somebody who was sitting around and they were discovered. That's an exception. You have to help yourself and talk to people. Make connections, and let yourself be known and seen, and do as many showcases as you can. And plays. And study. All that helps you get ahead.

If you had a sister, cousin, or some relative who wanted to start an acting career, what words of wisdom would you offer?

I'd tell them to be realistic. A lot of people come to town and they say, "I've been here three months and nothing has happened!" That's totally unrealistic.

I'd also tell them that it's hard work. You have to be persistent. It's hard work to find an agent. Everybody says "I need an agent but I can't find an agent because I don't have any credits!" So it's a big circle.

I think the biggest mistake is when people say, "My agent tells me that I can't do extra work anymore. But I don't have a job, and I don't know what I'm going to do. Still I can only do under-fives." Well, does your agent pay your rent? If you can earn $128 a day working as an extra on the soaps, why put yourself under that kind of pressure? If your agent is sending you out and you're busy with auditions five days a week, then that's another thing. But if you never hear from them, and you were told you can't do extra work because it will ruin your career, you just have to keep a level head and do what you feel is best.

If you are just moving to town and you get an opportunity to work as an extra on a film or on any television show, then do it and see who you meet and what it's like! Send your picture and resume out to agents and casting directors, and maybe you'll get extra work on the soaps, because there are five or six soaps in L.A. now. Also there's a lot of sitcoms, and they use extras as well. Overall, I would just say you have to do what's good for you.

The other thing that happens is that people I'll call to work will say, "I can't work because I have a bartending job at 12:00 noon." If you're trying to build a career as an actor you need to get a job where you are available during the day. Most shows shoot during the day—not to say that we don't have shoots that go until midnight. But if acting is your priority, you have to be available to work as an actor. If being a bartender is your priority or being a waiter is your priority, that's okay, but if you're here and you want to act, then try to get a job where you can be flexible with your hours.

When you get hired, the most important thing is to be professional. Be on time, bring the right wardrobe, know your lines, and just be professional. I have people that amazingly enough show up a half-hour late. I understand there are emergencies, but being late for your call causes real problems.

And whether you're working as an extra, an under-five, or a day-player, you're important. If you're not there on time, it creates problems for the whole production. A lot of people take that really lightly. They'll be booked as an extra and then they'll leave the set because they get an audition. If you commit to work, then make that your first commitment. Make that your priority for the day. Don't spread yourself so thin that you're trying to work on three shows and you're buzzing all over town because you don't want to miss the next gig. And once you get your foot in the door, be professional and learn as much as you can while you're on the set.

Becoming a Union Member

If you want to play in the big leagues, then you've got to be in the unions.

The Screen Actors Guild (SAG)

There is a long history regarding the development of the Screen Actors Guild, commonly known as SAG. Following in the footsteps of the Actors Equity Association (AEA), which formed in 1913 for theatrical performers, a small group of actors in June of 1933 sought to gain protection from the Hollywood studios, which were increasingly taking advantage of film performers through unregulated hours, substandard working conditions, and terrible pay. Their efforts to form a union were fueled in March 1933 by a 50 percent decrease in salary for contract players. By June, eighteen founding members came together and officially birthed what we know to be the Screen Actors Guild.

Since its formation, the guild has grown to approximately 90,000 members and continues to act in the interests of all professional actors through a process of collective bargaining with producers. Through years of continual negotiation, it has established detailed regulations governing all aspects of employment for union actors working in union projects.

As a new actor in town, you should realize that many actors in the early days risked their careers so that the benefits many take for granted today could be realized. Some of these include high minimum-pay scales, overtime pay, meals and rest areas, and assured payment for services.

As an actor in Hollywood, it is highly recommended that you at some point seek membership in the Screen Actors Guild; that is, if you want to have a career in television or film. Most feature films (the ones you see in theatres and many on video-tape), and television programs are union projects and can hire only SAG performers. (In truth, they can hire non-union performers for their first union job, but this happens rarely and will be discussed later.) Additionally, being a member of the union is important because it legitimizes you as an actor. It distinguishes you from the masses as a serious professional. Unfortunately for newcomers, getting into SAG is a difficult task, as certain requirements must be met.

Television shows taped on video, which include soap operas and sitcoms, fall under the jurisdiction of the American Federation of Radio and Television Artists (AFTRA). Likewise, voice-over artists who do radio commercials, Dee-Jays, and talk show hosts sign contracts that fall under AFTRA's jurisdiction. You will also want to be a member of AFTRA; however, joining is not a problem. It is an open union, as long as you have the money for your initiation fee.

For union theatre work, which is the only type of theatre work that pays, you'll need to be a member of the Actors Equity Association (AEA), commonly referred to as Equity. Though there is some Equity work in L.A., by far the vast majority of acting jobs are in television and film. Therefore, joining Equity isn't a top priority.

SAG's Eligibility Requirements

Becoming a member of SAG is one of the biggest hurdles many newcomers face. You can't just show up and join; you have to become eligible. Once you're eligible, you then have to pay a hefty initiation fee plus semi-annual dues.

Following are several ways a non-union person can beat the system and become eligible to join, as there is no standard route or typical path to follow.

1. Being Employed Under a SAG Contract. This is probably the fastest way to get into SAG. All you have to do is find a producer who will hire you for a principal, or speaking part. Easy enough? That depends. It can be very easy if you know someone in the industry who has the power to hire you—anyone from your director uncle, to the best friend of your mother's brother who's a producer. On the contrary, it can be very difficult if you don't know anyone in town. This is because, to get a union role, you typically need to audition for it, and to audition for it you typically need an agent to arrange it. The catch is that many agents don't bother to represent non-union people or send them to auditions. Interestingly, most producers and directors don't care whether an actor is union or not. All that matters is that they like your acting. So the problem in getting hired really lies with agents—the intermediaries—who often won't look at non-union people or submit them for union parts.

In the event you are hired to work on a union project, then the Taft-Hartley Law will be applied to you. It states that a non-union performer can be hired to work as a union performer, and then work union for another thirty days, but after that time period that person must join the union if he or she wants to work "union" again. Thus, when you are Taft-Hartley'd you become eligible to join SAG. To join, you simply need to have a letter from a producer of a SAG-signatory project that states he or she plans to hire you for his or her particular production.

2. You've Worked a Principal Role in Another Union. If you have been a paid-up member of an affiliated performer's union for at least one year, and you have worked at least once as a principal performer in that union's jurisdiction, then you are eligible to join SAG. The affiliated performer's unions are: AFTRA (American Federation of Television & Radio Artists), AEA (Actors Equity Association), AGVA (American Guild of Variety Artists), AGMA (American Guild of Musical Artists), and ACTRA (Alliance of Canadian Cinema, T.V., and Radio Artists). To join, you need to mail a copy of your principal performer's contract to the SAG membership office. Once your eligibility has been verified, you will be contacted to schedule an appointment.

3. You Have Worked as a SAG Extra Player for Three Days. As with being cast in a principal part, a Catch-22 exists when attempting to work as a union extra when you are non-union. The problem is that you're not supposed to do union extra work if you're non-union; but to be eligible to join SAG, non-union people have to do union extra work for three days. It sounds crazy and it is, but there are several ways to accomplish this. A surprising number of professional actors today were able to join SAG by working as a union extra for three days at some point early in their career.

Working "union" as an extra is simply a technicality, as both union and non-union folks show up to work together and perform the same duties. The difference is this: when extras come to work, they receive either a non-union or a union voucher, depending on their status, which serves as a time card and receipt for the day's work. If you are non-union, your mission is to get one of those union vouchers.

The number of people who work union and non-union on any given production varies by the type of project and the location. For the L.A. zone, SAG rules state that on television shows, at least fifteen extras must be union members. All the rest, above and beyond fifteen, can be non-union. On films, the first thirty extras must be union. After thirty, all others can be non-union. Thus, on a call for three hundred people for a film, only thirty have to be union. By those numbers, one can see that union vouchers are scarce and a commodity valued by non-union performers.

Below are several methods crafty non-union people can use to accomplish the challenging feat of obtaining union vouchers:

• **Method A: Utilizing Your Unique Skills.** One way to work as a union extra (when you're not) is to always pay attention to the unusual needs of the extras agencies. Many have special union message lines, that list the types of union people they need throughout the day. You should always listen to these, even though you may be non-union. Though generic types are often being sought, occasionally a more specific type is requested that is not so readily available. In such cases, non-union people are sometimes booked if appropriate union people cannot be found. For instance, out-of-the-ordinary requests include: surfers with specific haircuts and/or surf boards, jugglers, horseback riders, dancers with specialized skills, collegiate-level athletes, very short or tall people, amputees, and more. In addition, stand-ins are often needed who match exact sizes and have strong resemblances to principal actors. So tune in! If you have any specialized skills or look like a particular actor, you will be needed at some point in time. By paying attention to what is being cast every chance you get, you will be able to land some union extra work.

(Keep in mind that if an extras casting agency is simply looking for "union women in mid-twenties with brown hair," you probably have little chance of being booked if you are non-union. You might even upset a casting director. The obvious reason is that there are plenty of union women who fit that category.)

• **Method B: Befriending the Second Assistant Director on the Set.** When you arrive on a set as a non-union extra, there is still a possibility to work union. After you check in and receive your voucher from the second assistant director (or the second second assistant director or a production assistant), take note of whether there are any unclaimed union vouchers. This happen when union extras fail to arrive. If it's already twenty minutes past the check-in time and the assistant director is still clutching a union voucher, then tactfully inquire about it. You might be able to exchange your non-union voucher for a shiny new union one. (Be aware that some A.D.s hate to be asked for vouchers. Just be polite when asking and don't take it personally if their response is less than cordial.)

Smart extras even ask for union vouchers when they don't see any, because sometimes they are hidden or tucked away. The moral is: If you never ask, then you'll never receive anything. If you ask all of the time, then eventually you will get something. This not only applies to extra work but to every aspect of life as well. Little children are experts at this.

• **Method C: The Schmooze.** Get to know people! Above all, this is the easiest way to get your vouchers. You might even make some new friends in the process.

Every extras casting agency has visiting hours once a week. If you're intelligent and really craving those union vouchers, you should go as often as allowable. These informal sessions are great opportunities for casting people to get to know you and for you to express your interest in union work. They also give you a chance to practice your communication skills. Just be yourself, and always bring a headshot/resume with you so they have something by which to remember you. Learning to deal with these casting people will only help you when the time comes to deal with those who cast principal parts on television and in films.

Industry Interview:
Advice from Diana Carroll, Extras Casting Director at Central Casting, on Becoming SAG-Eligible

What would you say to newcomers who are trying to get into SAG by doing extra work? What are some ways to approach it and ways not to approach it?

This is a good question. I get this every day. I have people call me up out of the blue and say, "Can you help me get my SAG card!" My heart goes out to them. I'd love to, but I just can't help everybody.

The best and most professional way to go about it is to send a headshot and just a brief explanation of themselves and what they hope to do, and express that if there is anyway possible I can help them in the future, they would appreciate it. And usually in the end, I will end up helping them. It just happens that they will be in mind because they approached me so politely. Or they'll come in during visiting hours, and they happen to fit something I'm looking for, and of course, then it's easy.

Another way is that people happen to be on a set where some union people haven't shown up. This is called "speccing," and I don't really condone this, but I have seen people get their SAG cards this way. They'll find out about sets and the call-times, where they are, and go to a few of them everyday, and hope that a SAG person doesn't show up. They hope they fit the call and try to get on it. It's a very difficult way to do it, and usually ends up with rejection, but some people have done it successfully.

Or they'll be on a set as a non-union extra and they'll get bumped up because of a special bit or because someone on the crew happens to take a liking to you. There's a little favoritism sometimes.

So the basic way to do it is to do non-union for a while, and get to know some union casting directors by mailing in your headshots and doing it professionally, as opposed to just coming in and begging or coming in at an inopportune time saying "Please, Please, Please!" That only turns someone off when they are busy. You should come in on visiting days and profess that you're interested in getting your SAG card. Come in professionally, but don't beg, just say "If there's any chance, I'm always here" and leave a headshot. It takes persistence and it takes patience.

Once you do non-union for a while, you start getting that professionalism that gets noticed by us, because we go on the sets and we check-in extras on the set. Non-union casting directors and union casting directors work together too. If you get to know a non-union casting director really well, and they want to do you a favor, they'll come to us and say, "Please book this person. They're really wonderful and they really want their SAG card." And we always do it. It works out fine that way. That's the professional way to do it.

What to Expect When You Join

The cost of joining SAG is a one-time fee of $1044.00 plus semi-annual dues starting at $42.50 (based on your previous year's SAG earnings), paid on May 1 and November 1 every year. This is a hefty sum, but remember the union has a lot to offer. Currently principal performers (actors with speaking parts) earn a minimum of $522.00 per day. (On 7/1/96 it will become $540.00, and on 7/1/97 it will becomed $559.00.) This minimum is known as "scale" for day-players. There are also other minimums for three days, five days, and a huge set of tables that determine residual payments for movies, TV shows, and commercials that run more than once. Also remember that you are paying for the benefit of having assistance, should you ever have a grievance with your employer.

Regarding AFTRA

As mentioned earlier, AFTRA governs television programs shot on video, such as sitcoms and soap operas, as well as radio. Anyone can join AFTRA at anytime. The initiation is a one time fee of $800.00, plus semi-annual dues of $42.50 a year. Many actors do this when they first come to Hollywood, but it's really not necessary. Although you will eventually want to join AFTRA, you can work on an AFTRA program as a principal or extra for thirty days without being a member. After that, AFTRA will hold any future checks until your initiation fee is paid off in full. (However, if you land an AFTRA principal role and are non-SAG, then pay off AFTRA's initiation fee immediately so that you will be able to join SAG in a year. See number 2 on SAG's Eligibility Requirements). There is also talk of AFTRA merging with SAG, so who knows what will happen to dues when and if that happens.

The Benefits of Being in the Unions

Being a member of the unions has many great benefits, in addition to the most important ones, like having minimum contract requirements negotiated in advance through collective bargaining, and having assistance in the event of an employer dispute. Some of these include free assistance with income tax preparation (SAG's VITA Program), a SAG-AFTRA credit union that also offers members low-interest credit cards, casting lines by SAG and AFTRA that list casting announcements, and bulletin boards in union offices with notices posted by other members regarding apartments or houses for rent, automobiles for sale, airline tickets, and a few other things from time to time.

Another important benefit of being a union member is health insurance for qualified performers. In SAG, a performer must earn a minimum of $7,500 (in reported earnings from SAG acting jobs) within four consecutive calendar quarters to be qualified for free basic health insurance, which kicks in three months after the close of the qualifying quarter. Performers earning more than $15,000 in any four consecutive quarters qualify for additional benefits that include dental, mental health/chemical dependency, and life insurance coverage. AFTRA members must earn $7,500 in a calendar year to qualify themselves for coverage and earn $15,000 in a calendar year to qualify their dependents for coverage.

Another great aspect to union membership is access to agents and casting directors through guild-sponsored seminars and showcases. Actors can attend these free events by pre-registering in advance. The focus of some events is purely informational, while others offer actors an opportunity to showcase scenes or perform cold readings for industry people. In addition, another organization, the SAG Conservatory, offers classes and workshops, along with "question and answer" evenings with prominent casting directors in town. All of these events are also free of charge.

A Final Note about Gaining Union Status

It's important to remember that while becoming a union member is an important step on the road to being a successful actor in Hollywood, it by no means ensures that you'll suddenly become a hot commodity. Keep in mind that there are already approximately 90,000 members!

One of the drawbacks of joining the union is that, once you are a member, you are not supposed to perform non-union work anymore, excluding student and graduate films. Thus, some industry people suggest you at least get some experience under your belt before rushing to join the union, because a resume with no credits doesn't mean much, regardless of union status. Your credits and experience will still be very important. And since we're on the topic of resumes, it's time to focus on how to put together a professional-looking resume and how to get an outstanding picture of yourself that will hopefully bring you the attention you deserve.

The Screen Actors Guild is located at 5757 Wilshire Blvd., Los Angeles, CA 90036; (213) 954-1600.

The American Federation of Television and Radio Artists is located at 6922 Hollywood Blvd., Hollywood, CA 90078; (213) 461-8111.

CHAPTER SEVEN

You'll Need a Great Headshot

As a new actor in Hollywood, you will definitely need fantastic pictures of yourself, at least until you're very well-established and your work remains firmly planted in the minds of casting directors, directors, and producers. These pictures, most often referred to as "headshots," are your calling cards and you will go through hundreds, if not thousands, of them while seeking opportunities to work. It will be important to have headshots that show you looking your best, while at the same time, still looking like you.

If you are moving to L.A. from another part of the country, then you might wait until you arrive to have new pictures taken. You will find a greater selection of talented photographers who know what is acceptable and stylish, in terms of headshots. There will also be many more places where you can get quality reproductions at affordable prices.

How to Find a Photographer

Finding a good photographer is a relatively easy task. As with actors, L.A. seems to have a plethora of skilled photographers, and a few you'd probably want to avoid. Locating the right one for you will require some investigation on your part, but if you know where to look and what questions to ask, it won't be a difficult undertaking.

Probably the best way to find a good photographer is by referral. If you have a friend with a dynamite headshot, ask who photographed it. Perhaps you'll see some headshots of actors in an acting class or while at an audition. Be sure to ask them the photographer's name. Or if you have an agent or a friend in the industry, ask them too. They'll most likely be able to give you several names. This is the quickest, easiest way to find the photographer you're looking for. You won't have to be "sold": you'll already know that you or someone you respect likes the product.

Two more sources of photographers are *Drama-Logue* and *Back Stage West*, two weekly newspapers for actors in L.A. In addition to articles, casting notices, and reviews, these papers are filled with numerous photographers' ads, usually displaying a sample or two of their work. It's not a foolproof method of finding the perfect photographer, but it helps in locating a photographer that might suit you. You should also check theatre bookstores, such as Samuel French (7623 Sunset Blvd. or 11963 Ventura Blvd.), where many photographers advertise in a variety of actors' monthly, quarterly, and annual resource guides.

Your next step will be to contact the photographer and find out what types of packages are offered. In L.A., the cost of hiring a photographer varies a lot, and the expensive ones aren't necessarily the best! So have a price range in mind, and if the photographer's quote falls within your budget, then make an appointment to review their book. Their book, or portfolio, contains examples of their best work. Most reputable photographers have one.

You ought to meet with several photographers before choosing one to take your pictures. Sometimes people get overly excited about the first person they meet. Just remember there is no hurry. Taking a week to check out different people will not be wasted time. In the long run, you'll be glad you did.

There are several important topics you should cover with every photographer you meet. I've listed below many common concerns that should be addressed during your initial visit.

What Will the Session Cost? The cost of headshots varies tremendously, ranging from $50 to $500, and even higher. The more expensive photographers aren't always the best, so you really have to choose one based on quality, and not just price. Despite the big difference, the average cost usually runs between $100 and $250.

How Many Rolls of Film Are Included in the Session? Most photographers offer package deals, where they typically will shoot two or three rolls of you. Other photographers simply shoot on a "per-roll basis," from one to as many as you'd like. It's a good idea to do at least two rolls, so that you have a great selection to choose from. But don't go overboard—there is no reason to shoot ten rolls of film.

How Many Eight-by-Tens Will I Get? Most photographers will blow up one eight-by-ten of your choice for each roll they shoot. Thus, a three-roll shoot will yield three eight-by-tens, which is more than enough. You won't want to blow up and reproduce any more than that, because it gets extremely expensive, and for most people it's unnecessary (unless you are a character actor with many distinct looks). Some photographers don't offer any eight-by-tens in their packages, and if that's the case, then be sure to find out how much they will cost when it comes time to order.

Will the Shoot Be Indoors or Outdoors? Some photographers only shoot one way or the other; others are well-equipped to do both. It's really a personal choice for the actor. Generally, people with more of a "street look" or an active, athletic image tend to get their pictures taken outdoors, to complement their personality. Those shots are softer, and more lightly textured. People who tend to be more upscale, conservative, or glamorous usually go for indoor lighting, which is sharper, crisper, and filled with more contrast. However, there is no firm rule on which types of photos you need to have. It's purely a personal choice.

Who Keeps the Negatives? About half of all the photographers in L.A. will give you the negatives back after your film is developed. This is good because you can have headshots blown up rather easily, without having to ask the photographer to do it and then waiting several days. It's also advantageous because you have complete control over the negatives—you and only you can blow up pictures and use them in whatever way you please. They become your property.

Of the photographers who choose to keep the negatives themselves, some will charge you their cost for blowing up shots, without making any money on them. Others tack on a few extra dollars to the cost of each print. Be sure to ask the cost so that you're not shocked when the time comes to order.

How Much Do Prints Cost? Typically, a good original eight-by-ten print will cost ten to fifteen dollars, when reproduced on good paper at a quality lab. While you certainly could get it done for less, most photographers use quality film labs that can create a superior original from which you'll make cheaper mass reproductions.

How Many Different Looks Am I Allowed During the Shoot? This varies from photographer to photographer, but typically most suggest or allow one look per roll. You won't want to change wardrobe every five pictures anyway. You'll want to have a large pool of shots to choose from, so that it doesn't come down to, "Well, I like the clothes in those five shots, but none of the smiles are nice."

It's a good idea to know what specific type of wardrobe you want beforehand, rather than trying out many different looks during your shoot. Doing that will only make you more nervous and cause you to feel under pressure to present a perfect pose for every single shot.

Will the Actor Be Responsible for Hair and Make-up, or Will the Photographer or a Make-up Artist Take Care of It? Men generally wear little make-up during their photo shoots and their hair is usually low-maintenance, so this is not an issue for them—though it's still a good idea to cover up dark circles under your eyes and get rid of any shine on your face with some powder, regardless of your gender. Usually the photographer will take care of this.

However, women especially will want to clarify this issue with the photographer. Many photographers suggest that you come made-up beforehand, and they then add some finishing touches. In some instances, the photographer may recommend a make-up artist to assist, which can cost an additional forty to seventy-five dollars.

Is There a Satisfaction Guarantee? Most photographers will re-shoot your pictures in the event of a lighting or exposure problem, or if the style is not what you had specifically requested. But don't assume this, so be sure to ask. However, poor facial expressions or postures are your responsibility. Therefore, you'll probably be at a loss if you try to get pictures retaken just because you didn't come across as charmingly as you would have liked.

Choosing the Right Photographer

Overall, there are really three factors you should weigh when selecting a photographer. One of the most important is cost. You have to go with someone you can afford. Don't spend $500 if you don't have it, because you will have duplication costs as well. Granted, you might get some great pictures with an experienced and expensive photographer, but if cash is limited, there are still many photographers in L.A. who can take excellent pictures for less.

Another important factor is quality. On the contrary, don't choose someone just because they're fee is dirt cheap—you'll probably have to have your pictures retaken again by someone else. That is why it's strongly recommended that you visit at least five photographers before choosing one. You'll be coming from a much more knowledgeable and informed viewpoint when interpreting the quality of any particular person's work.

The third factor, often overlooked, is compatibility. Even if the cost of a photographer's services is within your range and the quality of work is exceptional, you'll be taking a risk by hiring him or her if you don't relate well. You must share the same vision and have a mutual understanding of how you want your pictures to come out, or it is pointless. If you don't feel comfortable or relaxed, the tension will inevitably come through in your pictures. Therefore, having some type of compatibility, whether on a friendly or professional level, will make all the difference in the world.

Appropriate Wardrobe for Pictures

Once you've decided on a photographer and have set up a time to shoot your pictures, choosing your wardrobe will be the next important decision. You'll have to ask yourself a few questions. What type of person are you? Are you a character actor or a leading man/woman? Are you a street type, or are you more refined-looking? Are you warm and fuzzy, or are you intense and commanding? You should think about these questions and take a few moments to think about what types of roles you are suited for. For now, forget about being able to play a wide spectrum of roles. Just think about how people will see you. Ask your friends for their honest opinions.

If you're more of a street type, you might wear a leather jacket, jeans, and a tee-shirt. More conservative-looking people usually wear dressier shirts, vests, sweaters, or sport coats.

Some go purely for a business look, with men wearing a coat and tie, and women wearing an elegant suit, dress, or sweater. By far, older actors tend to go for more conservative looks, while younger actors are more street-oriented. But don't feel as though the boundaries can't be crossed. Just go with what suits you.

Whatever you wear, make sure it has some style to it and be certain it makes you feel comfortable. That means: no out-of-date ties, jackets that are too small, bell-bottoms (unless you are extremely hip and trendy), or high-water pants. In terms of color, don't wear solid shirts that are similar in tone to your skin color. They blend too closely and get lost in one another. Don't wear any extremely busy patterns either, as they will detract too much from your face, which should be the main focus. It's better to wear textured clothing, or colors that offer a nice contrast to your complexion. Your photographer will probably offer you some suggestions before your shoot.

The Day of Your Shoot

Though you won't want to make a big production out of getting your pictures taken (because it only creates nerves), you should do several things that will help make everything flow nicely. First, be sure to get a lot of rest the night before. Make-up covers a lot, but it can't replicate the unique glow that a well-rested, relaxed face gives off. Second, try to exercise a few hours before your shoot. This creates a radiant youthful look, from increased circulation and endorphins released throughout your body. Third, give yourself ample time to prepare your wardrobe (and make-up, if necessary), and enough time to get to your photographer's location. Many photographers book clients in one- or two-hour blocks, so you need to show up on time. Running late will only make you edgy. And finally, relax and enjoy your shoot. If it helps, bring some music that makes you feel good and play it during the session. Do whatever it takes to feel comfortable.

The Best Pictures and Current Styles

After you've had your photo shoot, within a few days you'll get proof sheets of the negatives. Hopefully you'll be pleased with them. From these you'll choose the best shots, and there will probably be several great shots on each roll. When making your selections, you should look for pictures that capture one of two things: either your true personality, or the personality you want to portray. The first is much easier to do for newcomers, and probably much safer. Look for shots with natural expressiveness that aren't too posed. The second type, shots that reflect a certain image you want to portray (i.e., the hunk, the villain, the nerd), can be difficult to use as an actor if you don't really have a definite grasp on the types of parts you are well-suited for—and many newcomers don't. But if you're certain you're a villain or a demented scientist, then zero in on that particular niche.

It's always good to ask someone else for their opinion. Sometimes we're biased when it comes to judging ourselves. Therefore, consult a friend, preferably a working actor, as to which shots they like. If you have an agent, then they will probably advise you. Your photographer will more than likely point out their favorites too.

In your decision-making process, don't worry too much about having the "perfect" picture, because they really don't exist. Headshots are photography, and photography is art, and evaluations of art will always be subjective. No matter how good a picture might be, there will always be someone who doesn't like it for some reason. So just pick the ones about which you and your advisers feel most passionate.

The key is to have pictures that look like you, while you're looking good—very, very good. If you are considering reproducing a photo that looks marvelous but distorts your image in a significant way, whether it be through heavy make-up, an unusual hair-style (one-of-a-kind or super-poofy), or an uncharacteristic expression, you will be wasting your money. The reason is that casting directors and agents will be expecting to see the look on your headshot, and not anything else. So make sure that the picture looks like you!

But don't misunderstand. Your picture shouldn't depict you as mediocre, average, or boring. It has to catch the attention of casting directors as they weed through stacks and stacks of other headshots. Make sure your photo gives off a positive, honest, and likeable image. It must stand out by conveying an intriguing yet approachable persona.

For theatrical roles, you will want to have a headshot that conveys a somewhat serious, dramatic look, but not too overdone or melodramatic. Pictures that can express vulnerability and strength at the same time are great. A few actors can get away with a pouty look too. For commercial roles, you will want more upbeat pictures that express warmth and enthusiasm. You'll want to show off your smile and your teeth, as a majority of commercials need happy people. (But if you don't think you're a commercial type, don't be discouraged. There are plenty of spots that also call for character types—the more unusual and funny-looking, the better).

Three-Quarter Shots: A Recent Trend

In recent years, a growing number of actors have started using three-quarter shots in addition to traditional headshots. These shots are appropriately named because they typically display three-quarters of the body, from the head to the thighs or knees. They are particularly popular with commercial agents and commercial casting directors because they reveal more about one's appearance. Not only can they see your face, but also your proportions, weight, and overall presence.

It's a good idea to have a three-quarter shot of yourself in addition to the standard headshot. It will give you and your agent an option when submitting for a part. However, many casting directors say that a good picture, regardless of whether it's a headshot or three-quarter shot, is more important.

Reproducing Pictures

Once you've settled on one or two favorite pictures, you will need to get them reproduced in mass quantities, for auditions and mailings. In L.A., there are two common methods of duplication, photographic prints or lithographs, also known as lithos. Photographic prints are reproduced on photographic paper and look the best. However, they are considerably more expensive. The process involves taking a precision photograph of your eight-by-ten original, which becomes an eight-by-ten negative. From that negative, duplicates are created in mass quantities on either matte or glossy photographic paper. They come very close to replicating the original. Prices vary depending on quantity, but the average cost for an order of 100 glossies runs approximately fifty to seventy dollars. Matte paper, which some feel is a bit classier, is slightly more expensive. In addition, there is usually a one-time charge of ten to fifteen dollars for the negative, plus a five to ten dollar typesetting fee if you want your name to appear on the eight-by-ten. Most people do. (At most places, however, you can avoid this fee by typesetting your name on a computer yourself and bringing it in with your order.)

Lithographs are reproduced onto non-photographic paper, as heavy as card-stock, and are less expensive. You can get three hundred copies for approximately sixty-five to seventy-five dollars. The drawback to lithos is that contrast can be lost, sometimes up to 30 percent, which can make a great photograph look average. However, when using a reputable lithographer, the risk is diminished. If you are doing mass mailings—especially for non-union and college films, you might use lithos to save considerable money.

Where to Have Them Reproduced

There are many different duplication houses in L.A., and prices usually don't vary too much because there is tremendous competition. Below is a list of some of the photo-duplicators that many actors frequently use:

For Photographic Duplication:

- Duplicate Photo, 1522 N. Highland Ave., Hollywood, CA 90028. Tel: (213) 466-7544.
- Ipso Lipojian, 3108 W. Magnolia Blvd., Burbank, CA 91505. Tel: (818) 848-9001. Also at: 1237 N. Highland Ave., Hollywood, CA 90038.
- Producers & Quantity Photo, 6660 Santa Monica Blvd., Hollywood, CA 90038. Tel: (213) 462-1334.
- Quality Photo, 142 N. La Brea, Hollywood, CA 90036. Tel: (213) 938-0174.

For Lithographs:

- Anderson Graphics, 6037 Woodman Ave., Van Nuys, CA 91401. Tel: (818) 909-9100.
- Final Print, 1958 N. Vann Ness Ave., Hollywood, CA 90068. Tel: (213) 466-0566. Also at: 6305 Yucca St., Los Angeles, CA 90028.
- Graphic Reproductions, 1423 N. La Brea Ave., Hollywood, CA 90028. Tel: (213) 874-4335.

- Paper Chase Printing, 7176 Sunset Blvd., L.A., CA 90046. Tel: (213) 874-2300.

Industry Interview:
Advice from Michael Helms, Photographer, on Taking Good Pictures

Could you tell me about your idea of an ideal photo session?

The ideal photo session involves many elements. Before the shoot, you should meet with your agent and/or manager to decide what images are being sought. A stylist should be consulted for clothing and accessories. A hair and make-up artist should also be consulted. All too often, because of budgetary concerns, clients sacrifice some or all of these. With that in mind, here are a few suggestions:

Ultimately, actors should "be themselves." What you wear greatly affects how you are perceived. Therefore, it is important to wear clothing that reflects the "image" you are trying to project. Put your money where you make your money. If you look rather "momish" it would not be wise to compete with "beach bunny" types. Conversely, if you're young, blonde, and blue-eyed, the chance of being cast as a D.A. is slim. Ask your agent, manager, and/or acting coach—"What is my type?"; "How will I be cast?" We are all multi-faceted, but remember (especially those just starting out), lead with your strength. Decide what "looks" you want well in advance of your session, then dress accordingly for your photos.

There are a few things you should avoid simply because they rarely work well in photographs. Avoid solid white, deep "V" necks (unless a more sexy image is desired), tank tops, tube tops, sleeveless and short sleeve tops. Avoid busy patterns, i.e., plaids, paisley, polka dots, large checks, big prints; and leave your Hawaiian shirt at home. Generally, the idea is not to compete with your clothes for attention.

Hair and make-up also affect how you are perceived. Rarely can a client "do their own" and have it look as if it were done professionally. Make-up for a photo session (even very "natural" looking make-up) is not what you wear on the street. What the camera sees is different than what the human eye sees, so professional hair and make-up artists custom blend their products to enhance the faces of their clients.

Michael Helms can be contacted at (818) 899-8002.

EIGHT

Putting Together a Professional Resume

In addition to a great head-shot, you'll also need another very important selling-tool: a professional resume. Just like anyone else in the job world, you, as an actor, will need to compose a fantastic resume that will clearly and effectively help sell yourself to potential agents, casting directors, directors, and producers.

In the entertainment business, actors submit their headshots and resumes together. The resume is attached to the back side of the eight-by-ten picture, usually with rubber cement or staples. (Paper clips, tape, or glue that wrinkles the paper are not recommended.) The resume will include several very important things about you as an actor. First, it will list your acting experience, such as any film, television, theatre, and commercial work you've done. (It won't include non-acting employment, such as summer lifeguard jobs, congressional internships, or professional employment in any another field.) Second, it will detail your education and training as an actor, which includes any high school, college, and professional experiences. Finally, it will list any and all special skills you have, which hopefully will be needed sometime in the future.

The presentation and format of your resume is crucial if you want to be taken seriously. I can't tell you how many new people in Hollywood goof up this important step for just getting your foot in the door. So many young, intelligent actors with college and/or community experience come to this town with improperly formatted resumes. Others with little or no experience almost always have a poor resume too. The result is that you look like an amateur. And while in truth you might be an amateur, you won't want people to think you are. Therefore, you'll need to know the right way to display your credentials in a professional manner, whether you're the star in Small Town, USA or just starting out.

For younger, inexperienced actors, the thought of creating a resume can be an unpleasant one, to say the least, since often there is little or no information to give. If you are in this situation, don't panic! There are several honest ways to expand your resume, and they will be discussed at the end of the chapter.

Following is a breakdown of how to write a typical Hollywood acting resume. You'll find explanations of how to present information and why you should do it that way. There is also a sample resume immediately following to help tie all of this information together.

Your Name

This is the very first item on your resume. Many feel it should stand out, but not overwhelmingly. It can be a font size larger than the text or simply bolded or italicized, but whatever you do, don't make it one or two inches tall just to fill space. The general consensus is that gigantic names look funny to agents and casting directors. If anything, it might draw attention to the fact that someone doesn't have a lot of experience.

If you have a fairly common name and are non-union, you might want to check with SAG and AFTRA to see whether or not someone in the union already has it. The reason is that no two people in a union can share names that are spelled or sound the same. Thus, if your name is Hank Smith and someone else in SAG is named Hank Smith, you're going to have to use a different name when you eventually join SAG. Therefore, it might be a good idea to start using a stage name now that you won't have to change down the road. For example, if your middle name is Dean, you could be Hank D. Smith, Hank Dean Smith, Hank Dean, or really anything you want. It really doesn't matter, as long as no one else in the union uses it.

Union Affiliations

Underneath your name, any union affiliations are listed (e.g., SAG, AFTRA, AEA, etc.). If you are eligible to join a union like SAG but haven't joined (most likely because you don't have the money), then write "SAG-eligible." This helps to legitimize you in some people's eyes. If you have no union affiliations, then don't write anything. Keep in mind that most people won't be looking to see whether or not you're in SAG or AFTRA, except for some agents. A killer smile or mysterious eyes will grab someone's attention much better than any union affiliation.

A Contact Number

You'll need to include a telephone number where someone can contact you or your agent (if you have one). Instead of using a home telephone number, many actors opt for a voice-mailbox for messages, which generally runs eight to twelve dollars a month in the L.A. area. The reason is that in the event your picture ends up in the hands of a pervert, you wouldn't want to be harassed at home. This probably won't happen, but nonetheless it's just one reason why most actors (especially females) choose a voice-mailbox. Another reason is that you will never be caught off-guard. Murphy's Law dictates that when you're in the midst of an argument, or you've just stepped out of the shower, or you're stone-cold asleep, a new agent or casting person will call and want to speak with you. By having a voice-mailbox, you have the chance to be prepared and fully conscious whenever you are speaking to someone regarding your career.

Many actors also have pagers so that agents or casting people can reach them immediately. This is highly recommended. They are vital in this business, so plan on getting one. Some people own them and others rent. The cost is anywhere from $60 to $120 to buy one, with typical monthly fees about $10. Renters generally pay $12–$14 a month.

Your pager number is usually placed under the first contact number on your resume; that is, if you don't have an agent's number to list.

Vital Statistics

Get ready to reveal some of your most closely guarded secrets. Imagine applying for a job at a company and having to give them your weight!

Outrageous? Yes. But in the acting business, it's completely okay. In fact, casting directors need to know as many things about your appearance as they can to see if you're a possibility for a part.

Vital statistics include height, weight, hair and eye color. It is advised that you be truthful with this information, though with weight, a few pounds here or there won't make a difference. (No one is going to weigh you!) You will not necessarily help yourself by stating that you are much taller or slimmer than you really are, because casting people will discover the truth when you show up—and they will be expecting whatever sizes you've stated you're going to be. Parts are cast for people of all heights and sizes, so don't be self-conscious about whether you're the right size.

However, if you feel you want to be slightly taller on paper, then put down your height when you are wearing shoes with thick soles (excluding platform shoes!). After all, you'll be wearing shoes at auditions. With regard to hair, some suggest using descriptive adjectives to complement your hair color. For instance, instead of "brown" some might put "chestnut brown" or "dark brown." For blonde, it's important to specify "light blonde," "sandy blonde," or maybe even "golden blonde."

A side note: An agent friend kindly told me one time that "blonde" is for women and "blond" is for men. No one had ever taught me that, so be sure to use the correct spelling when submitting. (But keep in mind, most people aren't going to hold any one thing against you, especially something like the spelling of blonde. It's just that the more intelligent you are on your resume, the better it will reflect on you.)

Film, Television, and Theatre Experience

These are all fairly self-explanatory categories. While there is no rule carved in stone about how these should be listed, most people with a lot of experience tend to separate each category and then list work under each appropriate heading. Others who are fairly new sometimes combine them into "Film & Television" and "Theatre," and still others leave out "Film & Television" completely if they have no experience in that area. In L.A., film and television appear before theatre because that is the main industry here.

Be sure to include all experience, unless you have numerous jobs and plays to choose from. Most people generally list the most recent work first, especially for television and film. For theatre, most list the most prestigious work first (i.e., Broadway, Off-Broadway, Off-Off-Broadway, community, college, high school, and so on).

Also, if you have any industrial or training film experience, then either list it under "Film" or create a separate category for it. (Industrial or training films are used by companies to train employees or to instruct clients on the use of products/services. For example: the mini-movie you see on airplanes about seat belt safety is an industrial film.)

Commercials

On 99 percent of all resumes in this town, you will see something like "List available upon request" or simply "Upon Request" after this heading. This is because commercial agents don't want casting directors to be influenced by what you may or may have not done in the past. For example, unlike films and television shows, many ad agencies want fresh, new faces—not someone who's been overexposed in ten commercials over the last year. Therefore, it's wise to just say "Upon Request." (No one will ever ask for a detailed list anyway.) Conversely, if you've done nothing, you wouldn't want anyone to know that either, so "Upon Request" is a good filler. So most find it to the actor's advantage to simply say "Upon Request" when it comes to commercials.

You should know that at certain times you will never be considered for a commercial if you have a conflict, meaning you've done a commercial spot for a competitor. For example, if you just did an MCI commercial, you won't be considered to sell the True Rewards of AT&T.

If you are seeking commercial representation and you have commercial experience, you should by all means mention it when you contact the agent. Either explain all your commercial experience in your cover letter, or make a special resume which lists the experience (i.e., McDonald's, Xerox, Kellogg's, etc.). This will help you tremendously.

Training

Here you should list all professional study, college training, private coaching, and any weekend workshops or seminars that you have attended. If you have a degree, say so—even if it's in another field. (This is the only place to list your non-acting credentials.) Actors with only a college degree in acting, or just a few classes under their belt often list them all. Put down anything you can think of.

If you haven't had any training, then you should probably get some. While training isn't absolutely essential (as several of today's great stars have never taken an acting class in their lives), it gives you credibility. It makes a casting director feel safer when calling you in. It also can make you a much better actor. So train as much as you can afford to.

Special Skills

This is the final category on your resume. You should fill this with every activity you can do reasonably well. This category is most often referenced by commercial casting directors who need special skills for commercials.

Below is a listing of useful skills that actors have. While you won't need to know how to do all of them, knowing just a few of them might help you to get a part someday. Use this list to guide you in creating your own.

Sports: martial arts, basketball, football, baseball, ice hockey, tennis, swimming, surfing, soccer, bowling, billiards, fencing, horseback riding, gymnastics, tumbling, boxing, roller skating, rollerblading, weight training, golf, frisbee, archery, rodeo, etc.

Arts: dancing (ballroom, hip-hop, jazz, square dance, others), musical instruments, singing (opera/classical, cabaret, pop, rock, jazz, R&B), art (drawing, painting, sculpture), comedy (stand-up, physical).

Unique skills: juggling (2-ball, 3-ball, pins, knives, etc.), contortionist, magician, card dealer, firearms expert, auctioneer, yoga, stilts, tightrope, etc.

Dialects: the more specific the better. (e.g., "Kentucky" is better than "Southern," "Brooklyn" is better than "New York.")

Accents: (e.g., German, Russian, French, British, Spanish, etc.) You should only put these down if you are proficient at them.

What to Do When You've Got Limited Experience

There are two schools of thought when it comes to writing your resume. The first is that you should be as honest as possible: If you haven't had any experience, then be up-front about it and use your enthusiasm to get work. The second is that you should creatively write your resume, stretching a truth here or there, to make you look like you're not a total novice.

Most industry people advocate honesty for a couple of reasons. One is that it's simply the right thing to do. It shows integrity. Another is that if you're ever caught lying, you could ruin your relationship with a casting director. While most casting directors have never checked the validity of credits on an actor's resume (because what really counts is how well you do your audition), you might audition for someone who happens to have cast the production you inappropriately listed on your resume. Therefore, it's not recommended that you lie outright on your resume if you are lacking credits, especially in the areas of television or film.

The second school of thought encourages beefing-up your resume in creative ways. For instance, you could stretch the truth a little by including one or two "extra" jobs you've done. Such work is not really supposed to be on your resume, but many new people include their best jobs (not more than two, or it becomes obvious) to demonstrate they've at least had some experience working on a set. People usually list the part as "featured" or "bit" rather than "extra." If you decide to do this, be prepared to explain if an agent or casting director should ever ask about it.

Another option is to use "Representative Roles" as a heading, instead of "Film & Television." Under this category, list two or three movie or theatre roles that you have studied and would feel comfortable playing. Some believe this is a good way to give agents and casting directors a better indication of your "type." Obviously, choose parts that fit your age range and type. In Hollywood, as a newcomer, you're encouraged to play the parts that fit you. Rarely does anyone want you to become ten or twenty years older or play extraordinary, larger-than-life characters. They leave those roles to the stars. In time, you'll get your chance at them.

A third option, which actually borders on "outright lying" is to list under your "Theatre" section several credits (which include the name of the play, the character, and a theatre in which it was performed). Preferably, you should know these parts extremely well, in the event you're ever asked about them (and keep in mind, some people just want to make conversation when they ask about them; they're not necessarily trying to interrogate you). I've heard some respected agents and some well-known celebrities recommend this, while other agents and casting directors strongly discourage it. So the choice will be yours. Discover your own truth.

The Finished Product

Once you've written your resume, you should have it reproduced on a wordprocessor. Using a wordprocessor and printer to create your resume looks infinitely better than typing it the old-fashioned way. So if you have a computer, great! You're one step ahead. If not, consult a friend or a resume-typesetting service in *Drama-Logue*, or go to a copy store and rent one of the computers yourself. (Be sure to set the margins correctly for an eight-by-ten, rather than eight-and-a-half-by-eleven.)

Once you have a master copy, you should reproduce at least 100 copies. It's cheapest to do it at a place like Staples or Office Depot, where 100 copies are only two cents a copy.

Some actors opt for fancy colored paper, but in reality it makes little or no difference. Casting directors aren't going to disqualify you because your resume is on plain white paper! In fact, most actors use plain white paper.

Next, have them cut to eight-by-ten at a copy center. This is very inexpensive and looks much better than if you try it yourself with a hard-edge ruler and a cutting knife.

If you use rubber cement to attach resumes to the backs of pictures, only put a dab in each corner. This will prevent major wrinkles. If you use staples, one on the top and one on the bottom is sufficient. Too many staples only annoy casting directors when they catch, scratch, or nick other eight-by-tens in their pile of pictures.

Once you've got your pictures and resumes together, you'll want to start putting them to use. You'll want to keep a few on hand at all times, and you'll want to start sending them out to agents and casting directors. And have one for an acting teacher, who'll talk about your goals with you and how you might achieve them. Chapter 9 talks about the importance of studying your craft while you pursue work.

FIGURE 3   **A SAMPLE RESUME**

Jane "Newcomer" Doe
SAG/AFTRA

Height:	5' 7"	Phone: (213) 555-5555
Weight:	125	*or*
Hair:	Light Brown	(agent's name & number)
Eyes:	Deep Blue	

FILM & TELEVISION

THE LAST HURRAH	Jane/Lead	War Entertainment
CREEPY CRAWLERS	Lead	Creepy Productions
DIFFERENT PLACES	Featured	Worldly Productions
STORM	Lead	USC Student Film
READY, SET, GO!	Lead	USC Grad. Film
DOG CHASE DOG	Featured	UCLS Grad. Film

(Some actors list roles by name as well.)

THEATRE

THE SOUND OF MUSIC	Sister Jane	Grand Theatre
A VIEW FROM THE BRIDGE	Catherine	Hometown Theatre
THE SEA GULL	Nina	City College Theatre
THE RAINMAKER	Lizzie	City College Theatre

COMMERCIALS
List Upon Request

TRAINING

Acting Class	Joe Jones (L.A.)
	City College, B.A. Musical Theatre
Cold Reading	John Doe (L.A.)
Commercial Workshop	Jane Smith (L.A.)
Voice Training	Jim Actor (L.A.)

SPECIAL SKILLS
Gymnastics, Horseback Riding, Karate, Aerobics, Snorkeling, Square
Dancing, Juggling, Rollerblading, Ice Skating, Magic Tricks, Violin.

CHAPTER NINE

Studying Your Craft

Even though there are stars today who have never had one formal acting class, most industry notables will tell you that it's a smart idea to get some training under your belt here in Hollywood. Training of any kind can only help you! It won't get you the part, but it probably will give you more confidence in yourself and your acting ability, which ultimately will help in getting hired.

Many new actors in town show up with no training at all. Only an inspiration draws them, and that's okay. Others come with a long trail of studies from high school, college, and beyond. It's obvious that the latter individual has somewhat of a head start, but according to many acting coaches, even high school and college training tends to be somewhat basic. (Of course, this depends on where you might have studied.) While some fresh, new, college-trained actors are quite brilliant, many others lack a well-developed craft. Additionally, most aren't prepared for television and film, nor the audition process or cold-readings (auditioning with material just given to you). Therefore, you should strongly consider taking some classes in L.A., regardless of your high school or college background.

In L.A., you'll find many teachers offering a wide variety of study programs that range from short-term to indefinite. The courses explore and develop the acting craft in-depth, and can teach you more about "the Biz" than any high school or college class ever did. Many programs are also specifically tailored for actors seeking work in television and film, not just theatre, as in most high schools and colleges. Another plus to studying in L.A. is that agents and casting directors often look highly upon the actor who seeks to improve his craft by studying with a respected teacher.

Acting Classes and Workshops

Virtually every acting coach teaches his or her own particular variation of a method, some more in-depth than others. That means that there are hundreds of different styles to choose from! Your options will include "method" classes (which are usually variations of the Stanislavski System or the Lee Strasberg Method), scene-study/monologue classes, auditioning/cold-reading classes, improvisational/comedy classes, film-acting classes, commercial workshops, and dance or voice classes. All of these are good ideas, if you feel they can help you in some way. The problem is that often new people don't know where they need help, in terms of their acting skills. Therefore, it's best to ask around and get referrals from friends, agents, casting directors, or periodicals when choosing an acting teacher.

Whatever classes you decide to take, you will find that most meet one to three times a week, with the cost typically ranging anywhere from $100 to $200 a month. There are also some schools, like mini-colleges, that have one- or two-year acting programs. Obviously, fees for extended programs are much higher. While they can't hurt you, attending a one- or two-year school is really not necessary or by any means a sure way of getting your foot in the door. What matters most is that you can act, and secondarily, that you've studied with a reputable teacher.

Below is a more detailed description of the different types of classes you'll find in L.A.

Method Classes. You've heard of "method" actors. They study and utilize a method to help them in their acting. Thus, at method classes actors learn a particular method or system that is designed to give them a technical mastery of the craft. Most programs initially start with classes in fundamental exercises and culminate with the execution of polished scenes weeks or months later. You will find many different instructors teaching a variety of methods, although generally most teach some version of the Stanislavski System or the Lee Strasberg Method. There are also tons and tons of other "method" classes that have a variation, expansion, or combination, of methods. Plus, there are those who teach versions of the Meisner technique (not a method, but a technique), developed by Sanford Meisner. Whatever you choose, make sure that the approach offered is helping you!

Some famous method actors include Al Pacino, Marlon Brando, and Paul Newman. Famous Meisner students include Gene Hackman and Robert Duvall.

Scene-Study/Monologue Classes. These programs focus on developing acting skills primarily through rehearsal and refinement of scripted scenes. As with any class, it is important to have an established teacher who will be able to give you helpful and poignant insights. There are hundreds of scene study classes with all kinds of teachers, so find one with whom you feel comfortable. Many will let you audit a class for free to see if their style and approach to teaching suits you.

Auditioning/Cold-Reading Classes. Every actor new in town should take one of these classes, regardless of background. In Hollywood, your brief audition gets you the job, not the fact that you might be a brilliant actor from high school or college. Even if you are an established actor but feeling rusty you should take a cold-reading class. I can't tell you how important they are!

Concentrating on mastery of the audition process, most classes consist of weekly video-taped auditions with an instructor. Sometimes a guest casting director along with the instructor offers you wisdom on how to break down your script and refine technical aspects of your audition. Just be sure that the teacher is recommended and respected.

Improvisational/Comedy Classes. For those seeking to develop or polish their comedic abilities, improv/comedy classes are the way to go. Not just for stand-up comics, these classes have helped many actors land roles in commercials and sit-coms. They require some courage, but many find them to be extremely entertaining and uplifting. While no one will ever ask you whether or not you've taken one of these classes, it will help you immensely to have the additional training.

Film-Acting Classes. These classes usually operate like scene-study classes, except that the scenes are taped, hopefully professionally, as if they were appearing on television or film. This helps people fine-tune technical aspects. While some of these classes can be good, they sometimes offer newcomers little instruction on the process of acting, which is usually what they need the most. However, good film acting classes can, and will, sometimes provide you with nice material for a reel if you don't already have one.

Commercial Workshops. Sometimes these are taught by commercial casting directors as weekend events. Other times, independent teachers might hold six- to eight-week classes devoted entirely to the process of "commercial" acting and auditioning. These are great for refining your commercial technique on camera. But beware of any workshop that leads you to believe you have a strong chance of landing commercial representation just by taking the class. (Some classes invite agents to come to class one night.) Some students have gained representation that way, but I've heard from too many others that didn't. Therefore, if you take one of these classes, make your goal to develop a better auditioning technique, and let "landing an agent" be icing on the cake. Ask around for classes recommended by agents.

Dance and Voice Classes. Any class that expands your performing ability is a great thing. This is why many actors also learn to dance and sing. While not essential for success, classes devoted to other performing arts help you to become a double or triple threat when in the arena competing with other actors. Many actors have landed roles because they had that additional talent that allowed them to stand out from the crowd. Many actors find these classes to be great stress relievers.

Choosing a Teacher

The best source for finding a teacher is through referrals. Nothing beats a good recommendation from a friend. Lacking that, you will find a myriad of teachers advertised in *Drama-Logue* and *Back Stage West*. Listings of acting teachers and their backgrounds can also be found in several publications, including *Acting Coaches* and the *Working Actors Guide* at Samuel French Theatre & Film Bookshops.

When searching for the right teacher, try to meet with several before deciding on one. Most important is to have a teacher who is not only well-respected but capable of helping you. He/she must also be compatible with your personality and be willing to treat you the way you want to be treated. After all, you are paying them! Just like in every other profession, you'll find acting teachers with a wide range of personalities. Some are harsh, others are more gentle. Just find one that works for you. Finally, take a look at some of the students in the class. Find out if they are serious actors and if they are working. If they are, it will not only ensure that you get much more out of the class, but also indicate that the instructor is a good one.

You'll find that some acting coaches feel that college training is essentially garbage and that you should try to forget everything you learned and start over. Other teachers might feel your prior training has served you well and that you are ready to fine-tune your craft and work on scenes in a scene-study class. It can sometimes be a subjective call, depending on who you talk to. Therefore, talk to several teachers to see what course of action might be best for you.

A Checklist of Questions to Ask Before Enrolling in a Class

To help you find the most appropriate teacher, it's a good idea to get answers to the following questions before enrolling:

- How long has the instructor been teaching?
- What is taught/What is the format? Is there a method?
- What is the maximum number of students per class?
- How long is the course of study? Is it ongoing?
- What are the requirements for attendance?
- How often does it meet each week and for how long?
- What is the cost of the class?
- Are there any additional materials to be purchased?
- Are there any prerequisites for joining the class?
- Are there different levels? How will you be placed?
- Will assistants be teaching the class or the instructor?
- May you audit the class first before joining?

Don't Be Fooled by False Promises

In this town, there are a few people who prey on young, naive actors by promising them the world. Be aware that no legitimate acting teacher will ever guarantee you work. If they do, then you should probably turn around and go the other way!

Some organizations sponsor acting workshops taught by industry insiders—casting directors, agents, directors, producers, and the like—and while no guarantees are made, there is an implication that you'll get connected with the right people. The truth is that you might, but very often these are busy people (who see actors all day long anyway) who are simply trying to supplement their income, not trying to find new talent. Sometimes, but not always, they are horrible teachers too. Also, occasionally a casting director's name will be mentioned as a teacher, but instead an associate or assistant will show up to teach the class. Therefore, ask questions beforehand.

There are mixed feelings among actors and casting directors about these types of workshops. Some feel that paying to audition, which is essentially what many believe it boils down to, is unethical. Others feel that with so much competition, you have to do whatever you can to gain an edge over other actors, even if it means buying access.

If you decide to do one of these, then be sure to inquire about exactly who will be teaching and what kind of attention you'll be getting. Such investigation might keep you from feeling that your money has been wasted.

Keeping Up-to-Date with the Biz

In addition to staying in shape with acting classes and workshops, you'll also want to be "in-tune" with what's happening in the industry. Several trade papers that you should read on a regular basis to be an informed member of the entertainment community include *The Daily Variety*, *The Hollywood Reporter*, and especially for new actors, *Drama-Logue* and *Back Stage West*. *The Daily Variety* and *The Hollywood Reporter* are published daily and cover all types of entertainment-related news, including deals, mergers, grosses, stocks, executive shuffles, productions, and gossip. *Drama-Logue* and *Back Stage West* (published every Thursday) contain casting notices, interviews, stories; along with ads for instructors, workshops, photographers, and others. All of these periodicals can be purchased at any nearby convenience store, newsstand, or bookstore.

Though there is no need to become a database of information, it's really important to know what's happening in Hollywood. It helps your credibility when you're familiar with the various studios and their heads, film schools, arts organizations, current and future films, and stars who are the talk of the town. It shows you are an industry player, and not just the new kid in town.

In addition to reading papers, you should stay informed and knowledgeable by watching television and going to see movies and plays. As an actor, part of your job is to know the work of other actors, directors, and writers. It's good to know every show on TV, in the event that you get an audition for one of them. You'll feel much more confident going in to read.

So sponge up as much as you can about the industry, but maintain a sense of balance. Don't be so over-consumed that you live, eat, and breathe Hollywood! Just maintain an eager and enthusiastic attitude. You'll feel more and more like you "fit" into this town as you come to know more about it, and you'll find that the more you know about the business, the more people will take you seriously.

Industry Interview:
Advice from Eric Morris, Acting Coach, on Acting and Acting Classes

What is your impression of people who come to this town with college acting training? I know it varies a lot, but what is your overall impression?

Well, after teaching tens of thousands of people, I have a real cross-section. Here's my feeling, and it's a little bit elitist and a little bit hard: most of the people who teach in universities and colleges are academics who never really went out there and worked in the field as professionals. They are academics, they learned their stuff in college and then went on to get their M.A.s and Ph.D.s and M.F.A.s, and they stayed in academia. They haven't a clue about what goes on.

Also, I think being a fine or great teacher is a God-given gift, predicated on your knowledge and talent. The talent without the knowledge is as dangerous as the knowledge without the talent. But I find categorically that college-trained actors are ill-equipped to deal with creating reality in front of the camera or on the stage. There are only a half a dozen teachers I think in the entire country that I have respect for in terms of what they're teaching. I think there are probably hundreds of teachers who are ethical, committed, involved, and want to do the right thing, and are really committed to coaching and teaching and sculpting people, but they don't have a process. They haven't anything to teach.

So what I would say is, if you go to college and you want the degree that's all fine and good, but I've never had to use my degree (and I was an associate professor at USC hired for my attainments in the industry in the business). I was there for eight years, part-time. But if you want to go to college to get a degree or you want to get a background or you want to be well-read, then read a lot of plays, and get a good theatre background. The more power to you. But if you're really serious about being an actor, and particularly coming to California, you should find a really seasoned professional coach/teacher, not a college teacher.

After college, you should really spend two to three to four years training regularly, consistently with a professional, well-established teacher with a good reputation and a process. It's the only edge you have when you come to Los Angeles. The only edge you have is to be able to push your buttons with professionalism and a certain kind of mastery, and come up with a result. Because that's all they care about: what comes out on that screen. And if you don't know how to access your emotions, and you don't know how to create an inner, organic, authentic life on the stage or screen, you're in a pool of thousands and thousands of actors and then it becomes like a roulette wheel. Does the ball land on your number this time? Do you get a job because of that? To really call attention to yourself, and create and build a reputation in this business, you have to have an edge, and that edge is being a craftsman. Now matter what talent endowment you have, you've got to be able to access it.

I really want to reach people and communicate, and help people to make our business, our theaters, our films, better and more authentic and more meaningful. Because the richer our industry and our theatre is, the richer we all are. And everybody has to collaborate in that. You cannot take things out of the world without putting something back. You have to do that, and I'm really committed to that.

What advice do you have—mental, spiritual, physical—for actors?

Well, mentally, first of all, if you're going to go into this business, don't do it unless you need to do it. It's a calling, something you want to do. It's something you're inspired to do because you love it and you're going to make a commitment to it, a life commitment to it, not "I'm going to give this a try for one or two or three years." Listen, before Jack Nicholson did *Easy Rider*, he had been in the business eighteen years and had done thirty-one films, and nobody really knew who he was. Do you know what I'm saying? In the larger scale, we know who he was. But until he did *Easy Rider*, on the worldly level, nobody really knew who he was. So what I'm saying is that you can't come here for a year or two and "give it a try" because it isn't that kind of business. You might be here three, four, five years before they even know you exist! That's the first piece of advice.

The second is to look out for the charlatans. Parasites. People who want to take your pictures and manage you and coach you and shoot reels for you, and promise you work, and all these ads that sometimes appear in *Drama-Logue*. They survive parasitically on the young, impressionable, needy, unschooled, and naive actors. Look out for the charlatans! Don't go with a coach unless you check them out with Screen Actors Guild or you get references, referrals, you've heard of their reputation, or you've read their material. Don't go with an agent just to be with an agent. Find out who he represents, what he believes in. And don't go with an agent because he takes you because he likes your blue eyes. You want to be with an agent if he sees your work and he's turned on by what you do, and he has a good reputation and is recognized, accredited, and licensed to practice. Don't go with a manager. I don't think people should be with managers until they are at a certain place anyway. But don't go with a manger unless you have their credentials and know who they are. So many people out here want to reach into your pocket.

You should be well-prepared. If you don't come into town being well-prepared as an actor or craftsperson, you should get with a really good coach who has a good reputation, and there are some really good people out here—it doesn't have to be me. For example, Milton Katselas, Darryl Hickman, Allan Miller, Jeff Corey, and some of the people who teach my work, including my son. So there are some really reputable people that they should pursue and look up.

The other thing is, I've seen more people spin out in this town and fail because they did not recognize their financial responsibility. They got too deep in the hole and couldn't dig out. So finally, they had to get a job and give up pursuing. You should come here with some money if you can, at least enough to hold you six or seven months. Don't depend on it, but look for employment in that period of time. Don't over-extend yourself. Don't rent an apartment or condo that is too expensive, because this is a feast or famine business. You might get lucky and get two or three jobs and then not work for six months or a year. I know some incredibly good actors who have gone two or three years without a job. It had nothing to do with their talent. It had to do with being in the right place at the right time and being up for the right role. So fulfill your financial responsibility so that you don't get sucked into the quicksand.

Spiritually, mentally, and psychologically: keep optimistic and up. Any kind of spiritual involvement is good: yoga or other positive involvements. After you get some training, get yourself into a theatre company, audition for plays, and be seen. If you're going to get an agent, get into a play and invite them, so that they can see your work. Start working on creating a reel, which is a videotape that shows people your work. The first thing an agent will ask you is, "Do you have anything I can show anybody?" So start working on the reel as soon as you can.

It's a very competitive business, and I've seen too many people die of a phenomenon that I call "theatrical immortality." And the pheno-menon is that everybody has to work really hard and really struggle, "but not me, baby. It's going to happen for me!" That's a real dangerous preset. You have to work. You have to make a commitment. You have to be prepared. You have to keep positive about it and you have to fight discouragement and depression by keeping productive, active, and creative. And if you do all of that, somewhere down the line, opportunity will knock. Because it knocks more than once. Opportunity knocks so often that its knuckles get bloody. You've just got to be there for it. And don't take it personally. Rejection is part of what you are facing. Don't take it personally! It is personal and it is not personal. Of course it's personal: it deals with you. You may not get a part because you are too tall, too short, too blond, or because you've got brown eyes instead of blue eyes. Or it might be because you don't have the right quality for what their concept is. You may be perfect for the part but they have a different concept. So you can't take it personally.

In your opinion, when 100 actors audition for a role, out of that 100, how many have got the right stuff? And how do California actors compare to New York actors?

It could come down to something so minuscule as a vocal quality. You never know, but out of the hundred, I'd say it comes down to maybe 3 percent.

When I got here in 1954, there was the myth of the New York actor: that a New York actor was always better than a Hollywood actor. They were serious, well-trained actors. Well, I taught in New York for fifteen years, and they aren't any better there than they are here. It's a myth and a fantasy. It's not true. There aren't any more better actors there than there are here. As a matter of fact, there are probably more good actors here just by number. But what created that myth is the struggle, the commitment, the willingness to suffer for your art, the old Stanislavski addicts. But I have found some of the best actors in the world right here in Hollywood.

The best advice you can give anybody is to tell them to befriend somebody who's been in the business actively for five or more years. They can save them grief. They can save them a lot of grief!

Eric Morris can be contacted at the American New Theater, 1540 N. Cahuenga Blvd., Los Angeles, CA 90028; (213) 466-9250.

Industry Interview:
Advice from Julian Neil, Acting Coach, on Acting and Acting Classes

Could you tell me a little about the California mentality that you've noticed, in terms of actors and acting?

Many California people have an understanding of the craft, but they just want to be stars. They just want to make it—and it's possible because people can see you. For example, I have a student who the other day was working in a pizza place and the head of Disney saw him there and liked him. He thought he was incredible looking and so on and so forth, and is now setting him up with things. So, that happens and people expect that a little bit out here. I am leery of that because it doesn't give you the foundation of the craft and I think it's all about always being able to deliver.

So are you a strong advocate of theatre?

I think theatre is like classical music. If you can play classical music, you can play jazz, rock-and-roll, boogie-woogie, swing, it doesn't matter. It's funny—in other arts, dancers don't even get on stage unless they've trained for eight years. Musicians play their instruments every day for hours and hours and hours. But actors, a lot of them, not all, but a lot of them, feel like they can just not practice—not constantly work on and be opening up the instrument and stretching it, learning and developing. I think that's a big problem because acting is a craft, and as in any other craft, it's what is necessary. So I'm a big advocate of training and theatre, really knowing your craft and always working on it.

In terms of theatre versus film, if I move my hand largely, it's fine on stage, but if I do that on film, I'm out of frame. So there's a very different technique involved. With stage you're on two hours straight. With film, you sit around for two hours, and then you go for thirty seconds. So it requires a different technique and approach in a sense.

What important things in addition to the training, are important for actors to keep in mind as their working on their career and acting?

I think that being focused—incredibly focused—is a must. Most everything you do should be geared towards acting, if you really want to get a hold of it. However, I believe in balance. I tell my acting students all the time that they need to know classical plays (not only by Shakespeare and Strand and people like that, but Arthur Miller and Tennessee Williams, some of our American playwrights as well), but they should also be versed in music and literature and painting, etc. I think that is all very important: that you understand all kinds of crafts. Many times you can look at a painting or a photograph and you understand characters and you become a character just by that exposure. It gives you an experience that you then can translate through your instrument. And that's part of what I mean by being focused. What you do artistically and creatively ultimately feeds the instrument.

Emotionally, you have to understand that you can only do your part, and that so often there are so many other variables. The best actor does not always get the part. There are just too many other variables. So, learn to emotionally stay balanced with yourself and understand all you can do is do your part. It's about just doing the best you can each time—being able to stay focused, patient, and growing.

Spiritually, don't get caught in the illusion of the business. I think integrity is the most important thing. For me, integrity is not being able to be bought or sold, which means whether they offer you the Mercedes or they tell you to go be a waiter, that won't change the integrity of where you are creatively and your desire to have that creative expression. Be a contribution, and to me spiritually, this is the most important thing. See yourself as contributing something valuable to the industry, and therefore, to people that view the entertainment industry.

If you fall into the illusion of acceptance and rejection, it's a detrimental trip. You get tossed around. It's hell on earth. Every time they say you're "great," you shoot to the moon, and every time they don't give you the part, you fall to the depths. You're life will be hell. So I personally recommend a lot of yoga and meditation for actors, because it's very balancing and healing. It puts you in touch with yourself, and combines the body's spirit and mind, which is the instrument. We are our instrument. We don't put them away in a case, we carry them around with us. Just like I wouldn't want to take my sax and drag it on the cement and bang it around, we as actors, have to treat out instruments with the same respect. So eat good food and exercise. This is why California is great— the sunshine! These are things that help the body. So find those spiritual practices. It can be walking on the beach. It doesn't matter, just that you stay balanced and that you stay connected beyond the illusion, in a state of serenity and peace.

Also, we're in the business of illusion. Hollywood is like Detroit. They make cars in Detroit, and we make movies and illusion here in Hollywood. I think you have to be careful not to get sucked up into all of that.

As an actor and a teacher, how do you recommend that people go about finding an acting teacher?

One way is to get a periodical called *Acting Coaches* at Samuel French.

I have a spiritual view on it: that you find your teacher when you're ready, and you get the right teacher. But I think you should still look around. It doesn't mean that the first teacher someone recommends to you, is "your teacher." I tell all my clients that I'm not the teacher for everybody and I know that, and I expect them to know that. But I might be the right teacher for them, it depends. We need to see how it is.

So Samuel French is a good place to start if you know absolutely no one. *Back Stage*, *Drama-Logue*, and the trade papers are also places where you can get names or read testimonials from actors that you like. Agents often have a certain number of acting teachers too. Most agents will give you three or four different acting teachers that they recommend for their clients. That's another good way. Also, try asking at auditions or going around to the theaters and talking to people—"Who do you study with? What method is he/she teaching? How do you like it? Can I come and see it? Can you give me their number? Can I call and get an interview?"

I think you have to be systematic about it and try to get as much information as possible. And when you feel an affinity towards a teacher who is saying and doing the kind of things that you want to experience, and you feel they can really train you, then that's who you should start with.

As a director, what you do look for in actors? What turns you on and off? What inspires you to want to work with an actor?

There's an energy that comes from confidence. You can feel actors when they audition. You know when they're worried about what we the auditioners think of them and their work. It's a neediness, and an insecurity that we feel. And I will say that's a turn-off. Right away you've lost us.

So I'm always looking for somebody who is really able to bring out the truth of who they are. The more you can use yourself and your own truth, and you can do that without your own judgement, this is what comes through. Don't worry about what we are thinking. We watch actors who won't go into certain areas because they judge themselves, or they think they're going to look silly or that feelings make them weak. So they don't show their feelings or else they don't know how to.

A truth and a precision of craft—skill—is very important. It's a combination of both. Skill can be taught to anyone, and repetition is the mother of skill. So if you practice everyday, you will gain skill. And I want to see a skilled actor. But I also want to see someone who really knows how to bring life to something—that's the truth part—sculpted through the text given them—that's the skill part.

What would you tell someone who's just moved out to Hollywood? What advice or words of wisdom would you would offer about the way this town works?

You have to be prepared to support yourself financially. Finding a good foundation right away is almost more important than anything else. Finding a good place to live and a good job is practical advice. Get in a class so that you can be part of what's happening. Meet people who have been established and find a teacher who is established. Network, because in this town, it is very, very important. I would pick up the trades and books on agents, and again network. If you have a brother, or sister, or friend, or a distant cousin, or somebody you know, make the phone call. Don't be shy. If you don't ask it won't come to you. No one's going to find you in your apartment. They are not going to say "Oh, you finally came here!? Great! He's here!" So ask. The worst they can say is "No." And you're no worse off than when you started. So I think a lot of times, we want to stay humble. Humility is good. But we also have to be aggressive, and by that I mean, we simply ask for help. It's okay to ask for help. And to listen a lot and seek advice. Stick with the winners. Look at the people who are doing the kinds of things that you want to do, playing the kinds of roles or working in the kinds of arenas that you want to work in. Look for those things.

And don't be frightened of the town. It can be overwhelming. Get yourself a Thomas Guide so you can get around! These are practical things. In general, I say to anyone, if you can do anything else and be happy, do it. This is the business with the greatest highs in the world, but also very hard and tough, depending. Some people have an easier road. I look at it spiritually as karma, destiny, and those kinds of things. And if it's not going to be fun, don't do it. There's a certain sense of fun people have to have.

I also think that in this town especially, going places, meeting people, learning to do the schmooze are all important. Being places. Showing up. You have to start to just be places. And don't turn down an opportunity because of too many opinions, especially when you're new. Know less, I say, then you can experience more. Don't come with an attitude of "I know how to act. I know how to do this. I just need this and I just need that!" The people who come and say "I don't know anything. I just want to work and I'm willing to do. . . ." are the people who have a greater experience. They stay open enough to get the experiences, to be places, to do play readings, whatever. I'll give you an example: I'm directing a play that just opened and the actress in it has a wonderful agent now. She's an incredible actress, and a while back she did a reading, nothing more than a reading of a movie script—just a "can we get together in a room and read it for some industry people." Well it just so happened that there were a couple of agents who saw the reading and they signed her as a client based on that reading. That's how good she was. So I say, look at all the opportunities that present themselves.

Julian Neil can be contacted at (213) 955-1823.

Finding an **Agent**

I t is essential to be represented by an agent if you want to work as a professional actor in Hollywood. While you might be able to seek out work in student films and small independent projects on your own, you'll definitely need someone else pushing for you if you want to play in the big leagues of television and film.

What Agents Do and Why You Need One

In the simplest terms, an agent submits actors for roles, coordinates their auditions, and then negotiates their contracts when they are cast for parts. One reason that you, as an actor, need an agent is because only agents (and managers) have access to the Breakdowns, a service that many casting directors use to list roles they are casting. Also, having an agent legitimizes you by showing that someone believes in your acting ability. Additionally, an agent can open some doors by using his or her connections, which hopefully will land you more auditions and ultimately more work.

Getting an Agent to Represent You

Fortunately, it costs nothing to get a legitimate agent to represent you. All you need is for an agency to think that you have strong potential to make money as an actor. Any legitimate agency makes money only when the actor works, with the compensation being 10 percent of the client's earnings. This is regulated by the Screen Actors Guild and is standard throughout the industry. There are never any additional charges or fees that an actor can incur. This is great news to newcomers!

However, some say that every rose has a thorn, and that thorn is that it can be somewhat difficult to actually find an agent to represent you, if you are a newcomer here in Hollywood. The reason is that there are thousands and thousands of actors seeking representation. SAG members have a better chance than non-union folks, but even most of them have to work hard to attract an agent.

So how do you do it? How can you can get an agent interested in you? Following is a discussion of some of the most common ways actors, even those with little experience, have grabbed the attention of agents and landed representation:

Showcasing Your Talent. There are many theatres in Los Angeles where you should try to get the opportunity to showcase your talent. Every week *Drama-Logue* and *Back Stage West* have numerous listings (both Equity and non-union) for upcoming theatrical productions. So read the notices! Often auditions are open to the public, and all you have to do is show up. You'll be guaranteed the chance to try out for whatever part you want. When you are cast in a play, it's a perfect opportunity to invite agents and casting directors to come see your work. But make sure the play is a quality production that shows you in a good light. And make sure you have a sizable role that warrants their coming to see you. They won't be very impressed with you as "Crowd-member Sixteen," who's got one line in the Second Act.

If you feel you're pleased with the production, then send out postcards or flyers inviting industry people. Take the time to send something nice. A professional invitation runs circles around a sloppy handwritten note on spiral notebook paper. Some actors even follow up their mailings with phone calls to the people they especially would like to attend.

If an agent likes your performance, he or she may want you as a client! Casting directors, who frequent theatre regularly, might even call you in to read for roles they are currently casting! Lots of actors have been noticed this way. In fact, of all the methods of obtaining agents, this is probably the best way. The reason is that you are giving them an opportunity to see your polished talent. Additionally, you will be demonstrating that you are capable of getting work, as evidenced by landing your role in the production.

Mailing Out Pictures and Resumes. This can be costly and time-consuming, but it can be successful too. Though agents receive tons of mail on a daily basis from new faces, many actors have obtained representation this way.

Start by sending out pictures to about twenty or thirty agents at a time. Hopefully you'll get a call from several. With your picture, attach a brief letter explaining a little about yourself and that you are seeking representation. Short, direct, and polite notes are best because they seem most professional. Let some of your personality come out too, but don't go overboard! Silly and absurd notes often are inappropriate and ineffective—unless, of course, you are a very eccentric character type who might be expected to send something nutty.

If you have very little experience, you might consider going after a commercial agent first. This is because commercial casting is based more on looks than acting ability or experience, so agents will be less concerned about your background. Watch closely at all the commercials on television—more than half of the principal actors aren't even speaking, so a long theatrical background isn't always necessary. All that's needed is an ability to be professional coupled with something distinctive about yourself, whether it is stunning beauty, warm and fuzzy energy, unique skills, bizarre looks, or pizzazz.

Referrals. It helps tremendously if you have a friend or relative who is already signed with an agency. She can assist in getting your foot in the door to meet her agent. By no means will her connection guarantee you representation, but it's definitely an opportunity that many new actors have to work hard to get.

Remember, much of this business is knowing the right people and the right people knowing you. So if you have connections you might give serious consideration to using them. A friend saying "Hey, this guy is really great. I'd love for you to meet him," goes a long way.

When an Agent Calls You In: The Interview

If an agency is interested in you, one of its agents or owners will call you and usually set up an interview. If the meeting is for theatrical representation, you might be asked to prepare a scene or monologue (unless you already have a video reel of your work, which they'll probably opt to see instead). This is usually something most actors dread because the monologue takes place in a cramped office and you have to perform solo for several minutes to an audience of one person who happens to be judging you. To ease this situation, some agents will read sides with you, instead of asking you to do a monologue. This is actually more like a real casting session. Also, some agents will want to see you in a showcase, instead of having you read in their office.

If a commercial agent has called you, then you will most likely have to read commercial sides that will be given to you sometime during your meeting. Whatever an agent asks, it's best to try to accommodate his or her wishes, as long they are strictly professional. As a new person, you really won't have any clout to do things your way.

During your meeting, you will probably talk a lot about yourself: your experience, your acting background, your goals, your hometown, and your acting teachers. In addition, standard conversation starters like sports, the weather, Los Angeles, and current events will probably come up too. Most agents are really just trying to get a sense of how well you communicate and present yourself. Some agents really could care less about your experience; they just want to see if you have some undefinable sparkle in your eye, which they usually notice in the first twenty seconds.

After your meeting, you will probably have some idea about whether or not they are interested in representing you. If they are, they'll definitely tell you. If they aren't interested, or just not sure, they'll usually give you an excuse and say they'll get back to you.

If they inform you that they would like to represent you, but you still have other agency interviews scheduled, then tactfully put them off. Express your immense interest (even if it's only moderate) and let them know your situation. Most agents will understand and would never pressure you. In fact, most will encourage you to interview with other agents too.

If an agent chooses not to represent you, for whatever reason, be very polite and thank them for spending their time with you. Reasons an agent may not want to represent you are varied: It could be that they already represent too many people that are your "type." (But then you have to consider, why did they call you in the first place?) It could also be that you didn't click, that you reminded them of a bully in high school, or perhaps you're not as polished as they want you to be. Regardless, it is not the end of the world. There is an agent out there somewhere that will believe in you.

Signing with an Agent

In Los Angeles, actors are supposed to have only one agency representing them theatrically (television/film/theatre) and one representing them for commercials, though the same agency can represent an actor for both. Thus, you would never have two theatrical or two commercial agents at one time. It just depends what you want to do or what a particular agency wants to do with you. A high-clout agency might want to represent you only commercially, because they feel your theatrical credits aren't extensive enough. Sometimes agencies only represent actors in one area, so they can't cover you in both. As a newcomer, you'll take what you can get.

When you are fortunate to find an agency that wants to take you on board, they will either "sign" you immediately or operate on a verbal agreement, usually until you book your first job. Then they'll probably sign you. When you are signed, both you and the agency will sign a SAG Talent Agency Contract (either TV/Theatrical or Commercials), which will be valid for one year. However, after the first 151 days, if you have not worked for at least 10 days in the preceding 90 days, you may be released from a TV/Theatrical contract. With commercial contracts, if you have not earned $3,500 including residuals in the preceding 90 days, you may be released. (If your contract is a renewal contract, then the 151-day initial period does not apply.) Many agents don't like these clauses because they might work like a beaver for you for six months, with no compensation, and then you can leave them.

Though most actors prefer being signed because it solidifies a relationship and shows some kind of commitment from an agency, if you have obtained a verbal agreement instead, it's not necessarily a bad thing. Many agencies do this with relatively new talent and it's a way of setting up a trial period. Hopefully your agent will send you out on a number of auditions, and hopefully you'll book something, which will establish a deeper commitment to you by the agency. However, if the agent receives mostly negative feedback about you from casting people, then he or she will probably conveniently forget about you, and you'll have to go looking for a new one. Likewise, if your agent gets you only one or two auditions over a period of several months, you'll know it's definitely time to go searching for a new one. And since you only have a verbal agreement, you can leave whenever you feel it's necessary, without having to meet contractual obligations. All its takes is a phone call or letter.

Once You Have an Agent

Once you have an agent who is interested in representing you commercially, and/or theatrically, don't break out the champagne just yet. It won't mean a thing until you start going on auditions, and start booking work. There are many actors who have landed representation with a power agency and then waited six months only to go on zero auditions! The reason this happens is either because the power agent is not submitting you or because the agent is unknown, a poor worker, or has a bad reputation.

The time to start jumping up and down is when you are auditioning on a regular basis. This means at least once or more a week, or every couple of weeks during slow periods. Then you will know your agent is working hard and has a strong interest in promoting you.

To keep up your relationship and stay fresh in your agent's mind, it is nice to stay in touch at least once a week. It's especially important to do this if you are not being sent out often. As a premise for contacting an agent, many actors will call to check if any more pictures and resumes are needed. Other good topics of conversation include any roles you've heard about, or any classes or projects you're involved in. You will find that just a brief conversation is sometimes all that is needed to rekindle the fire.

It is vital to have a nice working relationship with your agent. If you can't stand the person, or if you feel very awkward or unwelcome every time you call, then it's obvious the agent is not the best person for you. An inability to communicate will probably lead to more trouble down the road. But don't feel as though you should be able to discuss with your agent, at length, details of your crisis-of-the-week. Agents are agents, not therapists, and most agent/client relationships are fairly professional. As you get to know them, they may seem more like friends and your relationship may become more open, but basically they are busy business people who are trying to make a living. Just keep that in mind.

A Final Note: Remember to Keep Hustling

Even after developing a solid relationship with an agent, many successful actors don't just sit around waiting for a phone call. They are constantly searching for work themselves. They scour the trade papers, send out pictures themselves, network, and do just about everything to get some exposure. They are true "hustlers" who will stop at little for an audition.

It will be important for you to develop and maintain such a mentality. Remember that professional acting is a business. Like any businessperson, you need to cultivate leads and contacts. This means going on as many auditions as possible and meeting as many casting directors, directors, and producers as you can. It's a numbers game: the more you show off your talent to people, the more opportunities people have to buy it.

Industry Interview:
Advice from Buzz Halliday, Owner of Buzz Halliday & Associates, a Talent Agency, on the Business of Acting

What advice would you give to new actors who are seeking represen-tation. How should they go about it? What should they do if they only have a few credits? What things can they do to help improve their chances of finding representation?

Number One: the actor should really want to be in this business. I mean, that "not to act" would be life threatening. You have to have that desire and have that determination of "this is what I am, this is what I have to do." That's got to be there. If you don't have that, I don't care what else you've got to offer. That is what will get you through some of the leaner and more frustrating times.

Number Two: You've got to believe in yourself. You've got to feel that you are truly talented and that you're not approaching this as a fantasy. The entertainment industry does not have one set path. Acting school is not like going to law school, where after graduation you pass the bar exam and work for a law firm. An actor can go to acting school but that does not guarantee your future as a successful actor. So you have to really look at the big picture—which it is—and really feel that "this is truly what I want to do and that I am really talented."

Number Three: An actor has to understand where they fit into a casting situation. If a young character man comes into my office and I ask him, "Where do you see yourself?" and he says, "I want to do romantic leading roles," right away I know that this is not somebody I want to invest any time in. He is not seeing himself.

If you are new in town, showcases are a terrific way of being seen. Do not choose a scene or piece that you fantasize about doing. This is your opportunity to show other people what you think you are right for now. If you are a "young upscale person," you do that kind of a scene. Please don't play an older person or do material that you can't relate to. You'll confuse people and casting people won't get a sense of your talents because they'll be watching your choices and not your acting ability and you've wasted a great opportunity.

What makes an actor better or more distinctive? The choices that you make. You have to help by showing yourself through your pictures, presenting yourself properly, and by choosing good material. Your life as an actor is filled with choices. Filled with agents, pictures, material, wardrobe, classes. . . . The list continues forever.

What do you look for in a client and what turns you off from a client?

I'm turned on by an ambitious person. I can sense it immediately. I'm turned off by somebody who I feel lies, who's got a game going, who comes in with an attitude about instant stardom. It's not necessary. That's living in a fantasy world. They saw it in movie, or they heard about it.

I'm sure that goes on, but if you're starting out and you don't know who people are, it's in your best interest to listen and ask questions. You should be in control of yourself and try to be in control of the situation so that you don't do something that you might look back on and regret.

What would you recommend to actors to stay active, to keep their creative juices flowing?

If you sit home waiting for your agent to call, it's going to be a very long wait. You have to read all the trades everyday and circle the names of people you know and who might also know your work. I'd watch every new television show at least once. Make a list of shows that you'd like to be on and films you see and be able to say, "These are the kinds of parts I want."

You have to be constantly working at your craft. Do a showcase or two at a reputable theatre. Join a theatre group. You should take a good cold-reading class, because auditions come up last minute and you've got to be able to feel comfortable winging it. Don't be afraid to find out what your peers are doing. Also, I don't know how many people do this, but I think probably one of the most constructive things you can do is to form a group. I don't mean a self-help group but a support group. The group could get together at least once a month. Talk about what you've been auditioning for, how you're doing with your agent, and anything else that's been happening. I'm aware that some directors do this. They hang out and have lunch together at least once a month and they've helped one another with leads. That could help with actors too. But I don't advise meeting with people whom you may be in competition with. In other words, they may not be telling you the truth and why affect a friendship?

What things should an actor keep in mind mentally, emotionally, physically, spiritually as they pursue their work?

The best thing, I think, is to know how to handle stress. I think everybody has to find their way of handling it, whether taking a yoga class, hiking, or learning another language—do whatever works for you. You have to deal with the physical part of yourself because there's so much mental stress in the acting profession.

I think it's terribly important to have something away from the business. It's what's kept me sane my whole life. You should always develop other interests because this business can become your life. It can just take over. When you are in a long-running situation like a television series, those people become your family and you have to become very careful, because the show will end and you could feel lost.

Actors can have a problem being well-rounded people. I actually had this problem early on when I first started out. I loved the business so much that the only things I read were about the business. I only hung out with industry professionals and I was becoming a very boring actor. I couldn't bring anything to my work except what I knew about the business. Every experience you have or create will add to the richness of the work. When you see some of the older actors who are around, why are they so interesting? Well, they have lived so much longer and lived so many more experiences, that they have that advantage over the young actor. If you get interested in other things, that's going to add to the wealth of your work.

Anything else you can recommend?

Oh yes, pictures are your passport! They not only have to look like you, they have to project the kinds of roles you feel you are right for. It's important for the actor to have control of his or her photo session. That has to do with choosing the right photographer. If you feel comfortable with a photographer, you should tell him or her, "This is what I need and this is what I want."

Industry Interview:
Sherry Robb, Owner of AFH Talent Agency, on Actors Seeking Representation

A lot of new actors arrive in L.A. and try to find an agent. What is your advice to new actors seeking representation?

The most important thing they can do is have a business-like manner in all their correspondence. They should also have a picture that isn't art gallery quality nor one that says, "Hi, I'm on a mantle-piece in New Jersey." Rather, it should be alive, natural, and it should talk to people. Agents should feel like they are actually meeting the person.

You should do a little research before you write your letter, too. I've gotten letters that say "Dear Sir," and I'm a woman. I've received letters that have my name spelled improperly. One simply needs to call SAG to get the agency listings and the correct spelling of the owners. It turns me off when I open letters and they say "Dear Sirs" or they have my name spelled "Cherry" instead of "Sherry." Right off the bat I think, "Do I want to represent this type of person?"

From the very beginning I look at actors' credits, but I also look at their demeanor. If someone comes in and is very positive, business-like, has a magic about himself or herself, and their pictures are great, it shows a level of professionalism.

I'm one of the agents who doesn't mind working with new writers and actors, so I could be biased, but I always judge a new writer or actor on their initial cover letter. If they've taken the time to do it right and it reads professionally, then something will grab me. I'll say, "This is someone I'd like to meet. This is someone I wouldn't mind getting to know better."

What I'm doing is becoming a partner with these people. I'm doing things for them and representing them out in the professional world, and they are also my embassador out there. If someone calls and says "I don't care if you take me or not, but I need an agent!" or "I'm the greatest!" then that's a problem.

By the way, don't use wonderful superlatives about yourself in your letters. It's much better if you say, "I met this casting director who said she really wants to interview me." Even if its your high school teacher or workshop leader that can say your acting is "magical" or that "you're particularly good in comedy," it helps. It's always better to have other people brag about you. Write down what people are saying about you.

If somebody, for example, The University of Iowa, Director of Theatre, says something nice about you, then you're suddenly aligning your name and your professionalism with someone bigger than you. You might be unknown but a university isn't. And it does grab attention.

Then there is the follow-up to sending your picture. Agents get hundreds of pictures a week. We try to open them whenever we can on a weekly basis, sometimes on a daily basis. But if you start calling agents, understand that the morning time is the busiest. Our messenger comes at one o'clock and at six o'clock, so if you call an agent early in the morning they are probably not going to have any time for you. They have actors that they are already representing that they need to service. So morning is just a bad time to call.

It doesn't work to keep bugging agents verbally either, because they really haven't made a relationship with you. What grabs me is when someone spends a dollar or makes a card and says, "I hope you had a chance to look at my picture. If not, here's a little postcard of it." Agents work very hard, and when a nice, pleasant card comes—not on an eight-by-ten because everything we see is a black-and-white, eight-by-ten—and says, "Thank you for taking the time to look at my picture," it's nice. If someone says "I know you receive thousands and thousands of pictures. Please take the time to look at my picture," I'll probably take the time out to look for that person's submission. I'm thinking that when we send that person out on auditions, they are going to send thank you notes to the casting people too, which will look good for us and them.

I'm always thinking, "Is this someone I want to be in business with." It's not just their look. There could be some gorgeous people with some great credits, but if they look like they are not going to be professional, it's not worth it.

We work everyday for no money. The money we get is when someone books a job. No one pays our paychecks unless we book actors. I can't afford to have clients who are unbusiness-like. For instance: people who don't return calls for four hours when we have an audition for them or people who don't staple the resumes on the back of their pictures on a regular basis. Each actor has one job to do and that is their own job. In order to make any kind of money, we have to focus on volume with a number of clients.

From the very beginning I also want to know if an actor understands what this whole thing is about. Do they stick to their drive? Are they taking classes? Have they gone to some training or commercial classes? Do they know how to read from a tele-prompter? Have they done everything they can to get ready to be launched into the professional world? If not, it's a waste of my time.

Also, some actors might just come at the right time at the right place. At this moment, we're looking for young teens up to eighteen and nineteen. So if someone calls and they happen to have the worst picture in the world and are unpolished, but they say "I'm sixteen and I'm a guy,"

I'll say, "Come over! What's your name? Fly in!" They happen to be at the right place at the right time. Additionally, we can at times have holes in our client list for real character types, older ethnicities, and comedians. There are so many breakdowns that have to do with those kind of people.

With regard to children, if you are a parent sending in a picture of your kid, just say things like, "We, as parents, will make sure our kids get to their auditions on time. This is a commitment we are ready to make." That's all that counts. We're not signing the kid as much as we are signing the parents. It doesn't matter how adorable you think your kid is. Of course, we look at that, but it's important to be professional and be ready to get your kids to auditions on time.

So in summary, there are four hundred ways to do everything right and look good, but it's the person with the right look at the right time, with the right attitude who gets representation. They don't have to be business experts—that's why there are agents—but knowledge is power. Therefore, if you know a little bit about contracts and read the rules and regulations when you join SAG, then your agent can only help you more. You'll be within an area of knowledge. For example, when your agent talks about being "Taft-Hartley'd," you won't say, "What's a Taft-Hartley?"

In L.A., Samuel French is a great place to go and buy books, and learn all you can about the business of acting. If you are in other parts of the country, the library always has some good books on acting. It's important to know what you are getting into.

Sometimes someone has no experience but there is something about them I just love from the minute they send me a picture. There's life, there's commitment, and an eagerness to learn. I want to be their partner and make a go at it, especially if they are willing to learn more and go to school.

Not all agents feel that way. I happen to feel that way because I feel that a lot of clients, when they become big, tend to leave smaller agencies. My experience is that the more you can instill and build confidence and loyalty in them, and help them to grow, the more they'll give you that back. But sometimes there is just that invisible belief in somebody. I've been around long enough to know when I think someone is going to be a star. There's something magical about them that attracts me.

I always tell people, I will work 50 percent for 10 percent, but I won't work 80 percent for 10 percent. We deal with over one hundred people. If they all do everything they have to do, it makes my life easier. I get more actors out on auditions every day that way. And every time actors can be positive it helps. Remember no one is paying an agent's paycheck, and the actor doesn't pay the paycheck right away until they hit it big. For example, even if you work one day, we only make fifty dollars. There are hours and hours we spend sending actors out where we're not making a penny, so take time to build your bridge.

You only have one chance to make a first impression. So, again, be professional. Those are the people with whom I tend to work best.

Industry Interview:
Onley Cahill, Personal Manager on Actors and the Business of Acting

What realistic advice do you have for actors who come here from other parts of the country?

Well, the first thing is not to get discouraged. People have very high expectations coming to L.A. They expect that within a few days or a few weeks they'll get a manager and an agent, and they'll be starring on a TV show. And it doesn't happen quite as fast as that. Remember that this is a melting pot of everyone coming from all over the country. So if you are a star in your hometown or even a large city, when you come to L.A., it's a lot different. The main thing is not to get discouraged. It doesn't take just three months.

Once an actor gets here, what can an actor do to help establish himself or herself?

The first thing is to check into a really good acting school. An actor has to work all the time. You'll get to make contacts, you'll get to work on your craft, you'll get to do showcases, casting people might get to see you, and producers might come in. The main thing is to network, network, network.

You'll get to meet other people who have access to other venues and other things that are going on. You really can just work with each other, forming a foundation that gets into other areas of the business.

The second thing is read the trades. It is very important because they tell you who is doing what and what's going on. If you don't have a manager and you don't have an agent when you first get here, you have to do all the work. Even when you have a manager and agent, you still have to work hard. You can't just sit back and relax. The trades will tell you who's casting for films, who's casting for theatre, and who's casting for anything. It's one way to keep up with what's going on in L.A. Read *The Daily Variety, The Hollywood Reporter, Back Stage West,* and any of the magazines that affect your business. You should be reading them every single day. Don't read them once a week, but every day so that you're familiar with what's happening.

What do personal managers do?

The reason for a personal manager is that managers can do things that agents and other people can't. First, they can sometimes get you an agent, and second, they can always follow up on auditions. They can call people that you know and that other people know and try to get your foot in the door. It's always something a little different. Managers can reach people because they've been in business a while. They can make a phone call for you. That's something not everyone can do when they first come out here because they don't know everybody. And personal managers are supposed to know everybody!

Also, the personal manager is like the babysitter, and the best friend of the actor. It's a tough job. Actors need a shoulder to cry on and to be happy with. They need to know how they are doing and they need a lot of advice. Actors have a very uncertain future. So everyday, it's nice to have someone you can call—and I do have people call me everyday—so they can hear a voice that sounds friendly. They need to be able to talk about what they did on their audition, or what they want to do tomorrow. It's also a way to pick each other's brain, because a lot of times they know people they've worked with and I happen to see something about it and we'll say "let's see what we can do about this project or this producer." It stimulates creative ideas between managers and actors.

Do you recommend that a new person seek a manager?

Well, I think it depends. Of course managers get a percentage of the profits, and if the manager is giving you good advice and getting you an agent, then it's worth it. Also it's good to have someone to talk to, to call, and get recommendations from regarding your career. It's very helpful.

Actors are creative people. They are not business managers. He or she is not a business manager and usually cannot go into a room and talk themselves up. You need somebody else to be your trumpeter. You need someone to say "This guy is fantastic!" That's what a manager does.

What turns you on to an actor? What do find appealing about someone you take on as a client?

I just see a certain dedication that an actor has. It takes a lot of inner strength to get through this battle. There are a lot of talented people out here and I see them every single day, and they don't always get the breaks. Success is one part luck, one part talent, and another part opportunity.

But when I see someone who has a certain amount of believability, I know that when they go out, everybody sees the same thing. A lot of people can't see themselves as other people see them. So I set them straight and then get them out there.

What are some important things actors should keep in mind as they pursue their careers?

You still have to do a lot of work on your own and network. You have to be out there. You have to go out to the parties. You have to find out who's doing what and how to get invited. The organization I always recommend is IFP West—Independent Features Project West. It's producers, writers, composers, and actors, and they are all independents. Independents are very big. There are also a lot of student filmmakers. If you have to pitch your script or you want to find a certain type of producer for your film, it's a good way to find someone. They have activities every single week. A lot of people start with them when they first come out here because they don't know anybody. There are openings for films, workshops, and a lot of famous speakers come. You get to talk to them firsthand, and that's important because its a lot easier to meet them in an informal setting.

Any other advice?

One more piece of advice is that when a manager asks you to do something, realize that it's very important. A lot of times, they'll say, "I want you to be at this party. There's a casting person that I want you to meet." You need to be there. We get invited to so many things and it's very important to be there to meet people. When you don't show up it's a "no-no." There could be the very person that your manager has been trying to get you to meet and you're not there! A lot of times actors will say, "Oh well, I can skip that. It's not important." But it is! So anytime a manager says it's important to be somewhere, you better be there or else you're not going to have a manager!

You can't just sit at home waiting for the phone to ring. You have to be out there networking to find out who's doing what and who has the next picture coming up. There might be a producer at a party who has something for you six months down the road. You have to be there, so they'll remember you.

Building Your Credits and Gaining Exposure

What's the best way to get people to take you seriously as an actor? It's very simple: work. A pretty face and great headshot will help you to get noticed, but when you can tell people you're currently doing a play, or you just finished a part on a television show or a movie, it really catches people's attention. You don't have to convince anyone that you're great, you can just tell them to go see your work.

Even performing in smaller-scale productions like student films, independent films, and cable television can be worthwhile endeavors that will help to kick-start your career and make you more of an attractive commodity in the eyes of talent buyers and sellers. And as a professional actor, that is an important goal. Therefore, this chapter will detail these and other important ways to build your credits and gain some exposure.

Student Films

For a newcomer to the business, this is a fantastic way to introduce yourself to the process of filmmaking. It's also the best way to acquire film of yourself for a reel, which can be shown to agents and casting directors.

Luckily, student films are prevalent in this town and very easy to find out about. All you have to do is pick up a copy of *Drama-Logue* and *Back Stage West*, and you're halfway there. Every week casting notices are posted by film students seeking actors for a multitude of assignments, which include short films, videos, and commercials. Most often these projects run anywhere from two to fifteen minutes in length, but occasionally you'll find a graduate student shooting a feature length film. And fortunately for you—the actor living in L.A.—most of these budding filmmakers attend one of the local colleges or universities, including University of Southern California (USC), University of California Los Angeles (UCLA), American Film Institute (AFI), Los Angeles City College (LACC), Loyola Marymount University (LMU), and California Institute of the Arts (Cal Arts).

You'll benefit in several ways by seeking out parts in any student project. First, you'll gain more experience with auditioning, which is an essential procedure with which every new actor needs to feel comfortable. You'll learn to deal with all kinds of people, all kinds of audition situations (improvisation, monologues, scenes), and all types of material. Second, if you are selected to act in a film, you'll get experience working with a crew, though probably a small one, and you'll learn the process by which film is shot—a very important thing to know before you're hired professionally. And finally, as mentioned, you'll get a copy of your work which can later be added to a personal reel to show people.

As you might expect, there is no pay for working on student films basically because students don't have any money. However, you probably can expect a sandwich and a soda for lunch, as some form of appreciation. The pay-off is really the experience, which is invaluable.

You won't have to worry about giving up too much of your time either. Since students have to attend classes during the week, they frequently shoot on weekends. This is a blessing because it won't interfere with your weekday auditions and/or job. Plus, most shoots don't last more than two to four weekends, so your time-commitment overall will be minimal.

Non-Union and Independent Projects

In addition to students, many independent filmmakers also advertise in actors' newspapers for films and videos they are producing. As with student films, often there is very little or no pay, maybe twenty-five to seventy-five dollars per day at most. (Sometimes advertisements will say "Possible Deferred Pay," but that usually translates into "Chances of ever getting any money from this thing are very, very slim.") But in the beginning of your career, your intention should mainly be to do these for experience and not for money anyway.

Just as you, the actor, are trying to acquire some film of yourself, the director very often is trying to develop a director's reel that he or she can show people. Sometimes the director also has hopes that the project might make it to film festivals or video stores, which would be nice for you too. In addition to getting some footage of yourself, you might get some great exposure!

Like college films, small independent films typically don't shoot for very long either—maybe a few days or a couple of weeks. Occasionally, I have seen announcements where actors are needed for up to two months with no pay, but that is a rarity. Most actors cannot do those because of time and financial constraints. So just look out for the jobs that you can manage to do, and send in your pictures every week.

Public Access Television

As you already probably know, public-access cable television shows have a reputation for being pretty bad. (Take note of the hilarious cable-TV spoofs that "Saturday Night Live" has done: Wayne's World, Coffee Talk with Linda Richman, and many others.) People more often laugh at public-access shows than actually appreciate them. But don't let that discourage you if you have an ingenious idea. As long as it's original, entertaining, and a quality product, it has every chance of helping your career. Even if no one ever sees it, you'll get experience in front of a camera, which can only help you polish your skills.

The sky's the limit with what you can do. In Los Angeles, there are fourteen cable franchise areas which are required to provide public access facilities and equipment at no charge (or very little) to users. In addition, all air-play time is free. The only restriction is that the material you produce must be non-commercial, meaning you can't be selling products or services. To get started, all you need to do is attend a seminar on how the process works, and additional seminars if you want to be able to rent video equipment.

There is a wide range of public-access entertainment airing throughout the day in L.A., including talk and variety shows, mini-movies, spoofs, and just totally bizarre programming. Talk-show hosts discuss anything and everything, including sex, spirituality, race, nationality, health, and hobbies. Actors produce a smorgasbord of half-hour skits, scenes, and video-movies. Occasionally you'll even see something so weird you won't know what's going on. Try channel-hopping and you will surely find some of these programs.

For more information on how to produce your own show, you can contact the L.A. Department of Telecommunications, Access Services Division, (213) 485-1354 or (213) 485-2751, to receive a brochure on how to get started. You can also contact individual cable companies listed below:

Cablevision, Chatsworth, CA	(818) 998-2266
King Videocable, Tujunga, CA	(818) 353-9304
United Cable TV, Van Nuys, CA	(818) 781-1900
Century Cable TV, Santa Monica, CA	(310) 315-4444
Century Cable TV, Eagle Rock, CA.	(213) 255-9881
Continental Cablevision, Hollywood, CA	(213) 993-8000
Continental Cablevision, Marina Del Rey, CA	(310) 822-1575
Continental Cablevision, Los Angeles, CA	(310) 216-3525
Continental Cablevision, Los Angeles, CA	(213) 730-9444
Buenavision Telecommunications, Los Angeles, CA	(213) 269-8266
Copley/Colony Harbor Cablevision, Wilmington, CA	(213) 513-1534
Dimension Cable, Rolling Hills Estates, CA	(310) 377-7207

Putting on a Showcase

Though it can be costly and time-consuming, some actors have had excellent success by putting together their own showcases. It's a way of gaining total control over a project, and ultimately your career. You and your cohorts pick the material, cast yourselves, rent the theatre, and do the advertising. In short, you do everything.

The most important rule to abide by when doing your own showcase is to do it professionally. In addition to having quality material and a clean theatre, you must also have adequate money set aside for advertising and publicity, which are frequently neglected by producers of small productions. Why go through all the trouble of rehearsing, renting space, building a set, and then not take time to draw people in? It's pointless, but it happens. Many actors have performed shows to an audience of one or two people on a Friday night! So make sure you have classy invitations and ample publicity in local newspapers to attract both industry people and the public. Consider hiring someone to create invitations and even a publicist to promote your production.

Realize too that if you want agents and casting directors to come, you will have to perform somewhere close to town. Very few people will drive to northern parts of the San Fernando Valley, but you'll probably get a high turnout if you do your show in places like Hollywood, West Hollywood, Studio City, or any of the neighboring vicinities. Of course theatres are more expensive to rent in these areas, but doing so might be worth it.

Many casting directors have said that they like to see new material too, so writing your own material isn't a bad idea as long as it's good stuff. High-quality material is vital or it will tarnish your performance. To ensure that it's brilliant, you should get second and third opinions of your material before you showcase it. If you decide to perform an already written work, you may have to pay a royalty fee which will be another added expense, albeit small.

Depending on the theatre in which you produce your material, you may also have to contact Equity to apply for showcase status, which involves submitting light paperwork. Many of the smaller theatres in L.A. fall under the AEA (Equity) 99 Seat Plan. However, some of the tiny theatres with thirty or forty seats don't fall under any plan, so you won't have to worry about such technicalities.

If you've never put together a showcase before, I would recommend hooking up with another actor who has—maybe a friend or someone from an acting class. It will save you a lot of headaches. They will know how to handle many of the details that come up.

Joining a Theatre Company

This is another way to gain exposure, while also making friends, improving your acting, and learning more about the business. Most theatre companies in L.A. have anywhere from twenty to fifty members. Some have more, some less. To join a company, you typically have to audition for a membership board or committee, and most companies holds auditions once or twice a year.

The standard way to seek out membership is to submit a picture and resume to the company, and then you will be contacted when auditions are held. Usually auditions consist of performing one or two monologues along with a brief interview. If you are accepted, which might be on the spot or after a few days, then there is almost always an initiation fee of approximately twenty-five to one hundred dollars. In addition, there are monthly membership fees ranging from twenty to fifty dollars. Also, you sometimes have to work a few hours a month for the company.

There are wonderful benefits to being in a theatre company. A good company will have many productions throughout the year in which its members can appear. Many groups also have helpful workshops on acting and the business of acting. Some even have play readings, to which industry people are invited. You'll also meet other actors with whom you can swap stories and develop friendships. One other benefit is that many companies are always seeking material, so if you are a budding writer too, you might have an outlet for your work.

Addresses and contacts for theatres and theatre companies, some of which have been around for years along with new ones that form on a monthly basis, can be found in resource periodicals at Samuel French. The year-end issue of *Drama-Logue* lists all theatres and theatre companies in L.A., and can be bought year-round for two dollars. Additionally, there are more comprehensive resource guides with addresses of all kinds that can be purchased. Also, some theatre companies advertise in *Drama-Logue* when they are seeking new members, which is one more avenue to pursue.

Volunteering Your Services

In the entertainment industry, there many opportunities to volunteer your services, where you can gain exposure. Some casting offices and talent agencies hire unpaid interns to work a few hours every week. The pay is obviously the learning experience and the connections you make. Production companies are always looking for help too. Even the Screen Actors Guild needs people to help coordinate events and seminars. There are so many places to which you can offer your services!

I really believe that great things can come from volunteer work. For example, a friend of mine volunteered to work as a production assistant for a week at a company that produces late-night erotic thrillers. Out of that came several paid production jobs. In addition, he not only learned a lot about behind-the-scenes work, but he got to know several casting directors, directors, and producers while working. It was a great experience for him.

So I would recommend calling or writing those people with whom you'd like to work. Keep calling people until someone says "Yes!"

Sending out Postcards

In addition to getting headshots reproduced, many actors also get postcards made of their headshot. Every few weeks, they send them out as reminders to industry people they have met or would like to meet eventually. Postcards are a nice, inexpensive way to make people aware of your presence in L.A., and doing such helps lead to employment sometime down the road, if not right away.

One of the smartest reasons for sending postcards is that they are much less expensive than headshots. The average cost for 500 is about sixty-five to seventy dollars. That's about thirteen to fifteen cents apiece! That's cheap—compared to headshots which can run as much as a dollar apiece! Another good reason to send postcards is that the required postage is much less than when sending an eight-by-ten. The savings really adds up when you're doing a mass mailing.

It's true that casting directors get tons and tons of mail every week, and that the chances of being called in from a postcard are slim. But it has happened plenty of times! I've heard many casting directors say they've called in actors from postcards when they happened to be looking for that particular type the day the actor's mail arrived. Some call that destiny or just pure luck. But even if you don't get called in immediately, sending postcards helps to slowly build your name recognition, either consciously or subconsciously, which someday might inspire a casting director to remember you when your agent has submitted you for a part.

When doing your mailing, it's a good idea to include a brief message on the back because it helps to reinforce that you're a real person and not just a picture. If you already know the individual to whom you're sending the postcard, then update him or her on what's been happening with your career. Say something like, "I just finished doing a play at Theatre XYZ, and I'm still studying with (Acting Teacher). I'd love the chance to read for you again sometime." If you haven't done anything lately, then just say hello and ask that they keep you in mind for any upcoming parts they may be casting. If you know the person really well, then be as personal or funny as you like.

Of course, if you've never met the person to whom you're sending a card, don't write a real cozy friend-to-friend message. That's totally inappropriate. Just be polite, professional, and concise. Write something like, "I'd love the chance to audition for you sometime" and then briefly mention any of your recent achievements. Anything you can say about your success will always boost the effectiveness of your message. Just use good judgement, don't be cocky, and remember to write neatly.

The Academy Players Directory

If you have obtained agency representation or you are a member of SAG, it's a good idea to include yourself in this publication. (Those are the requirements to be included.) The directory comes out three times a year in four volumes (men, women, characters, and children), with tiny pictures of hundreds of professional actors. While being included isn't a guarantee you'll get work, it can only help you. I've heard many reputable casting directors say they've thumbed through it, especially when looking to book actors on a last-minute notice. So contact them to find out when the next filing dates will be. The cost to have your picture included in one issue is approximately twenty dollars, and you must provide a glossy original. Academy Players Directory, 8949 Wilshire Blvd., Beverly Hills, CA 90211. Telephone: (310) 247-3000.

Hopefully you'll utilize some of these proven ways of building credits and gaining exposure. Combined with the work of your agent, they will help to get your foot in the door to meet the buyers of talent—casting directors, directors, and producers.

So what can you expect when one of these buyers calls you in to audition? The next chapter covers the whole process in detail.

The Audition Process

Your agent calls and tells you that you've got an audition tomorrow. Hurray! You've got your foot in the door! Now it's time to show 'em what you've got!

Taking classes, getting pictures made, and finding an agent were very important steps along the way, but the audition is the most important step in an actor's career. It is the determining factor that gets you the job. Sadly, many new, talented actors mess up their auditions because they are inexperienced at the whole process. It's one thing to be able to deliver a fantastic monologue that you've polished for months, but to give a stunning audition with brand new material definitely requires some practice.

You will need to become a master at it to succeed in this business. Though at first it may be awkward for you, in time auditioning will become easier and easier. Read on to gain a greater understanding of what you can expect.

The Elements of an Audition

One thing is certain about auditions: no two will be the same. Most of the time, you will read lines with the casting director; however, occasionally you may just meet and never actually go over any material. Of the times you do read, you might be video-taped; other times you won't be. You may chat it up for a few minutes before you read, and other times you'll pop in, read, and quickly leave. It really varies a lot, depending on both the personality and schedule of the casting director.

Despite these different situations, there are some common elements you can come to expect at an audition, which I'll try to explain. By being fully prepared and aware of what may transpire, you will have fewer butterflies and more time to focus on doing an excellent job.

The Call from Your Agent. The first aspect of the audition process is receiving a call from your agent. You'll be out and about in L.A., and all of sudden your pager will start beeping! It's your agent! He or she has some very important information for you about an audition. You'll be told the time, place, casting director, where or how to get sides (pages of a script that you'll be reading from) if it's a theatrical audition, and details about the part you'll be reading for. It is extremely important that you get down all of this information correctly. Always carry a pen and paper with you, or have them by the phone so you don't have to keep your agent waiting. (Agents tend to be very busy in the late afternoon.) If you have any questions, be sure to ask them at that time.

Usually your audition will be the next day, but be prepared for anything. Sometimes your agent will inform you that you have an audition in two hours! That means you've got to be able to drop what your doing and go see a casting director immediately. Smart actors keep a couple of changes of clothes in their car, even grooming supplies, in the event they can't make it home before their unanticipated audition.

After you jot down all the information, if you have a theatrical audition, you'll either have to go pick up your sides or have them faxed to you. There is a service called ShowFax which sometimes can handle that. If your audition is for a commercial, you won't have to worry about sides. You'll get them when you show up.

Spend a lot of time preparing for your audition. (Later in this chapter, tips on how to improve your auditioning will be discussed.) If you have a theatrical audition, go over the sides in-depth. Rehearse them with a friend or coach. Learn as much about your character as you can. If you have a commercial audition, spend time picking out an appropriate wardrobe for the call. With commercials, it's usually better to dress the part, in contrast to theatrical auditions where only a hint of the costume is necessary. If you aren't sure what to wear, then by all means consult your agent or any experienced actor you know.

Arriving at Your Audition. Make sure you show up on time for your audition! Being late won't necessarily eliminate you from being considered, but it's highly unprofessional and shows a lack of responsibility. Therefore, leave an extra half-hour early to compensate for any unexpected delays. If you don't already live in L.A., you will come to know that traffic delays occur frequently here, both on freeways and on connecting passageways like Laurel and Coldwater Canyon.

When you reach your destination, if you have to park on the street, put plenty of money in your meter. Auditions can sometimes run late, and you don't want to worry about whether your meter is about to expire while inside the casting director's office. Therefore, give yourself at least hour in the meter—preferably more—to allow for any delays.

You should walk into the casting office at your appointed time—not fifteen minutes early and not fifteen minutes late. Only show up early if you haven't yet seen your audition material. Otherwise, if you arrive early, take a walk around the block a few times or find something peaceful to do. The reason is that many actors tend to get cramped if they sit stationary in a casting lobby for a long time. There's an undercurrent of stress, usually emanating from other waiting actors, that can encroach upon you. It's better to walk into an office at your scheduled time, feeling vibrant and ready to go. So get some fresh air or have a cup of coffee. Do what ever it takes to maintain a sense of calm before you go in.

Signing In. When you finally walk into the office, be pleasant and friendly. Remember that receptionists in casting offices often become casting assistants, who become casting associates, who become casting directors. Even if someone is less than cordial, be nice. Some of these people are stressed out, others are just inherently unfriendly, but try not to let their attitude affect your audition. Remember that if they exhibit an unbalanced state, it probably has nothing to do with you.

Next, you should sign in. There will almost always be a sign-in sheet, where you fill out your name, agency, agency phone number, and some information regarding age and ethnicity. At SAG auditions, sign-in sheets are required. Non-union projects do as they please, though often they will have their own information sheet to fill out.

After signing in, just sit down and wait. If it's a commercial audition, sides or instructions (if there are no lines) will be available near the sign-in sheet. Typically, you'll have at least five or ten minutes to go over them. If it's a theatrical audition, you probably will have picked up the sides the previous day and already studied them with great diligence. Therefore, all you have to do is wait, or review your dialogue a few more times.

The waiting room will most likely have other actors waiting for their auditions also. If you're at a commercial casting facility, there could be five or six commercials being cast in different rooms, with as many as a hundred actors lining the halls and benches, lingering for their turn. If you're at a theatrical audition, the situation will probably be far less chaotic: maybe two or three other actors will be waiting to read.

Regardless of the situation, it is best to concentrate on your work rather than chatting it up with other people. This may seem unfriendly, but it affords you the opportunity to collect your thoughts and go into your audition totally focused. As long as you are polite, other people should understand.

The Actual Audition. When your turn arrives, your name will be called, possibly along with several others if it's a commercial audition. You will then be led into the audition room. If you have only had a minute or two to look over your sides, then you might politely ask if you can have some more time. Most likely your request will be granted, and another actor who is ready will go ahead of you.

Inside the audition room, there usually sits a casting director and sometimes an assistant. Also, a video camera might be present, though this usually happens for commercial auditions and theatrical callbacks only. It is important that you greet these people with a warm smile and confidence. Whatever you do, don't be arrogant—just be yourself. If they engage you in small talk, then kindly oblige, but be sure you have more to say than "yep", "nope," and "uh huh." Good topics are current movies, sports, news-of-the-day, tasteful jokes, and odd weather. You probably ought to stay away from how much you adore acting, and when speaking about your acting career, remember that you're not an "aspiring" actor but rather, you are an actor.

After some brief small talk, it becomes time for the audition. The casting director will probably ask you if you have any questions. If you do, then be sure to ask at this time. Casting directors don't mind intelligent questions. They want you to do well. If your audition is being videotaped, you might ask if they want you to look at them or the camera. Most of the time, you will direct your audition to the casting director, but it's good to know just in case.

If the camera is rolling, you will "slate" by saying your name and sometimes your agency too, and then you'll go straight into your reading. If it's a commercial audition, you might only have to perform an action, like placing a stick of gum into your mouth or pretending to taste some food. Likewise, it may involve dialogue between you and the casting director, which will be printed on a large board behind the camera. For theatrical auditions, you will probably do a two-person scene, and you will rely on your sides when delivering your lines.

If you have sides, they should stay in your hands during the reading. Although you want to impress the casting director, you don't want them to think you've memorized the lines completely and that you're giving the best performance you could possibly give. (Obviously, you're audition would be better with a few more days or weeks of rehearsal.) Casting directors don't expect your audition to be absolutely perfect, they simply want a great reading. So look down at the sides every now and then. However, don't go the opposite extreme by keeping your eyes stuck to the pages. That certainly won't impress them either. Just try to find a balance between the two situations.

Once you have finished your scene, the casting director might ask you to make some adjustments, such as making it heavier, lighter, etc., depending on your reading. Otherwise, you should thank them and then leave promptly. Don't comment too much on your performance and never ask for the casting director's appraisal by asking something like "So, what'd you think?" That is completely unprofessional.

Most likely the casting director will just thank you. If the casting director wants to have you back to read for the director or producers, either she will tell you on the spot or she will call your agent within a few days. You might be given new material, but usually he or she will want you to repeat the same scene. Also, if you were not taped at your first reading, then you probably will be taped during your second or third callback. And be sure to wear the same outfit to your callback. Obviously, it served you well in your initial reading, so don't change it.

The callback process can be challenging to say the least, especially if you are asked to return several times to read for the same role. For example, when you're up for a series regular part on a television show, you might first have to read for the casting director, then go on a callback for the producer, then for the director, then for the studio, and finally for the network. It's tremendous pressure. Anyone who gets through the process and gets the part certainly deserves it.

Auditioning Tips and Suggestions

Every casting director will tell you that it's somewhat difficult to define what makes up a fantastic audition. Usually it's a combination of many things, some that you can control and others that are out of your control. In this section, I'd like to focus on the things that you can control. Following are several universal qualities that should be included in any audition:

Presenting Good Energy. The most common problem with auditions is that they lack energy. Nerves take over, actors retreat inwardly, and they show only a fraction of their true personality. If you want to be "in the running," then you must display a passion about your work, a commanding self-awareness, and an absolute 100 percent belief in your abilities, all without cockiness or unappealing arrogance. You must also be relaxed and comfortable. Though calmness is an inward state of being that is cultivated from experience, one way to help increase it is by exercising and stretching prior to your audition, both physically and vocally. Go run a few miles and you'll burn off a lot of that nervous energy. Do some deep stretching and you'll enable vibrant energy to circulate through every cell of your being. It really does help.

You have to go into the room and give it everything you've got. Remember that it's *your* audition, and that it's your opportunity to give your interpretation of the material. Nine times out of ten, casting directors are not sure what they are looking for, but they do notice someone who is clear in their intention and who feels secure expressing it in a pleasant and meaningful way.

Many casting directors typically make up their mind about you within the first twenty seconds of meeting you. Partly, it has to do with your look, but a lot of it has to do with your energy, so find a way to present yourself uniquely. Do it with commitment. Good energy doesn't necessarily mean bouncing off the walls: if you're playing a depressed mother who's child has died, then you have to commit to that particular energy. And it doesn't mean that every word or line has to be that particular energy. You are trying to create an overall impression. Just be true to your character and make solid choices about the way you want to express yourself.

Casting directors really do want you to be brilliant. Of all the people in the industry, they are on your side. Their job is to find excellent actors for directors and producers, and they are hoping you'll make their job easy. In no way is it a "you against them" situation. When you realize this, some of the initial pressure of auditioning will disappear.

Have Strong Objectives. You need to have a clear understanding of your character before you go in to read. Being wishy-washy won't get you anywhere. You need to define as much as you can and be very specific with your choices before the audition.

One way to obtain information about your character is to ask questions when you pick up your sides. Be extremely nice to the receptionist or casting assistant and ask for any additional information that's not already listed in the Breakdowns. (You should get all of the Breakdown information about your role from your agent.) The receptionist might be able to give you some useful information, and sometimes will supply you with a script to read.

After you've read the script and analyzed the sides, try to determine as many qualities about your character as you can. Really get to know the essence of who he or she is. Below are a few questions you should definitely answer before attempting your audition:

- Who am I?
- Who am I talking to?
- Why am I here and why am I talking to this person?
- What is my relation to this person?
- What are my surroundings/environment?
- What is the conflict?

- What are my obstacles?
- How am I attempting to overcome them?
- What do I want?
- What was my previous moment before this scene, both physically and emotionally?

Obviously, the more specific you can be with your answers, the better off you will be. Therefore, read your script or sides carefully and extract as much information as you can. If you can't answer some of these questions based on the script, then fill in the gaps with your imagination. When you are done, you will have a solid definition of your character, and it will invariably pay off during your audition. If you don't do this homework, most casting directors will notice a shallowness and won't be impressed.

Create Transitions. Within every scene, there are usually one or two transitions, often called beats. These are opportunities where you can bring some real flair to your character. They are places where emotions can change and shifts in thought can occur. By taking advantage of them, you will elevate your reading from boring, flat, and one-sided to exciting and captivating.

You must specifically define these transitions. For instance, notice at a particular point if your character suddenly starts becoming jealous, playful, angry, or embarrassed. Maybe he has an ulterior motive that is now being revealed. Take note of when it starts to happen. But be careful not to create beats that don't exist in the script—just look for the ones that do and utilize them to their maximum. You'll add color, life, and variety, and will become much more interesting to watch. If you're not sure about where the transitions lurk, consult a friend or acting coach who can give you insight.

Be a Good Listener. Though you will have defined your character and the scene before your audition, you may discover during your reading that the casting director has an entirely different interpretation. Though yours may be clever, you'll have to listen and adjust to the casting director's viewpoint. After all, good acting involves reacting to another person. So listen closely and flow with the casting director's interpretation by not forcing your pre-planned outcome. Allow the scene to go where it goes, from one unanticipated moment to the next, by being flexible and spontaneous. Allow what the moment brings. Think of your preparation as homework for a test, but respond to the test with what it asks for, not your premeditated response.

Display Good Technical Skills. Not all of your auditions will be videotaped, usually just commercial auditions and theatrical callbacks. But when you do find yourself looking into a camera, you will need to display good technical skills. A lack of technical awareness will hamper an otherwise excellent reading.

The most common problems are too much head movement and too much eye blinking. Frequent bobbing of the head is usually found in young stage actors not used to the confines of a camera. This can be remedied with practice in a good cold-reading class. Eye blinking, which is usually the by-product of nerves, is remedied by becoming aware of it and then practicing control over it. It's disappearance is proportionate to how comfortable you feel while auditioning.

Another problem is facial or verbal commenting. For some reason, actors tend to be the worst judges of their performances. If you were unsatisfied with your audition, then please don't comment negatively about it to the casting director in any way. That is unprofessional. Just ask if you may do it again. By throwing in your own opinion, facially or verbally, you are not allowing the casting director to make up their own mind, and it only works against you in the end. Not only might it influence the casting director, but it also makes you look insecure.

A Few Other Miscellaneous Hints. First, try to stay away from using props in theatrical auditions. Most casting directors hate props, unless they are specifically necessary for the scene to transpire. For example, most agree that your using your hand as a gun is much better than using a real one.

Second, don't try dialects or accents unless you have mastered them. A mediocre attempt will cast a shadow over your whole audition. It will make you look like a novice.

Finally, make sure that you correctly pronounce any names, places, or foreign expressions that are found in the script. If you mispronounce a word when reading a line, it shows that you didn't take time to learn as much as you could about the material. Very simply, it makes you look less intelligent than the next person who comes in and pronounces it correctly.

After Your Audition

Okay, you're done. You've given the casting director the best you could. Regardless of how it went, you should leave feeling good about yourself. Be happy that you had the courage and initiative to go and seek out an opportunity, thereby placing yourself in a vulnerable situation that most people are too afraid to even consider. If you feel you gave a great reading then celebrate! Evaluate your performance and catalog it for the future. If you feel you did a poor job, don't beat yourself up. You wouldn't kick and dent a Mercedes if its engine made a peculiar noise, would you? The best thing to do is note what you could have done better, and then work on it. Think about ways you can improve. That's all you can do.

Auditioning is a complex process that requires a lot of practice. It can be very stressful at first, but like anything else, it becomes easier with experience. So audition every chance you get! Think of auditions as opportunities to act, not as opportunities to be judged!

If the casting director wants to have you back for a callback, you'll know within several days. After that time, you probably can assume you weren't right for that particular part. But you never know where things can lead. The casting director might remember you and call you in for other projects in the future! You just never know. So stay optimistic regardless of whether or not you were called back.

I recommend sending a thank you card after each audition to the casting director for whom you auditioned. You should thank them for giving you the opportunity to read, especially because probably less than 10 percent of all actors that were submitted by agents were called in. I don't think many actors do this, so you'll definitely make a small mark by writing. Besides, true gratitude is a good thing.

A Few Words about Open Calls

From time to time, you may hear about "open casting calls" for certain roles in a television series or movie. An "open casting call" means that anyone can come without an appointment or audition scheduled. They happen very infrequently in L.A., as compared to a place like New York City, but you should still be aware of them.

If you go to one, then go early! Usually hundreds, if not thousands, show up and wait for hours to be seen. Unfortunately, it seems that in

L.A. some of these are publicity stunts and the roles being offered end up going to "name" actors anyway. The goal of such events is really to generate a lot of hoopla about the particular film or television show.

One example is the part of Robin in *Batman Forever*. A major studio held an open call here in L.A. in 1994 looking for a "street-smart, Hispanic" Robin, and auditioned many, many young unknown actors. Chris O'Donnell ended up playing the part, along with an all-star cast. Call me crazy, but was the studio really going to consider an "unknown" for a such a blockbuster movie? I think not, but only they know for sure.

Nevertheless, don't be discouraged about open calls. If you think you fit the description for a part, then go anyway. Even if the part goes to a star or the movie never comes to fruition, at least you'll get more auditioning experience, and you might even walk away with a free token. (I got a baseball cap at an open call for the TV series "The Untouchables"!) You never know what could happen—you might get the part.

Industry Interview:
Advice from Mike Fenton, Casting Director (*E.T., Raiders of the Lost Ark, Back to the Future, Total Recall, Aliens, Getaway, Arachnaphobia, Congo,* and many other successful films) on Actors and Auditioning

There's a lot of preparation for an actor before they walk in your door. Could you tell me about that?

The preparation is to have a picture and resume that are professional. New actors should find out from other actors, agents, or managers what format their resume should take. Their photograph should be an eight-by-ten, double-weight matte finish shot—preferably a headshot, for the motion picture business. Photographers couldn't figure out anything better to do, so they decided that people in the motion picture business wanted to see three-quarter photographs. That's nonsense. People in the motion picture business want to see eyes. Therefore, close-ups are better. The photo should be current. A change in hair, facial hair, or weight dictates the necessity of having new pictures.

With any luck at some point, actors will have to devise and put together a videotape, but that's another part of the story.

What do think distinguishes a really good audition?

I don't see auditions. All we do is interview people, unless we're actually putting people on tape for a particular project. So an audition is nothing more than sitting down and chatting.

Auditions can be very interesting. I'll give you a little story. I went to New York for a film called *Blown Away* and I was looking for a young man to play a particular part. A young man showed up two days before anyone was going to meet the director. He gave me his picture and resume, and I looked at it. The resume had been changed. Under special skills and abilities, it said "Long-Distance Runner." Obviously, the agent had told this kid that I'm a long-distance runner. He also put on his resume that he went to "States in Cross-Country." So I said to this young man, "How did you do in the States?" He told me that he won. I said, "Oh, what was your time?" He said he didn't remember. He was out the door faster than if the door had been revolving.

If you're going lie on your resume, you had better have the information and lie accurately. He didn't have a clue what cross-country running was. Not a clue. If you won, you'd know your time for the rest of your life. You'd go to the grave knowing what your time was. It's like any other sport: If you swim the 100-meter butterfly, you will know your times for the rest of your life.

The guy was a liar, and I don't like liars. When I find someone has lied on their resume, it's the end of the interview.

Could you tell me a little about what really stands out about an actor. Is that hard to define?

There's no way anyone can define what makes a star. I've heard that question for thirty years. You don't know.

When I first met Madeleine Stowe, she came in and sat down, and there was something about her that was just arresting. (Joe Rice sent Madeleine Stowe to meet me. He called and said, "I've got this fascinating young woman you must meet.") I'm not sure whether it was her eyes, her face, or her body. But when you put it all together, she became a package. She became a woman who was attractive, alluring, sensual, and bright, with a very good education. A very smart young woman.

I'm very interested in an actor's formal education. A formal education indicates to me someone who wishes to be a professional. There are a number of people who come to Hollywood and think they are going to fall off the turnip truck, be struck by lightning, and immediately become stars. Therefore, they don't even begin to study. They don't even try to become professionals. I think that a person like that might get lucky and get a job in television, but they will never have a career. Actors who have real careers are usually actors who by and large have formal education and professional coaches with whom they have studied.

Many of our best actors have gone to England. They've gone to the National Theatre. They've become members of the Royal Shakespeare Company. They've studied at LAMBDA. They've studied at RADA. They've studied at Central in London, and they study constantly. And that is really the bottom line. They study and continue to study. Believe me, Al Pacino and Bobby De Niro study when they are home in New York. They study with professional acting teachers. They hone their craft. They are always prepared.

When I look at a resume I want to know if someone has studied with an acting teacher who I feel is one of the top professionals in the game. If they have, then all of a sudden it elevates that individual.

Do you have any other suggestion for an actor moving out here?

I don't know if this will necessarily help them, but it is imperative in Hollywood for artists to have agents. They cannot succeed without an agent. If they can't get an agent, then they have to get a manager. They need to get someone who can open the door—at least so they can get their foot in. Because without a foot in the door, or without the door being somewhat ajar, they can never make it. You cannot come out here and send pictures and resumes to casting directors and expect to have a career. It just won't happen.

You probably get many calls every day from agents asking you to see clients. How often do you see those clients?

Well, it depends on how busy we are. Currently, we have a number of pictures starting in the next several months. Right now, we are trying to set the leads, so all of our time is spent working from lists. At the moment, we could care less about the smaller parts. It's a rude thing to say, but you can't make a movie by casting day-players. You make a movie with the people who get the audience to buy the tickets. Therefore, we spend much of our time putting together lists and making offers to entice stars into projects. That is a never ending task. It goes on constantly.

And once the leads are cast, do you have your assistants bring in actors?

No, Allison, Julie and I cast the movies together. I would not run an operation where I had an assistant do the casting work. In my opinion, that would be unfair to the producer.

Finally, is there anything else you want to say?

Acting is one of the single most thankless professions that a person can attempt. It is heart-rending. Actors are so fragile that when they get rejected, they just about blow their brains out. My suggestion is that for any actor, the crux of the matter is that they must love acting.

They can act anywhere in the United States. For them to come to California and vegetate, and not even have the opportunity to have a door open for them, in my mind, is a great waste of time. I think that actors should realize that they can make a living probably anywhere in the United States easier than they can in Southern California. It's important for actors to realize that if they live in Atlanta, New Orleans, or St. Louis, and are making a living as a big fish in a small pond, they are better off staying there and continuing to have a life, rather than uprooting themselves, coming to California, and finding only frustration.

A ton of movies are being shot all over the country. For the smaller parts, the studios don't want us to haul actors from California to New Orleans, for example. They would prefer we use people in New Orleans. Actors have a much better opportunity for really meaningful roles being right where they are, especially if they are the big fish in that pond.

There's one other thing, and this is perhaps very rude. Motion picture stars are attractive people. For the young artist seeking a career, the first thing they have to do is look in the mirror and be very realistic.

Yes, there are exceptions, but for the most part, to really have a career in the motion picture business, one has to be relatively attractive. When we look at the stars of movies, by and large, they are very attractive people. They have some sort of charisma, something that we can't bottle.

We can't put our finger on it. If it were possible for an agent, casting director, or talent scout to recognize the magic of an individual and say "That person will be a star!" and then they emerge as a star, that would be one of the greatest gifts that any human being could have. But I defy you to find somebody who can meet an individual walking into their office and can say in all honesty, "That person will become a star." It's almost impossible to do because we don't make the stars, the people who buy the tickets make the stars. For example, we used Jim Carrey in a movie a number of years ago in Canada. He played a small part and was very good in it. But fifteen years later, all of a sudden he's getting $20 million a movie! What a great business!

Industry Interview:
Advice from Tony Shepherd, Vice President of Talent and Casting, Spelling Television Inc., on Actors and Auditioning

To give the readers an understanding of your job, could you tell me briefly what your duties entail?

Basically, I oversee the casting of all the shows that Spelling Television produces. My primary focus deals with series players and people who are around for more than a day or two. However, I do oversee the day-player and guest-starring roles, but the focus is primarily new project development and ongoing series players.

What advice do you have for actors in terms of auditioning? You've seen hundreds and hundreds of actors, and I'm sure you've seen a lot of both good and bad auditions. What advice do you have that would help actors improve their auditioning?

I don't know how many bad auditions I actually see. You'd be surprised how few bad ones there are. I think that when you work on the kind of shows that we do, most of the people who come in the door have been around a while. I think they've eliminated some of the preliminary mistakes that new actors make. So I think I see more good auditions than bad auditions. However, we don't see a lot of great auditions, which is the key.

To be successful in the audition process, more than anything actors need a total sense of self. They need to understand how they fit into the big picture and how all the pieces of the puzzle fit together.

Actors come here to L.A, and there are a thousand closed doors, surrounded by a bunch of tall brick walls that people have to try to scale. Hopefully they'll find the door that you can open behind that brick wall.

After an actor settles down in this town and deals with all the B.S., and once they finally walk in the door of a Warner Bros. or Spelling Television, or Columbia, Paramount, Disney, or wherever, they have to be prepared to meet the challenge. That means thoroughly understanding the business, understanding how the audition process works, understanding the craft of acting, being ready to face the challenge.

One of the things I say when I go around the country and speak to actors is that there is probably not a single person who comes to this town who doesn't know somebody who knows somebody. There's an old saying, "It only takes two phone calls to reach anybody in the world." Think about that. We were going through an example one day, and somebody said "What about Bill Clinton?" I responded, "I'd pick up the phone and call Linda Bloodworth-Thomason." I don't know her real well, but I know her well enough, and she could pick up the phone, call Bill Clinton, and I would get to Bill Clinton. It takes two calls to reach anybody in the world. So the theory is if you want to go sit in the president's office at Warner Bros. and cold-read for him, chances are you would have the ability to do so. And I'm talking in the ethereal, figurative sense.

Fine, that's all well and wonderful, but the day you walk into that office, and whether it's the president of Warner Bros. or the casting director who's casting a low-budget fifty thousand dollar movie, the actor has to be ready to face that challenge. The question is: do they have everything and the entire package put together that makes them ready to face that?

How would you define that package?

I think there are eight different elements that make up an actor. The first four elements of the truly complete actor are 1) a drive and determination to make it, 2) an openness and honesty as a person, 3) a willingness to take a risk, and 4) a total 100 percent belief in himself/herself.

The other four elements are what makes up the actor: 5) the actor's look, 6) the actor's talent, 7) the actor's personality, and 8) the actor's discipline. You put those eight elements together, and if everything is clicking, all eight of those elements will kick in and the actor will get the job.

Someone asked me once to give an analogy to what other job in the world is like being an actor, and that's easy: a baseball player. Becoming a baseball player is almost identical to becoming an actor. Think about it. Many are called, few are chosen. There are a lot of professional baseball players out there but very few make the major leagues. The most successful player fails seven out of ten times, which means that on average they get three hits out of every ten times up at bat. And in terms of the ability to do what they do, they have to practice the craft. You can't expect a baseball player to hit a home run and win a game at the bottom of the ninth if he doesn't take batting practice every day. Likewise, you can't expect an actor to walk into a room, do an audition, and get the job if he doesn't work at his craft everyday, which means taking classes. So if you take those eight elements of an actor and you put it together with the baseball analogy, it gives you an overall picture.

I think you can break down the talent, look, discipline, and personality a little bit more specifically: Contrary to what the average guy on the street thinks, there are people who make solid livings in this business who are not stunningly beautiful. If you happen to be blessed with extraordinary youth and extraordinary beauty, that's great. It will get you through the door. But once you're through the door, you've got to be able to stay in the room. Without all the other elements (like talent, discipline, personality), careers will lack longevity. It's my hope for any actor that their acting careers last longer than their youth and beauty.

Talent is the only lasting thing in this business. If you're good at what you do, if you're a good actor and you have the ability to put the work out there, whether it's a showcase or a theatre or wherever, someone someday is going to see it. The cream does always rise to the top without question. Talent is the only lasting thing. It's the only thing that will remain.

What can you say about the profession of acting?

Being an actor is a frustrating business at best, for a myriad of reasons. Number One: actors continually work at the craft and continually study. The average actor will probably put five to ten thousand dollars a year into classes and training in the beginning. And they'll get into a workshop mode after that, without a guarantee that they'll ever earn a dime at the craft.

If you're a lawyer and you take a seminar, it will add to what you do, and therefore allow you to bill more hours. There are no guarantees in this business—none whatsoever. If you pass the law bar, finish in the top half of your class, and you go to a decent law school, you will get a job. But there's no guarantee you will get a job as an actor.

One of things that I think is a real cold-hearted reality for actors is if an actor goes to school in any state besides California, Illinois, New York, Florida, or Texas, which are really the main talent centers of this country, when they come out here they are going to have to unlearn everything they learned in college.

People frequently say to me, "You travel all over the country speaking to actors. You must speak at colleges and universities often." The truth is very rarely. Very frankly, colleges and universities don't want to hear what I have to say because I'm basically teaching the antithesis of what they teach in the classroom. There's no substitute for an education, but what colleges and universities in this country do is teach an actor how to teach acting. In most cases, theatre departments are preparing people for a career as a teacher.

That's right, go to graduate school, get an M.F.A. . . . .

And teach away! So the first thing I tell actors to do after they move here is to find a class. It doesn't have to be ten weeks, or even two weeks. It could be one day or a weekend. Go to UCLA, USC, and take a class in the business of show. It's called show "business" for a reason.

I think the actor has to come into Los Angeles with two separate agendas: their business agenda and their creative agenda. One should not interfere with the other. I believe that taking classes is critical, and if it comes down to eating or taking a class, you take a class because you'll feel better anyway since you won't be as fat! (Laugh) That's Number One.

On the business side of things, you have to come in with a series of goals, and you have to try to achieve those goals on a step-by-step basis. When I speak to actors, I ask how many people have a personal definition of success. Out of a group of approximately seventy-five people, ten will raise their hands. I'll also ask them why they want to be actors, and maybe twenty will raise their hands. We live in a world that's full of people who don't know what they want and will go through hell to get it.

You have to have a career plan. You need a definition for success. You've got to know why you want to be an actor. With success, which is a really important thing for the actor, early on the rewards are few and far between. I tell actors that my own definition for success is that it's not how far you've gotten, it's the distance you've traveled from where you started. So if you are taking a step every day towards your career, you are becoming a success. Let's face it, there isn't going to be somebody with the proverbial contract and pen in hand waiting for you every day. You've got to create your own success. You've got to take control of it.

There is a really hard concept for actors to accept: that acting is something you should want to do so badly you're willing to do it for nothing, and get so good at it that people are willing to pay you for it. I think that the day that an actor accepts this concept, and really truly from his heart believes it, is the day that dealing with what goes on here will be better. It's really hard for actors to accept because they're saying, "Look, I could happily act in Des Moines, Iowa, but I came out to L.A. because I want to be paid as an actor." Well, if you're looking to come out and be paid for the work—yes, you want that—but that's not your reason for being here. You've got to totally love the craft and totally love the creative side of it, which makes the business all worthwhile. You're going to get knocked around so much on the business side. If the creative side is not where it's supposed to be, you're going to be in big trouble.

What can you say about finding an acting coach and the right "method" for you?

In terms of studying acting, I do believe that though your best friend next door, John Actor, may swear by his teacher, and you may be the best of friends—you may live together, you may be lovers, you may be husband and wife—but his teacher may not work for you. It's a very individual thing. I rarely meet an actor who has studied with one teacher their entire career, because you can only take so much out of somebody and then you want to add to that from someone else. The best "method" of acting is taking a little bit of this one, and a little bit of that one, and a little bit of this one, and put it together into the "method" that works best for you.

When you're watching an audition, what really turns you on about an actor's performance? What are you looking for?

It's that undefinable something. I'll be honest, I get asked that question at every single interview I do. And I'll give you the same answer I give everybody else: In the broadest sense, if I could isolate that, I would put it in a bottle, put it on a shelf, and sell it for $150, and then retire because every actor would buy it. It is that undefinable something. It really is. When the right actor walks in the room, it is definitely a combination of actor and role.

I have a perfect example. A young actress came in here yesterday, who we had seen previously for "90210," and she read for a role that she wasn't right for. We brought her back to read for a pilot that we're doing, and she walked in the room, and it was just like sparks were flying from the chair. She is so right for the part. She is talented, has the perfect look, is the right age, and has a great personality that comes through the work. There is enough of who she is that she can put into the work and make it real and believable. It's the perfect combination of actor and role. Her "90210" reading was very nice. But she wasn't that part. She was this part. And it's not that she was typecast, it's just the perfect combination of actor and role.

I think the actor's job is to take all these various elements and put them together into one neat little package. And going back to baseball: you spend hours working on your swing, where your feet are, where you keep your hand, how you see the ball, all those things. You try to put those into action every single time at bat. The truth of the matter is that no matter how good you are, you're not going to be successful every time. The same is true with the actor. Everything he does at an audition may be absolutely right, but it may not be the right combination of factors.

Physically, obviously, you've got to fit the silhouette. If you don't fit the silhouette, no matter what you do, it's not going to get you the job.

Are there exceptions to that rule? Yes, there are. Here's an example: Joey Tata is a series regular on "90210." He plays Nat, the guy who owns the Peach Pit. I have known him for many years and he is a close personal friend of mine. He has had a long and distinguished career, with over 700 hours of film. I've always said that if you look up "character actor" in the dictionary, you'd see Joey's picture. In the very first season of "90210," about four or five episodes into the show, they were looking for a character to run this Peach Pit. The way they described this role to me initially, it sounded like it was perfect for Joey. I told the casting director that I wanted Joey to read for the producer. (This was on a Monday, and the audition was on a Thursday.) Come Wednesday, the concept of the role was changed to be a kind, old grandfather type, not a smart-talking ex-actor—what the role is now.

I'll be honest with you, had he not been my friend, I would have canceled his audition. But I said to Dianne Young, the casting director, let him read and if he doesn't get it, I'll explain that they changed the concept of the role. Well, the bottom line is that he came in and they loved him so much, they changed the concept back. That doesn't happen every day, but it's a valuable story because it's certainly about bucking the odds, and there's great tales of perseverance. I guess the bottom line to it is: no matter how right you are, how good you are, how right it's working that day, there are elements that are out of your control.

Red Skelton once said, that in any business two plus two equals four. But in show business, it equals, six, five, or eight, but never four. The reason you have to write a book and the reason I go all over the country talking to actors is because for every rule there is, there are 125 exceptions.

In what way do you recommend that actors approach a life in show business here in L.A?

I believe in the most conservative step-by-step approach to this business that you can take. But I tell actors around the country that some of them may find themselves in Los Angeles one day, and they might approach the business exactly as I tell them to, and it might not work. Then they might go out and do the direct opposite of what I tell them and end up on a series in three months. There are no guarantees. I know good actors who have come here and been out here for six to seven years, plugging away, and still don't have an agent, don't have a SAG card, and can't get a job. And I know actors who have walked into this town on April 1st, and on April 30th have an agent, their SAG card, and already have two small roles, and they are off and running. There are no rules, and it's very frustrating. And as a wise doctor friend of mine said, "To be forewarned, is to be forearmed," and the best thing you can do is come into this town with as much information as possible.

I certainly recommend that when you're considering coming here, you don't just say "On January 14th, I'm moving to Los Angeles." When I'm speaking to actors in another part of the country I'll ask how many are thinking about moving to Los Angeles. Out of seventy-five, maybe forty-five or fifty hands will go up. Of those, only half have ever been to L.A. before. How do you know you want to come to L.A. if you've never been to L.A. before?

Hollywood is a place where you spend more money than you make on things that you don't need to impress people that you don't like. I've always described Los Angeles as being a circus without the tent. This is a scary place. It's very different. You've got to come out here and take a look around. You've got to make a trial visit. Go on the Universal Studios tour—it may be the only studio lot you ever get on. Look around and see what the city is about.

In your opinion how has Hollywood changed and how is it different from the rest of the country?

Hollywood, first of all, is a misnomer, because there is no Hollywood. Hollywood is the land of make-believe. There are a number of things actors should realize. First of all, in 1965 or 1970, approximately 85 to 90 percent of all motion pictures and television shows were shot in Los Angeles. It's now only 20 to 30 percent.

You know what I tell experienced actors who come here: experienced actors come to Los Angeles to relocate from here to somewhere else. Every year you'll get that influx of actors who come here for pilot season, hopefully with agents. (Why an actor would come here for pilot season without an agent is like leaving a diabetic in a candy store.) They come here, find an apartment, move in, they're here two months, then they get a pilot. But the pilot says they have to move to Vancouver or Florida, or San Antonio, Texas. That's one thing that's different.

But also, the city itself. How many cities do you know in this country where you can see beautiful manicured lawns, gorgeous houses, and unless someone told you that if you walk down the street at night, you're going to get shot, you wouldn't you know it. Some of the most beautiful areas in the city are incredibly dangerous.

There's also that problem of understanding what the sense of community here is and the lack thereof. I have a little bit of a unique perspective on this. I was born and raised here. I've lived a lot of other places too, and because of the seminars I teach, I've had the benefit of seeing almost every major city in the country. There is nothing that can prepare an actor for L.A., especially actors who come from parts of the country where people stop and talk to you on the street. There's nothing that can prepare them for what they are going to face here. For some it can be frightening.

I met a young actress recently who had moved here from Cincinnati, which is a big city, but it's really different from L.A. There's virtually no entertainment community there. She came out here totally on her own, not knowing a soul. She managed to start working immediately doing B-movies, and did that for six months and then realized she'd done twenty B-movies, where she wasn't wearing clothes in about half of them. She had realized she had come to an impasse in her career and was trying figure out what she could do.

When she got here, she was mortified at what she found. She was used to walking down the street and people saying hello, being able to go out and shop at two-o'clock in the morning, without having to look over your shoulder. When it comes to L.A., it's a whole different environment.

People have to be comfortable here. I tell actors that they should bring as much from where they come as they can. There is something about coming home at night and seeing that chair from home, that carpet, that picture on the wall, whatever. The little things. It's having those little creature comforts around you.

Another suggestion is that if at all humanly possible, move out here with somebody. It helps. At least you have somebody you can share those experiences with.

Also, once you find a place to live, find an acting class. Even if it's temporary, you've got to be surrounded by people who do what you do. Even if you move out with someone, you don't know anybody here. What happens when the first Saturday night rolls around and you're sitting alone—and this can be an incredibly lonely city. You need to have people around you.

Actors, although competitive, do share a common bond. When you hit that acting class, strike up friendships. But when it comes to the business, talk very little and listen very much. The reality is you don't want to give too much information, and you want to take as much information as you can get. It takes some practice. I can give you ten examples of actors who have whispered a little too loudly in their acting classes about auditions, and then people overheard them, went out and got the jobs. Right, wrong, or indifferent, it happens.

Finally, bring a car if at all possible. The reason is that it's probably 25 to 30 percent more expensive here than the rest of the country to buy a car. It's the old "supply and demand." If you do have to buy a car here, then you are better off doing it out of L.A. County, maybe Orange County or Ventura County, where it might be less expensive.

CHAPTER THIRTEEN

Getting the Part

Hopefully after you learn the ropes of auditioning and you practice at it, you'll go out into the real world, audition your heart out, and soon be hired as an actor here in Los Angeles! Someone might want your services for just a day, maybe a week, possibly a month, or even in a starring capacity in a motion picture or television series. Whatever it ends up being, be happy about it. Any credit, big or small, will help to advance your acting career.

As a new actor, there are a few things you should know about being hired. These include understanding your contract, how it's negotiated, how you should be prepared for your job, and how you can publicize it afterwards. This chapter aims to cover all of these important details.

Your Contract and How It's Negotiated

As mentioned in chapter 10, your agent will be negotiating your contract for you. Fortunately, this is not something that will be drawn up from scratch or that requires a tremendous amount of work. Remember the helpful unions, SAG and AFTRA, which were established to protect actors? Well, every few years a union negotiating committee renegotiates a standard agreement with all motion picture/television producers and the networks. The agreement applies whenever an actor is hired, and it covers significant things like minimum wages, overtime, per diems, and a wide variety of regulations governing working conditions.

For example, the agreement clearly spells out the minimum wages (called "scale") that a union actor is to be paid when working in television or in theatrical films. The minimum wages for principal performers are as follows: Daily Performers earn $522.00 per day. (On 7/1/96 it will become $540.00, and on 7/1/97 it will become $559.00.) Weekly Performers earn $1,813.00 per week. (On 7/1/96 it will become $1,877.00, and on 7/1/97 it will become $1,942.00.) There are also other salary provisions for stand-ins, extras, stunt coordinators, and residual payments.

The parts of the contract that will actually have to be negotiated are few. These include your actual salary (which will either be scale or above), your credit or billing (where your name appears), and a per diem (a daily allowance, if you are shooting out of town). When it comes to negotiating salary, your agent will not have much leverage if you are totally unknown as an actor. Many new actors or relatively new actors receive "scale plus ten," which means SAG minimum wage plus an additional 10 percent to cover the agent's fee. Even some established actors, but not stars, are sometimes forced to accept scale wages if they want to work at all.

Over the years, production companies have been paying less and less to day-player and featured performers as they shell out larger and larger sums for the stars. In other words, in some productions there are one or two actors making several million dollars, and most of the others are earning scale.

One positive for actors, however, is that new networks and channels are developing, which ultimately is leading to more product being produced. That means there are more acting jobs on the market for all the actors here in L.A.!

Understanding How Deals Are Made

Deal-making can be very simple and also very complex. As I mentioned, for most acting jobs, the negotiation of the contract is very quick. The only time it can get complex is when you are a star or you are up for a major role. Star-level talent agencies, with the assistance of entertainment lawyers on staff, will ask for as much as they can get for their clients who earn millions of dollars. In addition to sky-high salaries, they negotiate things like special living quarters, special meals, percentages of profit, and even things like having a golf or batting cage on the set. These things are not relevant to newcomers, so for now, I'll explain how deals are made for most actors in the business.

As a newcomer, in the beginning you typically will be hired for parts that last from only one day to a few weeks. When a studio or production company is interested in you for a particular project, your agent will be contacted. Usually the casting director will call and say that you are wanted for a role (usually the one you auditioned for, but not always). They will also specify how many days you are needed for.

Determining Your Salary

Many times the casting director will tell your agent how much the production company is willing to pay, if it hasn't already been disclosed in the Breakdowns. For example, at the top of a Breakdown casting notice for a particular project, it might say "Salary: Scale + 10%." That lets agents know what the production company is willing to pay for the parts offered. Therefore, there won't be any negotiating and agents won't submit actors who only work for amounts higher than what is offered. This opens the door to newcomers who almost always work for scale.

Other times, the casting director will ask your agent for your day-quote—your daily working rate—before disclosing how much money the production company might be willing to offer. As a new actor, you probably won't have a day-quote, because a day-quote is established by working on projects where you've made more than scale. Your agent will either tell them that you have no quote or give them your quote if you have one, and then the casting director will present it to the producers of the project who will then put together an offer.

Whenever an offer is presented, a good agent will usually try to get more money than proposed. Agents will say, "Listen, she worked on *Movie XYZ* and got X amount of dollars, so she should at least get that now." The casting director will then try to verify that previous salary. However, that still might prove to be pointless. If the production company is only willing to pay a certain salary, the job will go to another actor if your agent won't accept the offer. That means you might lose the job because you and your agent tried to get you more money! Bargaining is part of the business, but in today's world where competition is fierce, most actors are willing to take lower-paying jobs than they are used to (as long as the casting director won't tell anyone that they were paid less than their day-quote). If you need food on the table, you take what you can get.

Some new actors think it unfair that stars and celebrities make so much money, and they—struggling actors—often only make scale. Here is the reasoning behind it: big stars are not paid twenty million dollars because of their tremendous acting ability. They are paid huge sums because they have an ability to attract an audience that will pay millions of dollars to come see a movie. An "unknown" actor has no power at the box office. An unknown can't draw in the masses to see a movie. Therefore, that actor is usually paid scale, or slightly above, for his or her acting services only, not any box office power. Can you understand the rationale?

What about Billing?

Where and how your name appears, billing, helps to give you name recognition and also satisifies you and your relatives who might be watching you. Since most newcomers are hired for small parts, billing is usually not a big issue. It's usually left to the producer's discretion, as to where your name will appear. In film, featured players with speaking lines are listed in the ending credits, along with crew members, sound-track credits, and other miscellaneous credits. However, if you have a nice supporting role or you are co-starring on television, your agent might want to discuss billing. If you've landed a really big part, your agent will also have to discuss where, how, and if, your name will appear in advertising. But for most roles that newcomers get, billing is very straight-forward and not even necessary to negotiate.

A Per Diem

One other element that might need to be negotiated is your per diem, which is an additional daily allowance. If the movie is shot outside of Los Angeles—and more and more are these days—you will receive a per diem. The current SAG travel allowance minimum is $70.00, used to cover additional meals and living expenses. This is not usually a debated issue, although some agents have been able to negotiate high per diem's for their actors, sometimes up to $200.00 a day or more. That's a lot of pocket change! But like billing, it's usually not necessary to negotiate it when it involves a relatively new actor who's only hired for a few days.

Getting Ready for Your Job

After your contract is negotiated and you are officially hired, there are still a few more details that need to be attended to before you start work. They are:

Getting a Script. You'll need to get a copy of the script. One will either be delivered to you, or you will pick one up before your first day(s) of work. If the part is tiny, you might actually just get to see the script the day you show up. For example, if you yell out only one word in one scene, getting a complete script in your hands is not of the utmost urgency. On the contrary, if you've got twenty lines, plans will definitely be made for you to get a script immediately.

Getting Dressed. You'll also have to work out wardrobe details. Sometimes the production company will provide your attire, especially if you're working on a period piece. Other times they might want you to bring in your own clothes, especially if you have a very small role, in an effort to save money on costume rentals. This is all cleared up with a simple phone call to wardrobe. Depending on how important you are and how important your role is, you will either have to make the call yourself or you will get a call from wardrobe. The discussion will probably take only a few minutes, and will cover things like shirt sizes and wardrobe colors. So be attentive and make sure you know your measurements.

Once these details are straightened out, you just have to work on the acting aspect. Make sure you learn your lines. Constantly forgetting or stumbling over your lines on the set is something you won't want to do. Therefore, practice, practice, practice. Try to foresee all possible circumstances—though if you could do that you might not be in this business! Prepare different ways you can deliver your lines in the event the director says "I want you to try it differently." Also be aware that your lines may be changed overnight. Yes, that's right. The writers might change, add, delete, or swap any of your lines and not even tell you until you show up. You'll arrive ready to go with your scene only to find out that a new one has been written. So plan for this possibility, though it's more likely that it won't happen. Developing an ability to pick up new material, learn it fast, and deliver it well on cue will only help you.

The Day You Go to Work

Make sure you set a couple of alarms to wake you up the day of your job. Can you think of anything worse than oversleeping for something you've worked so hard to get?

Next, go over your lines as you get ready. Get warmed up! Stretch, exercise, eat right, and practice. But don't drive yourself crazy—you have to make this business fun! When you get ready to leave, another good idea is to have the production office's phone number with you, in the event you have any unexpected delays. And as with auditioning, make sure you leave for your destination early.

If you are shooting on a studio lot, your name will be on a list at the front gate, and you'll be allowed to enter. You'll also be given directions to the stage where you are shooting. If you are working on location, you could be shooting anywhere from downtown L.A. to Long Beach. So keep that Thomas Guide handy!

When you finally get to the set, the first person you'll probably be looking for is the second assistant director—not anyone else. He or she will have your contract, in addition to some brief tax forms for you to fill out. You'll have to sign these papers sometime during the day. Be sure to look over your contract to see that everything is correctly stated. Check for your name, your ID numbers (telephone, social security, address), your salary, per diem, billing, and anything else that might have been negotiated by your agent. Otherwise everything on it should be okay. Remember it's a standard SAG contract, so you won't have to worry about the fine print.

Next, you'll probably be directed by the second A.D. to one of several places. Most likely you'll go to your trailer or dressing room, but if they need you soon, you might be ushered off to wardrobe or make-up. You'll notice that big stars generally have bigger dressing rooms or trailers. If you are only working for a day or two, you might only get a fourth of a trailer! The general rule is the bigger the part, the bigger the trailer. That's just the way it goes. However, when it comes to make-up, everybody usually shares the same make-up room.

The second A.D., or one of his or her assistants, will keep tabs on you throughout the day. It's their job to know where everyone is at all times. To avoid any unnecessary all-out searches for you, it's best to stay just in your designated area. Of course, you should feel free to visit "craft service," the food table, for some munchies. (A side note: you can always tell the budget of a film by the expansiveness of the craft service set-up. A major feature film production will have money budgeted for all kinds of goodies: cereals, fruits, veggies, snacks, cookies, drinks, and even vitamins. A small budget movie might only have cheese balls. Yikes!)

Working on Television Is Different from Film

While all of the above information applies to both television and film, you should know that there are some differences when working in each medium. On movies, you generally will show up for your part, wait in your trailer for a few hours or even most of the day, and come out when they need you. You'll probably have only a brief rehearsal if it's a small part, maybe a couple of runs through your scene and then you'll shoot. Obviously, this is for small parts. If your part is larger, it will be a little different. You will get to know the cast and crew, and feel much more at home on the set.

For sitcoms, you typically are hired for the week if you have a co-starring role, and sometimes three days for smaller parts. Most rehearse for four days, and shoot on the fifth. That gives you the opportunity to become closer to everyone on the set. Dramatic serials shoot more like movies, filming different scenes on different days of the week. Thus, you'll be called when they need you, without four days of rehearsal. Soap operas shoot a full episode everyday, which is the toughest job of all. This is why everyone says that soap work is the hardest. Most soaps rehearse the full episode in the morning and tape in the afternoon, with usually only two or three takes per scene. So make sure you know your lines! (Soaps do use cue cards though, because it can be very difficult for cast members to perfectly memorize pages and pages of script every day.)

You're On!

Depending on which director you work with and in which medium, you may get a lot assistance or virtually none. Film directors seem more apt to discuss your work with you, offering suggestions and guidance, as they can shoot one scene for days. Television directors seem more intent on getting the show finished on time in an acceptable state. But it really depends on the director. There are plenty of exceptions in both mediums.

If you are on a movie, you will have to shoot the scene several times from several different angles. Then it will all be edited together. You'll start with a master shot that opens the scene with all actors in it, and then proceed to shoot close-ups of each actor. Most television serials, such as medical or legal dramas, shoot this way also. Sitcoms and soap operas shoot with four differently located video cameras that tape the dialogue simultaneously. This is why their shooting schedule is much more rapid.

That's a Wrap!

Okay, you've given an Academy Award–winning performance and now you're done, or "wrapped" as they say. You'll be thanked and then all you have to do is sign-out with the second A.D. They will have your call-time for the following day if you are scheduled to come back. Go home and revel in your experience.

Publicizing Your Success

Publicizing your job is important, but overly celebrating it is not only a little tacky but also like "counting your chickens before they hatch." You can only definitively celebrate your moment in the spotlight once that film or television show airs and you're still in it. If you had a sizable role, you will probably still be included. Smaller roles, especially in films, can occasionally end up on the cutting room floor if the scene wasn't crucial and footage had to be cut. Think positive, but be prepared for that possibility. Hopefully that won't happen to you.

In the meantime, it's nice to casually inform any industry people that you meet that you just finished working on this movie or that television show! Work breeds work. Directors, producers, and casting directors love to hear actors say that they are working. It gives more power to that actor because it shows that someone was interested in hiring them.

But before you contact anyone about going to see you or watching you on television, make sure that you are definitely still going to be seen and that your performance warrants watching. If you only have a line or two, then be up-front about it. (No one but your mother and your agent will be overjoyed to see you pop on screen, say "Madam, here is your drink," and then disappear for good. It's a nice credit to put on your resume, but realistically no one will remember it as a stunning performance.) On the other hand, if you have a meaty role, make some phone calls, send out some flyers, or take out ads in the trade papers.

Most television shows don't cut footage very much, so a part on TV will probably stay in the final product. Motion pictures, however, tend to cut out a lot. Therefore, contact the production company or go to the premiere first to make sure you are still in before you do any mass publicity. I know stars of movies who have gone to sneak previews and were absolutely stunned at how many scenes were cut. The moral of the story is your true achievement comes when you are still in the final product.

If you really want to do some major publicity and you have the money, then hire a publicist. They specialize in promoting actors and artists to the public, and can create campaigns for actors at all different levels of their careers. They range from mailings to all out media blitzes, and can cost you anywhere from five hundred to thousands and thousands of dollars a month.

The Snowball Effect

Booking your first job in L.A. is a nice feeling. For some, it takes a couple of weeks, for others, several years. No one can decisively say when it will happen, but with persistence your efforts will eventually pay off.

You will find that after you book your first job, it will be slightly easier to book your second, and third, and so on. I call that the "snowball effect." It happens partly because your confidence level goes up. It radiates through your entire aura. Another reason is that casting people take you a tiny bit more seriously. After you've worked for someone else they respect, especially if your role was in a critically acclaimed project, it will become easier to get into their offices for auditions and general interviews. They won't necessarily be begging to hire you. They'll just give you more acknowledgement. Some will give you an opportunity to read for bigger and better roles that otherwise would have been offered to someone else. Of course, getting the job will usually still depend on your audition.

The snowballing of your career is a gradual process, with many turns in the road. Some actors book five or six jobs in one year, and then don't work at all in the next. So working isn't always a guarantee of future employment. But in truth, it can be said that the more work you do, the more you will be respected and appreciated, which usually will create more opportunities for you in the long run.

CHAPTER FOURTEEN

Pertaining to the Wallet

Unfortunately, living in L.A. as an actor isn't as simple as showing up at the set, doing your role, and then relaxing in the California sunshine until your next booking. Yes, L.A. is the real world, which means you'll have to take care of, among other things, the financial matters of your life. This includes preparing for your taxes, living within your means, understanding unemployment (if you should ever need it), and saving money in whatever ways you can. When you become rich and famous, you'll have plenty of people take care of all of these affairs for you, but for now you should know how to manage them yourself.

Handling Your Taxes

No one likes taxes. In fact, the thought of preparing a tax return makes most people cringe. As an actor, you'll have to start keeping good records and saving receipts, since you'll be able to take many legitimate deductions by having them. I strongly advise that you hire an accountant, preferably one well-acquainted with actors and entertainers, to prepare your tax return for you. Not only will it save you time, especially if you have somewhat complicated taxes, but it will protect you from a tremendous headache and probably save you more money than if you did it yourself. The typical $100 to $200 dollar fee is well worth it.

In order to maximize your deductions, you will need organized receipts of acting expenses and mileage records. Deductible expenses include accounting fees, admissions and tickets to movies and plays, agency and manager commissions, business gifts, copying/typesetting fees for resumes, acting lessons/coaching, hairstyling, make-up/cosmetics, pagers and cellular phones, voice-mailboxes, photography, picture duplication costs, postage, *Academy Players Directory* fees, union dues, theatre company dues, publicity, trade magazines and books, wardrobe cleaning expenses, and any other expense that is solely related to acting that cannot be attributed to personal or other use.

You should also keep receipts of auto expenses, such as gas and repairs, as well as a mileage log for business miles driven. Your accountant will tell you that to derive a total figure for auto expenses, you can either take the total business miles driven during the year and multiply that by a standard per mile figure (currently thirty cents), or you can total up all your auto expenses and then multiply that by the percentage of business miles driven out of the total miles driven during the year. Which ever comes to a higher dollar amount will be used as a deduction.

Thus, it's so important to keep good records. Get a file cabinet or a special drawer so that you keep all of your receipts in one place. The more organized you start out, the easier it will be next April when you are scrambling to do your taxes.

The VITA Program

Once you are a member of SAG, you'll be able to receive free tax assistance if you want it. Volunteer members of the guild who have been trained by the IRS help other members prepare their tax returns. You can register to attend a small class held at the Guild in the months prior to every April 15 filing deadline. The program is called VITA (The Volunteer Income Tax Assistance) Committee. For more information contact the Screen Actors Guild.

Living Within Your Means

It sounds like common sense, but you'd be surprised how many actors seem to lack time and money management. Many actors start to slowly spend more than they earn, resulting in serious financial worries down the road.

This over-spending encompasses all aspects of life. For example, some people live in an apartment that they really can't afford. Some people come out to L.A. and rent a one-bedroom apartment that costs $800 or $900 a month. That's okay if you have a constant income, but a lot of actors don't. Living in a cheaper place, that's perhaps $500 to $600 a month could save you several thousand dollars a year.

Another bad habit that some actors develop is that they eat out too much. Ten or fifteen dollars at an average restaurant for one meal can buy food at a grocery store that could last several days. It's nice to go out to eat, but you should also learn to cook if you are on a limited budget. Think grains, beans, salads, and fruit. Not only will you save money, you'll start looking healthier too.

The same goes for socializing. In L.A., not only will you spend at least five dollars and up to twenty dollars just to get into most clubs, but you'll easily spend another twenty on drinks. (And if you have a date, that could be double.) So be smart. While it's important to socialize and make contacts, just be aware of how much you're spending.

Finally, watch your credit cards. Charging a little here and little there won't add up to much at the end of the week, but at the end of the year, you could easily accrue an extra debt of five or ten thousand dollars. Charge cards are convenient, but don't let them get too convenient. In other words, if you don't really need something, then don't buy it.

Learn to develop a practical way of thinking when it comes to money. You'll have plenty to spend when you're starring on television or in features, so for now just lead a simpler life.

Unemployment

Many actors have sought assistance from unemployment when times were just too lean to handle. There is mixed sentiment about actors using this program. Some actors feel they shouldn't have to take jobs outside of their chosen profession. Others say you should take any job you can get when you have to pay bills. For your sake, I've gathered the appropriate information on unemployment and you can decide for yourself.

The Unemployment Insurance Program is administered by the State Employment Development Department for citizens of California. If you file a claim and qualify for unemployment, you will be awarded weekly assistance based on previous earnings during a prior twelve-month period. This assistance will be for up to twenty-six weeks during a benefit year of fifty-two weeks.

Your payments will be modified on a weekly basis if you have any reported earnings during that week. Also, in order to qualify you have to fill out a form every week that reports any work you have performed and lists all attempts at seeking employment. (They want to make sure you're trying to find work.)

Unemployment has saved many actors from destitution. However, it's also encouraged some to be a little less tenacious in their quest for success. But if you need help, call your local employment development department office for assistance.

Saving Money in L.A.

As an actor who might be living on a limited income, you'll want to save money any way you can. This applies to nearly every aspect of your life, from food to resumes to clothing.

Below are a few money-saving tips that I've learned or that have been passed on to me by fellow actors.

Resumes and Other Stationery Supplies. Get your resumes copied at Staples or Office Depot, where you can get them for as low as two cents apiece, in quantities of 100 or more. It's much cheaper than using major copy chains, which typically charge seven cents or more per copy.

Of course, you'll have to make a trip to a major copy center to get them cut to eight-by-ten size, since Staples and Office Depot don't usually have cutting machines. Cutting charges typically run under two dollars for the whole stack. Making the two trips is worth it if you run off a lot of resumes and are tight on cash.

When in need of envelopes, rubber cement, or any other supplies for your desk, head to Staples or Office Depot again, or one of the major club warehouses, like PriceCostco or Sam's. You'll find items in bulk quantities at all of these stores, which saves you a lot of money. And as an actor, you will definitely go through 100 or more envelopes in no time, so buying in bulk is definitely the way to go.

Raid the 99-cent Store! Do you need laundry detergent, trash bags, soap, shampoo, toothbrushes, toilet paper, or batteries? No problem. The "99-Cent Stores," a chain of stores in L.A., have just about anything you could possibly need—and never need. Many items are day-to-day disposables you would normally buy at a supermarket or drugstore, other items are less functional—like straw hats and porcelain figures. Nonetheless, cruising the aisles of a 99-Cent Store can be a highly entertaining experience!

Food. You'd be surprised how many actors use coupons in line at the grocery store. Since most of the major grocery store chains like Ralphs and Vons do "double coupons," there is tremendous possibility to cut your grocery bill by at least a third, if not a half, by clipping coupons.

Every Sunday, the *L.A. Times* is packed with coupons of all kinds. Clip them if you need to save money. You could save an extra twenty dollars next time you're in line! Granted you might feel like a tight-wad, but if you are trying to save money, who really cares what the person behind you thinks!

Yard Sale Mania. It would be hard to drive anywhere on a Saturday or Sunday in Los Angeles and not see at least several yard sales. There are hundreds and hundreds of them every weekend in L.A.! Signs are posted at every intersection, "Yard Sale Today, Great Stuff, Turn Right!" Some sales are tiny, others are humongous.

The main reason for scoping out any of these would be for furniture. If you've just moved into town and you have little money, yard sales are great places to find desks, mirrors, chairs, and even beds. You'll also find a lot of junk, but if you know what you're doing, you might even make some money rummaging through it. I know a couple of actors who own booths at antique malls, where they sell for good sums of money recently acquired objects, which were purchased cheaply at yard sales.

Clothing. As an actor who is trying to present a professional image, you should wear the nicest clothes possible when you are meeting industry people. Wearing nice clothing not only makes you feel good, but it makes people take you more seriously. While, in truth, you can't judge a book by its cover, people in this town tend to do exactly that.

Therefore, find out when the upscale clothing like Armani, Hugo Boss, Valentino, Mondo, Donna Karan, and the like, is going to be on sale. Don't pay full price for these clothes! Everybody from struggling actors to studio executives loves to get them on sale, and quite often do. Bullocks (the West Coast version of Macy's), marks down some of these items as much as 50 percent several times a year. Another fine, upscale clothing store, Ron Ross, in Studio City, has a semi-annual sale twice a year, with mark-downs up to 75 percent off. If you go, show up the day the sale starts, because everyone arrives when good clothes are 75 percent off.

Hopefully, money will be one of your lesser concerns while you pursue your acting career. If it gets to be a major problem, then take time out to resolve it. It's not a crime to get a temporary day-job for a month to pay your bills if you have to. Granted, your acting career will be on hold, but you need to take time to straighten out your financial situation when it needs attention.

Finally, now that you understand the nuts and bolts of the business, let's focus on one of the most important things to create during your first year in Hollywood: a positive existence.

CHAPTER FIFTEEN

Creating a Positive Existence

Having covered the basic steps you should take during your first year, it's now time to talk about how you can create an existence that will be conducive to success.

When contemplating your reality, are you going to look at your glass as half empty or half full? Are you going to focus on your problems or on finding solutions to them? It's so easy to sit back, complain, and proclaim to the world that you are a "victim." It's so easy to blame someone or something for why your life isn't working out the way you want it to. Such negative thinking never really gets you anywhere, except into a deeper depression.

The acting business will probably challenge you like nothing else, and for you to succeed you'll need great strength—physically, mentally, emotionally, and spiritually. Let's take a look at what I mean specifically.

A Healthy Physical Body

You will be challenged physically a great deal as an actor. The challenge is not so much the acting, but rather it's juggling one or more jobs, running to auditions on a moment's notice, going to acting classes, going to see your agent, and taking care of everything else in life simultaneously. If you don't eat right, exercise often, and stretch, in no time you will start to look exhausted and emaciated. Not only will you lose weight, but you probably will start to develop any one of the following unappealing conditions: big, dark circles under your eyes, pasty skin that's prone to infection, droopy cheeks, an expanding jelly roll around your midsection, muscle twitches and spasms, and an overall wounded and depleted-looking aura. Now if you are a character actor and that's the look you want, then great! But I have a feeling that's not the look you want to project.

Therefore, take care of yourself! I'm not suggesting that you try to look like a super-model. Just treat your body like it's priceless—which it is. Nourish yourself with healthy foods (I suggest vegetarian) and stay away from processed foods from cans or jars. Those tend to lose much of their nutritional value while sitting on grocery store shelves for several months.

Whatever you put into your body, make sure you do it in moderation too. A lot of actors tend to drink heavily, so if you drink, keep it under control. And drugs? Don't even think about it. Doing drugs is the surest way to get you off your path as an actor, not to mention ruin your body in the process.

With regard to exercise, it can take any form. You don't have to join a gym (which is a very L.A. thing to do) and start training on a daily basis. You could go hiking in the Santa Monica Mountains (Will Rogers State Park and Coldwater Canyon park are great places). What about dancing around your apartment to your favorite tunes for fifteen minutes? Have you tried kundalini yoga? Do whatever you enjoy. Understand that exercise will revitalize your body in the long run, not make it more tired. It will also give you a cheerful disposition.

A Balanced and Focused Mind

Because of the hectic schedule that most actors lead, it's easy for the mind to get distracted, agitated, and bent out of shape. Worrying about finances, worrying about how you did at your audition, worrying about whether your agent really likes you, worrying about that funny noise in your car, and worrying about when you're going to be a star are just a handful of concerns many actors have.

The key to living an easier life is to simply stop worrying. No one puts a gun to your head and says "Worry!" It is wasted energy and really just a bad habit. Be conscious and aware of what's going on in your life, but try not to dwell on anything for too long. Use discernment in making decisions and deal with circumstances as necessary.

People, especially actors, tend to worry so much about things that are out of their control. For example, this is a common situation many actors fall into: after leaving an audition, actors will replay the audition over and over in their head until they have a splitting headache, as if it's going to change their reading. It's in the casting director's hands once you walk out of the room. All you can do is evaluate your audition and contemplate how you can improve future ones. Therefore, don't go home and nervously run the whole scenario through your head a hundred times. Relax and try to maintain some balance.

Practice watching your mind, not only after auditions, but in every situation in life. When you notice your mind heading into high gear—getting frantic, upset or angry about something—ask it to calm down. Nothing in life is worth getting terribly disturbed over. Your negative thoughts bombard your body like invisible missiles. They weaken you physically, depleting your energy tremendously. So watch out for those nasty little thoughts.

They are most noticeable in a moment of extreme anger or hurt, but be aware too that negative thoughts in the subconscious and unconscious are common too. For example, when you are driving on the freeway, are you subconsciously thinking, "I hate this damn traffic! It's so hot and smoggy! No one better say anything to me when I get home!"? Such thoughts can happen easily, causing you to frown and grimace, and nearly explode at things that ordinarily wouldn't disturb you. Therefore, try to be aware of your complete self at all times. Try to find something to appreciate in every moment. It can be done! Not only will you be happier, but other people will find you to be a much more appealing and attractive person. You will light up a whole room if you sincerely develop an enthusiastic love affair with life.

With regard to focus, when you've got a job to do, then just do it. As an actor, don't try to memorize lines with the radio on, the television blasting, and a beer in your hand. Focus on whatever you are doing, rather than attempting to accomplish several things at one time. If you have a major audition tomorrow, then don't focus on something else scheduled in three days. Give 100 percent to the task at hand. A little focus goes a long way.

A Stable Emotional State

Understanding your emotions, accepting your current state, and being able to change it for the better, requires a tremendous amount of introspection. As I've said, acting can be a very challenging business and many actors are prone to depression. The thought of, "Am I ever going to make it?" runs rampant among actors. If you think that thought enough, consciously or subconsciously, it can lead to a profound sadness in your being. You begin to question everything in your reality. At that point, you have to decide whether or not you really love acting. You have to understand what your motives are and be very honest. It's okay to want fame and fortune, but if there's no passion for the creative aspect of acting, then you'll need to find something else to pursue.

Another source of deep emotional pain in many people, actors included, pertains to regrets about past events. People often contemplate what might have happened if they had only done something differently. The only way to heal such pain is to look at every incident in your life as a learning experience, something that you can grow from. For example, getting back to auditions, you can learn and grow from an unpleasant audition and become a better auditioner because of it. A bad audition is not the end of the world. Likewise, in life, you can grow from any experience from which you still feel hurt or pain. Ask yourself what you can learn from that experience. How are you a better person because of it? Look at every unpleasant experience as an opportunity for growth instead of just a bad thing that happened to you. If you really contemplate the value of any past situation, you will find some answers.

Understanding and realizing, not just accepting, that everything in life can be a learning experience will bring great ease to you. Remember that it's not about pretending that an apparently bad thing is a good thing, but rather truly discovering how people and all of humanity can consciously grow from every situation in life.

Another important thing to do for your emotional well-being is to set aside time for little things that make you happy. Do you enjoy going to the movies, taking a walk on the beach, playing a sport, or going on a long drive? What about reading, painting, or spending time with friends? You have to set aside time for these important things. If you are unhappy, you will only become unhappier sitting around thinking about your unhappiness. These little fun things help to elevate you.

Probably the best way to thrust your life into instant joy is to get someone to tickle you for five minutes. Laughter is healing. If that's too much to handle, then try going to a comedy club or watching stand-up on television. Some cancer patients have claimed that a healthy dose of laughter every day healed them! Some might question that, but no one can dispute that laughter makes you feel good. So laugh your heart out at how funny life can be!

A Spiritual Self

I think it's important to recognize yourself as a spiritual being. I don't necessarily mean you have to go to a church, temple, or other spiritual center once a week. You just have to feel that you are important, meaningful, and have a purpose in this world. You have to know it—not just believe it—twenty-four hours a day, seven days a week. It's true that going to places of worship once a week can help to cultivate this feeling, but I've been amazed at how many people seem to lose their spirituality when they are not sitting in a pew.

I believe that there are infinite spiritual paths to fulfillment, so I'm not about to recommend any particular one for you. I think that everyone's spirituality is unique, so you have to practice whatever brings you the most love and joy, and whatever allows you to spread the most love and joy out to the world.

Try to be a positive contribution to the planet. Love and serve all of humanity as best you can. Your life out here in Los Angeles (a city that needs healing desperately) will be much more peaceful if you recognize that everyone is a spiritual being just as important as you, from the stranger at the street corner to the casting director in front of you. If you develop a helpful attitude toward everyone in your reality, it will help make this a much better place for everyone. And think about the fact that you, as an actor, are wanting people to help you to become successful.

Can you honestly expect others in the entertainment industry to assist you, if you yourself are not a helping person? Food for thought.

You Are Here to Have Fun!

Wherever you find yourself in life, whether in Los Angeles, your hometown, or another part of the world, try to make it a rule to have fun with whatever you are doing and with whomever you're with. That's my bottom line. Why waste precious time being unhappy? You have a choice. Either change your attitude if you are unhappy, or find someone or something that makes you happy.

When you are on your deathbed, you aren't going to be thinking about the movies you starred in, the business empire you built, or the best-selling novels you wrote. You'll be thinking about the loved ones in your life and the joyful moments you shared with them. Those are the things that matter the most. Worldly possessions and large sums of money won't have any value. Therefore, nurture friendships and relationships, and try to have fun. Your life will feel much, much more rewarding.

SIXTEEN

Advice from Established Film Actors

There is a tremendous wealth of information to be had from talking to actors who are very established in the business. Not only do they have practical knowledge, but more importantly, experiential wisdom, which they have collected over the years, and which can help new actors stay balanced and be prepared as they pursue an acting career.

This chapter contains interviews with three successful actors, Mariette Hartley, William McNamara, and Michael Harris. They are all very different, in terms of age, background, and the types of roles they play; but all are honest, sincere, and passionate, and have worked many times in a "starring" capacity in both film and television.

Mariette Hartley is an Emmy Award winner and six-time Emmy nominee. As a stage, screen, and television actress for more than thirty-five years, she has starred in a myriad of films, including *Ride the High Country* and *Encino Man*; television series, such as "Peyton Place," "The Incredible Hulk," and "WIOU"; and acclaimed television movies, including *M.A.D.D.: Mothers Against Drunk Drivers* and *Silence of the Heart*. William McNamara is an accomplished young film actor, having starred in a number of features, including *Stealing Home, Texasville*,

Copycat, and many others, as well as several major television movies. Some of Michael Harris's credits include *Sleep Stalker: The Sandman's Last Rights*, *Bar Girls*, *He Said She Said*, and many other film and guest-starring television roles.

Industry Interview:
Advice from Mariette Hartley, Actress

You've had a long career. Could you tell me some of the things you've learned about the business, and some things that you feel new actors need to know?

As an actor, what you really need to know is that this is what you want to do more than anything in world. But also listen to the truth about yourself. I never surrounded myself with "yes men." I always wanted to know as much as they could tell me. What was the truth? If I was trying to sing, I wanted to know that I wasn't making a total ass of myself. I knew that I had people around me, including a husband and a manager, who were very honest with me.

Another thing I had to learn is who I was, because in this town they try to make you into anything that you aren't. To find your center in the midst of this town in today's world—and I'm a mother with children in the midst of this town—is very, very hard.

You do have to have a deep spiritual base. Wherever you can find a deep spiritual base, make use of it. This is the kind of advice that nobody ever gave me, because nobody knew to. You have to have that. Find a church. Find something other than this business, because my discovery is that you can't act unless you have a life, and you can't have a life (supporting yourself by acting) unless you act!

I did this for myself and I would also recommend this to anybody: get busy writing if you can. Do whatever you can to shore up your own talent. If you can't support yourself writing, acting, then get another job. Don't be too proud to get another job. I did. When I was starting out, I went to I. Magnins and worked in budget dresses and found that I could sell. I then went back to acting and came back in a totally renewed way.

Get into a theatre group. Start doing scene work. Also, you don't have to just be a good actor. You also have to have an incredible sense of publicity and commercialism. It's very important. You have to do that too. In the beginning, you're your own one-man band. It is a business.

Most people know you from television, movies, and those Polaroid commercials. What's your feeling about the commercials—did they help you?

In those days commercials were not hip to do. But as much as I resisted them, it was the commercials that put me on the map.

Today they are very hip, and I would recommend to anybody to get a commercial agent for narrations, voice-overs, etc. (It takes a long time to get into voice-overs, because there's a small group of people who only do those.)

How did your strong theatre background and training prepare you for film and television?

My feeling is that if the break happens you've got to be ready for it. So I never stopped working and training. I never stopped toning my instrument. I was always in a group. I was always taking singing lessons and I always did scene work.

I think there are tremendous advantages to having a theatre background. There's a style that happens. You learn to work on the arc of the whole story. In films you sometimes do the last scene first, and you've rarely had a chance to rehearse it. That's what makes it so fake. How can you get there from here unless you've really rehearsed? When I did *Silence of the Heart*, I insisted on two weeks of rehearsal, and we had two weeks, and it turned out to be a wonderful movie, because I knew where I was going to go. I could get there. I had done all the work.

The thing I love the most about acting is the process of rehearsal. It's so exciting. It's when the birth happens. It's when the excitement of trying things is really alive. It's so exciting when something evolves.

There's a disadvantage to theatre too. When I was a kid, you got going for a result in theatre. In movies, your acting is a much more internal journey. It really is in your eyes. Carroll O'Connor taught me that when I did *The Last Hurrah*. And I keep learning that. And you don't learn that on stage.

The balance of the two mediums is so exciting!

What important things should actors keep in mind as they proceed?

My commitment as an actor is to stay as available to my feelings as I possibly can. I don't know how you portray feelings unless you allow them to become available to yourself—unless you know what the feelings are.

I came from a community where nobody talked about feelings. We worshipped secrets, and that was how we got along. But in 1963 after my dad died (from suicide), I surrendered to therapy and it was the beginning of my life. I deeply needed it.

There are all kinds of therapy for struggling actors, because we crash and burn. It's a very hard business to be in and to stay in with hope. You're dashed to the rocks constantly. You are constantly open to rejection. Where do you go, unless you drink? I can't do that and work, but there are a lot of actors that do drink and take drugs. Where do you go to keep filling yourself up and nourishing yourself? Where do you go so you can go back and nourish your children? Go where you can get help. I have no qualms about saying "How do you do this?" or "Could you help me and teach me how to do this?"

I used to have an enormous kind of pride, which was "I'll do this myself!" That way is such a lonely journey. You don't get to meet people. You don't get to learn things. You're continually embracing only yourself. It doesn't work.

I've been a member of a church since 1963, that's gone through many changes. It's so exciting now. I also found friends in other support groups. The baseline is: you cannot do it yourself.

In addition to the arts, you're also involved in charities . . . for instance, the Foundation for Suicide Prevention. . . .

And that happened by accident. That happened through my life. That happened because I did this movie-of-the-week called *Silence of the Heart* which is about a child's suicide. After being a survivor of my father's suicide for twenty years, I was introduced to the fact that there were many other people that this had happened to. I had no idea. Now I meet thousands and thousands of survivors all over the country. They forced me to start talking about it because I was visible. I was a celebrity and I could finally bring a highly visible public spotlight on the topic of suicide. And we've been bringing in thousands and thousands of dollars for research.

I think it's something very important to touch upon in the book, because actors do have a tendency to get depressed. Creative people do. There's a whole study coming out now about creativity and suicide. That's when priorities have to get straight. If I found out that I could never act again, I better have another choice somewhere along the line. Whether life will show me or whatever. But to have acting be the be all and end all, saying "If I'm not a star, then I'll die!" is not good. When you're on your deathbed, from what I've heard—you do not remember your last job, you remember the last time you held your child's hand. So take time to smell the roses.

When I wake up in the morning, the first thoughts that come into my head are "Thank you. No matter what happens today, if I appear to not be grateful for it, please forgive me because I don't see the whole picture yet." It really helps me a lot. And then I get down on my knees. That's the beginning of the day. It's an amazing journey.

What I would pray is that there is a balance between expectation and fantasy and reality. A lot of actors have a lot of trouble with that. People need to know that building a career takes time, no matter what other people say to them. It's one thing to come here hoping to become a star and being willing to work, but I think people have to know the statistics. There are about 3 percent of actors who make over twenty-five thousand dollars a year. The rest of the people make, literally, seven thousand dollars a year or less. Poverty wages. But if I was new in town and knew that, I don't think I would get scared because I know my mission is acting. Everybody has his or her own journey, and that's the exciting thing about life and about being a human being. Actors are going to fall down, they are going to dust themselves off, and they are going to start all over again, if they really want to do this.

Industry Interview:
Advice from William McNamara, Actor

Could you tell me a little about your background?

I lived in New York City. I went to boarding school since I was twelve, so I was never really around any drama or theatre. Theatre wasn't very cool—guys dressed up in girls' clothing wasn't very cool.

I always wanted to be an actor when I was really young, but I didn't really know how to go about it. My mom wanted me to go through high school and finish college first. After that, she said I could do whatever I wanted, but I had to complete college. So I ended up at Columbia University in New York, which made my mother happy, and also gave me access to New York City, which had so many teachers, photographers, agents, and commercials.

At Columbia, I took enough classes to get by, the minimum requirement, and meanwhile I started studying acting. Ben Stiller was in my class. We were both terrible. Now he's a big director. I got an agent, J. Michael Bloom, and I started going on commercial auditions. I started booking commercial after commercial. My first year I did ten commercials. So I made about a hundred grand! I was nineteen or twenty years old.

Soon after that, I'd heard about a place called Williamstown, a theatre festival—summer stock—so I auditioned for that and got in for the whole summer. My agent said "Oh my God! This is when all the commercials are happening!" But I didn't care. I wanted to go to Williamstown to try it.

What Williamstown did for me was amazing. It was three months of doing Shakespeare, Chekhov, and something different every week. I got to watch Christopher Walken every night in *A Street Car Named Desire*, because in the daytime I worked, but at night I had to serve refreshments in front of the theatre. Like an apprentice.

So I did that, and came back to Columbia. Three weeks into my second year at Columbia, I booked an acting job, which was a movie called *The Beat*. It was only a four-week-long shoot, so I decided I would go to Columbia and explain that I would take four weeks off. I actually rigged it so that I'd get credit for what I was doing. On-the-job credit. I had to keep a diary.

So I did the movie, but then I never went back to school, and I don't really regret it. Maybe it's because I didn't have very good teachers at Columbia. I had pretty bad freshman teachers, which I guess are bad at any university. But you'd think Columbia would be better.

Then I got a mini-series that shot in Morocco and Rome for about five months. That was more of an education to me than anything else, and I made a lot of money. In *The Beat* I made nothing, but when I went to Morocco and Rome I was getting paid a weekly salary that was humongous. I was twenty or twenty-one years old.

Then I did another Italian movie when I was over there, which screwed everything up for me, because I was offered the brother's role in *Bright Lights, Big City* but couldn't do it. I had already committed and shot film on this cheesy Italian thriller. But I met a really good friend of mine, a really wonderful actor, who taught me a lot about Shakespeare. He was a very great English actor named Ian Charleson. He's dead now— he died of AIDS. Died of AIDS doing *Hamlet* in London. He was the guy in *Chariots of Fire*—the priest who wouldn't run on Sunday. He was a very, very well-known English stage actor.

So I lost *Bright Lights, Big City* because of it. Then I came back to New York. Then I booked a movie called *Stealing Home* with Jodie Foster and that was a big studio movie, so that was a big break. Then after that, I did an after-school special, and some TV movies.

The first time I came to L.A., after *Stealing Home*, I had signed with CAA (Creative Artists Agency). I had done one or two movies with them, small roles that they had put me in, and then I got a movie called *Texasville* that Peter Bogdonovich had directed. It's a sequel to the *Last Picture Show*. I played Jeff Bridges's son.

At the same time I got that, CAA packaged a terrible television series called "Island Son" with Richard Chamberlain. It was his comeback to episodic television, and I played his son. It shot in Hawaii for a year, so that basically screwed me up for a long time.

When I came back to L.A., that series was canceled. I couldn't even get an audition for a feature film or anything. It was pretty terrible. I think I moved back to New York City, and got serious. I got in a really good acting class. I was a professional observer at the Actors Studio.

Then I came out here to L.A. once in a while because the business is so shut down in New York, there's probably hardly anything going on now. As far as making a living, it's really hard in New York. So I'd come out here for a week at a time, and that's how I booked those TV movies.

Then I moved back out here after those movies. I made enough publicity from them and enough money, that I thought I'd take another shot at Hollywood.

How did you support yourself early on, before your commercials?

Well, I worked at a nightclub in New York City called Area, down in Tribeca. I worked on the weekends, because you make a lot of money on tips. I was a bar back—that means you carry all the dirty glasses from the bar to the kitchen, and then you bring all the clean glasses back. In a popular club, you're back and forth. It's just straight non-stop work all night. And I worked at a little restaurant called the Bank Cafe, and made tips there as a waiter. That sucked.

Prior to becoming an actor, every summer I spent working for Twentieth Century Fox as a production assistant. So I worked on movies. When I came out to L.A., I worked at the Fox studio, so I kind of got the other side of the business. I knew what to expect. I knew how actors were treated.

In fact, the last movie I worked on, I worked in the casting process too, with Marcia Shulman who cast *The Beat*. So I already knew her and I knew how the whole process worked.

You can't take anything personally. And the casting process really is insane. People really are not cast because they're too thin, too fat, too big of a smile, not enough of a smile, lips are too thin, lips are too fat. It really boils down to that sometimes.

What other important things should actors keep in mind, emotionally, physically, spiritually? What should they be prepared for?

Well, L.A. can be such a scary place. Whenever I found that I was losing ground or not gaining any ground, I immediately left. In my opinion, it's a really bad place to be when you're not having any sort of success. I'd rather go wait on tables and be anonymous in New York City.

I think it's important for an actor who wants to be a serious actor to get started in New York. At least you can afford a ticket or stand in the back for a Broadway show. You can pay for standing room for about six or twelve dollars, or be an usher and see the show for free, just to be around that.

So you think theatre is really important?

Seeing it is so important. That's what's so inspirational. Every time I see something on TV—like last night there was a thing on HBO about all the black comedians who've made it and they showed Whoopie Goldberg's first thing she did on Broadway with all those characters that she played—and I'm like, "I saw that. I was sitting out in the audience." It's funny. And that was one of Whoopie Goldberg's first big breaks.

I saw so many great plays. I saw *Burn This* with Malkovich four times in a row. I thought he was so awesome. I saw this incredible play called *Breaking the Code*. I saw a play called *As Is*, which is like the original play about AIDS.

New York City is so much more inspirational than Los Angeles. With L.A., you come out here just to get an episodic or to get on a soap, or whatever. And I think that it sort of narrows the scope of things.

Also, the competition out here in Los Angeles is so tough, because everybody from the United States and from Europe is now here. Now all the European actors are coming to L.A. This is the only place where the film business is doing so well. It's like the number two or three business in America—the entertainment industry.

So what would you tell a friend in a nutshell, about what to expect in L.A.?

I think the most important thing is to be prepared, or trained. If you're going to do community college, do an extra two years of community theatre. Do it for as long as you can before you go insane. It's almost like telling an Olympic swimmer that you don't need to train until you're at the Olympics. These guys train for four years prior to their one swimming race, or whatever race they have. It's the same kind of attitude and mental commitment you have to have here, because L.A. is like the Olympics of the entertainment business. It's so competitive. You've got all these people from all over the world trying to get work.

The best thing to do is not be so eager to get here. Put all your eagerness and that energy into that training prior to getting here.

Sometimes an agent will take you on, and send you out on three auditions and then call the casting director and say, "What's the deal? Give me the bottom line. I just got this guy. Should I keep him?" And if the casting director says, "You know what? He wasn't prepared, he never brought his head up from the pages, he was nervous, and blah, blah, blah" then that agent is going to drop you. So the best thing to do is put all your energy into training before getting to Los Angeles. If that means making the circuitous route, and that means going to Chicago, New York, even Dallas, then fine.

If you're coming from some small town, it would be much more important to do some kind of summer stock or theatre all over the U.S. There are places to go.

And if you have nothing to write down on your resume, then you're definitely not going to get an agent—forget about getting an audition. But if you've done twenty-five plays, even if it's regional theatre, you're much more likely to get an agent.

Another suggestion is to go to a really good college with a great theatre background—NYU, SMU in Dallas, and a lot of other great places. Then, you fulfill your parents' wishes and have them pay for your preparation.

And learning how to audition?

Yeah, in New York City before I ever even went on a commercial audition, I studied for five months. I booked the first commercial I ever auditioned for. I was trained so well. It's all about the preparation. That's what it's all about.

What do think makes a good actor a really good actor? What qualities make them stand out?

A lot of the actors that I admire are the ones that when they are working on film or TV, you don't see the acting. It's totally invisible. The better actor isn't necessarily the guy that can recreate what it's like to be coming down off heroin. It's more or less, the guy who can come into the room and say to the secretary, "Do I have any phone calls?" and you believe him. That is so much harder to do than a technical exercise of what it is to come down off of heroin.

So I like actors like Steve McQueen, who was brilliant at doing absolutely nothing, underplaying everything. He was so real and so attuned to the details of what reality is. I love actors that pay attention to the detail.

Also, I love actors that make what they do really interesting. They've always got something else going on. Take the actor who comes into the room asking for messages: at the same time he'll look over at the candy tray thinking about if he wants a piece of candy or not. Always thinking about really making it real—always having another objective, instead of coming into the room acting, saying "Do I have any messages?" and then looking at the phone.

Another actor I've always loved is Don Knotts, on "The Andy Griffith Show," one of my favorite television shows of all time. Everybody was so real on that show, it's mind-blowing. But the great thing about Don Knotts is that he is so committed to what he is doing, however ridiculous or absurd it is in a scene. He was so committed to that absurdity that you totally bought it. You totally got sucked into his energy. Also, he had a sense of humor about everything. He didn't mind looking ridiculous.

Industry Interview:
Advice from Michael Harris, Actor
When you were starting out, what were some of the obstacles you faced?

Part of the problem in starting out as young actor is that nobody knows who you are. The other part of the problem is that you don't know who you are either. You are in your early twenties and you're full of talent and energy and self-righteous indignation, and you've obviously got a really healthy ego or you wouldn't even think of attempting a career like acting. But the question is, "What have you done?"—not as an actor, but "What have you done in your life?"

You don't really know who you are until later on. Some people do, and sometimes that makes a big difference in how people perceive you. If you don't really know who you are and you haven't really established a persona with yourself, it's really hard for anyone else to see you. For me, I had a lot of ideas about who I was, but I was in such a state of change. I was not a young leading man on the inside. (I don't know if I looked like that on the outside.) But on the inside, I was never a young leading man, so I was never right for the parts I was right for—because I wasn't right on the inside for them. So I was at a loss. I wanted to play parts of guys who were in their forties, wild character roles.

So that was one obstacle that I came up against: I didn't yet know who I was.

How do successful actors become successful?

I think there are two ways that that happens. It either happens right away and you're hurled into success and stardom in a film that happens to gross $300 million, and you happen to be the person that Rob Reiner or Steven Speilberg points to and says "You!" Or you're on the TV series of Aaron Spelling or Norman Lear, and you're like "Boom!" You made it, you were here for three weeks and you got the gig and now you're famous and rich! This may be the end of your career too. But nonetheless it happens right away.

The other side to that is the people who come and they stay and they don't leave. They continue to work and not work, work and not work, for some extended period of time, between two years and thirty years. Eventually at some point they become a cumulative success.

And that's actually the majority. . . .

The majority of people who make a living as an actor are in that category. Of the SAG membership, I think under 5 percent make a living as an actor. And under a quarter of one percent become rich or wealthy.

So I guess those are important odds to keep in mind. Not that you should discourage people if they have a passion. . . .

Oh, I think you should always discourage people! [laugh]

I met some executive at Universal when I was seventeen when my hair was down to the middle of my back. I was wearing a lot of jewelry and I said "I want to be an actor, yeah!" and the guy said "Well, if there's anything else you'd like to do as much as acting, then go do that."

The only people who are going to make it here or even survive are the people who don't have another choice of what to do. Even with those people, no matter who they are and no matter how special they are, there are going to be at least a hundred thousand other people exactly like them who are just as good as they are. So if they don't really love it and really want to get involved in the process of trying to become an actor, they should forget it because the odds are huge.

And just because you're talented doesn't mean anything. Everybody's talented. Nobody's out here who's not talented, except for some few successful people that we all know. . . . Some people's talent is just who they are. That's their talent. It's something about what they give or how people see them. That's their talent. Their charisma is their talent and that's just as valid as being Robert De Niro or anybody who is a highly skilled, inspired actor.

If you had a relative coming out here to work on a career, and they needed to know how Hollywood works, in a nutshell, what would you tell them? What key things should they keep in mind?

I would tell them, go home! Go back to the incredibly nice life they had before they got the stupid idea to come to Hollywood to start an acting career!

The most important thing to know about Hollywood is that it doesn't matter who you know or how good you are, and it doesn't matter what you know. None of that matters. You could know everybody and still have things not work out. You could be at all the parties and still not be able to survive as an actor.

Hollywood is like Las Vegas. It's just like Las Vegas. It's built on the same premise of chance, for actors. It's not built on hard work.

So if you're a gambling type of person, it's the place to be—

And if you like the game, and don't mind losing more than you win in the hopes that you might hit the jackpot, then that's okay. If you don't like that game, and you're not into that process of losing more than you're winning and just trying to manage the losses because you might get lucky eventually, then rethink it.

SEVENTEEN

Advice from a Writer/Producer and a Publicist

Often new actors learn about the business from other actors, which is very helpful and practical, though sometimes it can be limiting. For that reason, throughout the book, I've included interviews with agents, casting directors, teachers, and others to help broaden your perspective on the industry. Now it's time to take a step further and hear from a highly-respected writer/producer, Earl Hamner, and a prominent publicist, Michael Levine. Publicists and producers are very important people in Hollywood who every actor should get to know.

Industry Interview:
Advice from Earl Hamner, Writer/Producer ("The Waltons," "Falcon Crest")

What would you tell new actors moving to this town? In other words, what should they expect emotionally, financially, and psychologically while living in Los Angeles and the whole Hollywood environment?

To an actor coming into town, I would say that the preparation should start long before you get here. Ideally the best thing would be to be born into a very rich family! That way you have financial stability. That seems to be one of the problems that most people that I know face when they come here: how to make a living. I would come with some kind of substantial nest egg, something that would mean that I wasn't desperate, so I didn't go to auditions with the feeling that this is "all or nothing."

Failing a rich mother and father, I would be prepared to find some kind of job. There's no stigma in coming to town and taking a job as a valet or a waiter or waitress, or any kind of so-called menial job.

The other day I was at lunch at Warner Commissary and I asked the waiter, "Are you an actor?" He said, "No, I'm just out here to look around." I thought "Well, this is the most astonishing thing in the world! Here is a waiter who is *not* an actor or aspiring actor!"

I would also tell newcomers to remember that acting is a business and to prepare for it like you would for a profession. Going on an audition, be as professional as possible with the preparation of the material. Try to give it your best shot the first time you read it. Don't say "If that wasn't right, I'll read it for you again." That shows some self-doubt. It is best to give it everything you've got in the one reading. Then if the casting agent, director, or producers suggest that you read it again, then of course you would, and take any guidance they will give you. But don't offer to do it again because it might diminish what you gave them in your first reading.

It sounds calculated and self-serving, but I would also, in preparation for the audition, learn everything I could about the people for whom I'll be auditioning. When you get there, a director would love to hear "I saw your work last week. That was very interesting what you did." We are all human and a quick sincere compliment to any one of the people participating in the audition can be quite meaningful.

At the same time, those people who are auditioning you are very busy and one of the worst things you can do is to come in and start a conversation on your own. If the director, producer, or casting agent initiates something or a friendly kind of overture, then by all means respond. But at the same time, remember that these are busy people and don't overdo it. One of the worst auditions I think I've ever been in is where we couldn't get the person to read. This person kept talking and talking and talking, and finally the director said, "Would you kindly read?"

Just keep in mind how busy these people are. They are professionals and they have been there over and over again, and chances are that their judgement is going to be very professional. If you get the job it's because you've done a good job and because it's what they are looking for.

Also it's a very good idea not to take it personally if you don't get the job. It's not that you were rejected. It's simply that you didn't meet the requirements. A lot of people get all broken up over the fact that they didn't get the job. It has nothing to do with your interpretation of the role. Maybe the age is wrong or the look isn't right, or maybe the director took an instant dislike to you. There's no reason to take things personally.

Another thing that I've learned from going to auditions and from casting many people is "Don't do anything bizarre." I remember one role I was casting: it was for a young fundamentalist minister. The actor strode around the room as he read the lines. He jumped up on the table. He shouted and he gesticulated, and he scared the hell out of everyone else in the room! Of course he didn't get the part.

Also, I've found that—this may just be a personal preference—people who dress for the role in an exaggerated way frequently are wrong for the role. If a girl comes in who's going to be a tart and she's got on a short leather skirt and a low cut bra, I think she didn't need to dress the part. If a man comes in and he's trying out for the part of a cowboy, and he's got on a plaid shirt, chaps, and boots, it's just ridiculous. It's much more business-like not to try tricks.

I've done a lot of casting and I've been in some casting sessions that were absolutely thrilling. When I was doing "Falcon Crest," the actress Ana Alicia came in and was so terrific that she held us all spellbound. It was rather a sexy scene, and Ana did it with such finesse and with such good taste. A scene of that kind could have gone overboard. It could have been embarrassing to her and to us, but it was so perfectly done. When she left the room we all looked at each other, and the director said "I want to work with her!" I said, "That's the role I had in mind!" Ana is a consummate actress.

I had that same experience with the actress Ronnie Claire Edwards, who plays the role of Corabeth on "The Waltons." She plays the store-keeper's wife. She was so perfectly right for the role. She understood the role. She did it short, sweet, in, out, and left us speechless with admiration and pleasure. It was just wonderful. It is just so thrilling when an actor comes in and gives you a character right away.

So how could you sum up what you look for in an actor during an audition?

A direct approach to the role. Nothing tricky. Nothing bizarre. Just a very honest appraisal of the role, and then fitting into it, sort of loosely. Don't define it rigidly because the director wants his interpretation, but just like a loosely fitting garment, if that makes sense.

You are the classic story of someone who grew up in a small town—you're from a small town in Virginia—and you eventually found yourself out here in Hollywood as a successful writer and producer. Could you explain what inspired you to be a writer and how did you get from there to here?

I have no idea of why I became a writer, except that it was the only thing I ever wanted to do. I think I would have failed miserably at any other thing that I might have tried.

I've wanted to write from the time that I could hold a pencil. I always kept a journal, and whether a writer, or actor, or producer, or whatever we become in this business, I think that keeping a journal is invaluable. For a lark, I once took a course in acting and the textbook was *Six Lessons in Acting* by Stanislavski. One of the lessons is called "Memory of Emotion" in which he tells you that you don't have to murder somebody to play a murderer. Perhaps once inadvertently you killed something—say you ran over a raccoon on the highway—but if you can remember the feelings of having killed the live thing, then you can draw on that memory to play someone.

So the journal I think helps you to look back over your own experiences and when you need that experience in acting, you can draw on your memory.

But, yes. I've been wondering about how I've got from the hills of Virginia to New York. It was a passion to write and it drove me to overcome a good many obstacles, such as being quite poor with no hope of ever going to college, with no hope of really getting beyond those mountains in Nelson County, VA. But I had a passion to write and I had a passion to see things and go places, and I did. I went from the University of Richmond to the army, and was fortunate that I was stationed overseas in England and in Paris. Then after the war, I went to the University of Cincinnati. I graduated there and I started writing professionally as a radio writer in 1948. At the same time, I began writing novels and one of those became a bestseller. In 1954, I married Jane, who was an editor at *Harper's Bazaar*. We lived in New York for ten years and then moved to L.A. in 1961. I freelanced for a year and then I was fortunate enough to sell, "The Waltons," which was on CBS for ten years. Then I produced "Falcon Crest" for ten years and now all these years later, I'm seventy-two years old and I have twenty minutes to live, and I'm a very happy old man!

How would say that Hollywood has changed since you first came here?

I came here in 1961. It was a fairly innocent time. There were shows like "Mayberry RFD" and "Green Acres"—a lot of family shows. It was a kinder, gentler world. As I watched from 1961 to 1995, it became more restricted because it became more of a hard-edged business. People became less interested in quality and more interested in mass appeal, which of course means a lowering of standards. I'm not shocked and I'm not surprised, and I'm not even dismayed to see the progress of more frankness in language and in displays of nudity. That happened along with the whole society, as it has become freer and more relaxed.

I always promised myself that when I became a senior citizen, I would be tolerant of young people. I wouldn't say, "This terrible younger generation!" I wouldn't be judgmental and I'd try to stay young with the young people. But I find that now I go into the networks (because I still pitch ideas—I'm still producing a show in Australia and I'm developing another "Waltons" special—we just did one last year), and I feel ancient. I look at the young people who are in positions of authority and they seem younger than my children. And they are! I find a reluctance on their part and I understand it, but I don't forgive it. Because they look at me as if I am their father, and of course, they don't want their father coming in and telling them how to run things. And it disappoints me.

I have a concrete example: When I first came to Hollywood, Rod Serling was a friend and I sold some "Twilight Zone" scripts to Rod. He liked what I did, and I did a good many of them. Years later, I ran into another person who was a story editor on the "New Twilight Zone." I said, "I hear you're on the "Twilight Zone." I know a nice old writer who would love to write episodes for you." He said he would get back to me. A few days later he came back and said, "They don't want any of the old guys." I thought, "Well that's foolish. But that's alright. I'm still happy doing what I do."

Other changes in Hollywood are that all of the big studios have sold off their back lots. To my great dismay, Warner Bros. is turning the area that used to be the "Waltons" set into a parking lot. They are not destroying the house; they are saving the framework and they are going to move it over to the ranch. When we do revivals or specials, it will be available to us. But we have to move it to leave the original locale. I feel great affection for that area. Will Geer, who's dead, lives there. He's there. You can feel his spirit. I have such memories associated with that area from that time. I can see Richard Thomas when we were just starting out in 1972. I can see all those actors, like Kami Cotler, who was six when we started the series. She is now a grown woman teaching school in Virginia.

Is there any one thing during your career that you've learned either about yourself or about other people in this town or about show business that might be helpful to pass on to a new person?

Yes, and I can illustrate it with a story. There's a moral, which is to be arrogant. This is a town where hundreds of actors get off of airplanes, trains, and buses every day. The town is flooded with actors and would-be actors. The competition is incredible, as you know. For every role there are probably fifty people who could fill that role. But because of your agent, your talent, or some past show piece you've done, you are there to try out for a part.

It's a town where you have to shout to be heard. You have to make your presence known. And when I say to be arrogant, it goes back to a willingness to display what your talent is. When I was in New York right after World War II, I had been writing radio scripts. Then television came, and I would go to see television producers. I found there was a prejudice against radio writers. They would say, "You have been writing for the ear. You can't write for the eye *and* the ear."

So after some rejections I went to see a friend named Mark Smith, a story editor. That was in The Golden Years of television. There was a show called "The Theatre Guild on the Air" and it was sponsored by United States Steel. I went to Mark and said, "I'm not getting jobs. I've written books and I've written for radio, but I can't get a job in television." Mark said, "Well, what do you want me to do?" I said, "I'd like to show you what I can do. Give me the same assignment that you give your very best writer and for no money I will take the same assignment and I will write it better than your best writer. I simply want to show you what I can do." He said, "Well, if you are that arrogant you must be good. I won't take you up on your offer, but I will give you an assignment." So I've always found that a certain amount of arrogance, if you have the talent to back it up, can help.

There's one other thing I would say to actors: if you don't make it here, there's no disgrace in going home and using your talent there. Sometimes, I think it's probably better for actors to not come directly to Hollywood, but to go to Philadelphia, Cincinnati, New Orleans, or San Francisco and work in theatre while you're honing your talents. At the same time, if you're a young person and you have the youth and the looks and the energy, it seems a shame not to use them. But if you're getting along in your years and you aren't making it, don't be ashamed to go back to Cincinnati and open an acting school or take up ice skating, or get married, or have 2½ children, or God forbid, become a normal person.

Industry Interview:
Advice from Michael Levine, Publicist, Owner of Levine Communications Office, Inc.

Could you tell me how you got started in this business and how you've come to be where you are today?

I was born in New York City and moved here in 1977. I always felt very pulled and called to L.A. and to Hollywood. It's not something I really understand fully, except that underneath my vocational dreams was to in some way participate in the entertainment industry or in Hollywood. So for me, Hollywood was not a vocation, but an avocation—like a calling to the priesthood. So I came here, and then in 1983 I started a P.R. firm.

Could you explain to the readers of the book the importance of having a publicist?

Well, public relations is kind of like gift-wrapping. I tell people that if I give someone a gift and I give it to them in a Tiffany box, the gift has a higher perceived value in their mind than if I gave it to them in no box, or a box of less prestige. And so that's what we do as publicists—we gift-wrap things. In the culture in which we live, we gift-wrap our movies and TV stars, our politicians, and our corporate heads, and even to some extent our toilet paper. We gift-wrap everything and gift-wrapping is very important.

Then it's another extension of the whole advertising process, I guess?

The difference between advertising and public relations is in advertising you pay for it, and in public relations you pray for it.

You work with a lot of different people in show business: actors, writers, directors, producers. In your opinion, what distinguishes the successful people you know?

Well, I've studied this quite a bit and I do work with some fabulously talented and successful people. The truth is that people who fail in life both personally and professionally have two roots: most people fail because of fear and most people fail because of irresponsibility.

First we'll talk about fear. Either consciously or subconsciously, people who fail are often scared or frightened. This isn't always a conscious thing, it's often subconscious and their fear holds them back significantly. They're afraid. They're terrified. Again, it's not always a conscious thing, often it's subconscious.

The other thing is that irresponsibility is a big reason for failure. And the truth is, many people—most people as a matter of fact—to a greater or lesser degree, are flaky. Now that doesn't mean people are all equally flaky. Some people are terribly, terribly flaky—they kind of fall into the "four-square not-very-functional," and some people are mildly flaky. One of the things about flakiness, though, that is hard to diagnose is that nobody thinks of themselves as flaky. The most flaky people think they are not flaky.

So fear and irresponsibility are the two things that hold back most people from becoming successful.

What do you recommend to new actors in the business who have few credits or maybe limited training that you come across who are trying to develop a solid career in the business?

Well I think that even this book is helpful. I think that information in the beginning is very useful. I think that we need maps. Without information, it's kind of like building a house without a hammer and nails. Now it's possible to build a house without a hammer and nails. I just am not sure it's the most efficient way.

It's possible, of course, to stumble across the right combination of things, but I think that in the beginning the first responsibility is to get a map together. Through the accumulation of information, it's possible to draw a map. That's why I think a book like this can be useful.

So I guess that includes talking to as many people as possible?

Yes, but I have to guide people in this area. I think that talking to people can be useful, but it depends on who you talk to. If you're seeking information about mental health, and you stumble upon Charles Manson and you ask him some questions, I think it's probably not a good idea to talk to him. On the other hand, if you were walking down the road, and you were to stumble upon Scott Peck, the author of *The Road Less Travelled*, I think it would probably be a good idea.

It depends on who you talk to. My observation is that often people in Hollywood talk to too many people. Particularly creative people, or actors, talk to too many other actors. I think that one of the biggest problems that actors have is that they don't know any business people. And business people don't know any actors. I think this is a tragedy and a real problem.

What insights can you give about the nature of Hollywood and how it works?

Well, I think that the entertainment industry, which is generally referred to as "Show Business" has an interesting title. It's two words: "Show" and "Business." It's not called "Show Art," it's called "Show Business." I think it's overwhelmingly a business; I know it's overwhelmingly a business! I think that to the extent that creative people can come to make peace with that, unfortunately despite their very best efforts, it has as much to do, if not more, with who you know than what you know. And that's a painful realization for people. I think those are some possible insights on how to get through this unusual obstacle.

If a friend of a friend, or a brother or sister, was coming to this town to begin an acting career, what words of wisdom would you tell them?

The first thing I would remind them of is that all journeys begin as internal journeys, and that they need to have a serious understanding of their real calling in life, and what it is they want to do. If there is anything else they can do besides act, I'd recommend they do it because it's a very difficult life. On the other hand, if they are convinced that this is the only direction God is calling them in, then I would pursue it.

There's a saying that we should "both pray and row to shore," and I think that we should both pray and row to shore. Not only check out what's going on with the spiritual part of yourself and what you're being called to, but prepare yourself. "Rowing to shore" means working actively on making sure that you get to your destination. One of the best ways is by getting information.

CHAPTER EIGHTEEN

More Advice from Working Actors

Your success will come from the knowledge you acquire and how you apply it with determination and a strong work ethic. This chapter has interviews with three working actors—Jimmy Wlcek, Veanne Cox, and Brad Greenquist—whose personal stories and situations are shared by many, and whose successes are inspiring because they show the great reward of perseverance.

Jimmy Wlcek has starred in three different soap operas, "Ryan's Hope," "One Life to Live," and "As the World Turns"; several television commercials; and can be seen in *Steel Magnolias*. His first major "break" in the business demonstrated how the audition process can be like a rollercoaster. Veanne Cox starred in the 1987 Broadway production of *Smile* and in the 1995 Broadway revival of *Company*. She has also had supporting roles in several films and numerous featured guest-starring roles on television shows, such as "Seinfeld," "Love & War," "Hope & Gloria," and many others. She is the epitome of a hard-working actress, someone every new actor should emulate. Finally, Brad Greenquist has starred in several features, including *The Bedroom Window, Pet Sematary,* and in many other made-for-TV movies. He offers insight that is practical, sensible, and helpful for every new person in Hollywood.

Interview with Jimmy Wlcek, Actor

Could you tell me a little bit about your background?

I got my first agent in 1984 in New York and I didn't get my first gig until 1986, which was a "Tales from the Dark Side" episode. That gave me some confidence. In the meantime, I was always auditioning for commercials—never got one.

In 1987, I auditioned for a part on "All My Children." When I met the casting director, she didn't think that I had a womanizing quality. She told my agent, but my agent convinced her to let me read for the part, and she liked it. Then I read for the producers and they liked it. Then I screen-tested, and all the feedback was "You did it! You hit the mark!" I was excited. And I thought I got it.

In the end, I didn't get it because I wasn't old enough. I was devastated. I went to Texas to visit my mom and sisters, and I figured I'd not bother with acting anymore because I was never going to get that close. When I came back, I got a phone call saying they sent my tape over to "Ryan's Hope," and then they just gave me the role. And that's how I got "Ryan's Hope."

So for instance, if you're auditioning for "Days of Our Lives," and they don't take you because you're too young, too old, too blonde, too short, but they liked you and they know somebody in their network is looking to fill a certain role, they'll submit that tape over to that show. So that's how I got "Ryan's Hope." It was pretty easy. I just went in there, and they pretty much wanted to give it to me.

At the time, I was working for Keebler Cookies in New Jersey in a warehouse loading trucks—mostly graveyard shift. It took me three months to get adjusted to my new job on television and feel like I belonged and deserved getting paid for it. I just felt that I should still be loading trucks.

In the beginning, I just wasn't that good. My confidence was nowhere. Then I got adjusted very well. I loved the show, and it's been my favorite experience ever since.

After the show was canceled, "One Life to Live" created a role for me. I wasn't too happy with "One Life to Live." In nine months, I asked to be let go because I was up for a series called "True Blue," which was canceled after thirteen weeks. Grant Show got my role. I had to ask to be let go before they would screen-test me.

Then I did a play Off-Off-Off-Off-Broadway. Eight months later I got "As the World Turns," and I did that for two years. Then a whole year after that, I came out here to L.A. for pilot season. I've had the chance to do several really good commercials.

If you had a little brother who wanted to start an acting career, what would you tell him about Hollywood?

Well, first I think you've got to give it at least three years. They say if you can get one pilot in three years, you're lucky.

You have to study too. They say that New York actors are usually better actors—more serious—but I find that untrue, because in any class that I've audited or been in out here, the actors are phenomenal and hard-working. So you really have to be in a class, and reading plays, and doing scenes, and working on your craft very hard.

And don't ever take any rejection personally. You have to be tenacious. You can't let people sidetrack you. There are a lot of people who want to mess your head up and try to discourage you. I had one experience when I was starting out where somebody in an office said, "Why do you want to be an actor? Do you really want to be an actor?" He really wanted to see how much confidence I had with that question. And I think I gave it to him. I didn't back away saying, "Well, gees, maybe I shouldn't be an actor." You've got to know that you want to do this and that you're willing to give what it takes.

Tenacity is the key word. Time and hard work. You can't think that you are going to come out here and be a star. Think craft. Think, "I just want to be a good actor. How can I grow as an actor?" Take each thing as a stepping stone—an episode here, a commercial here, a soap, whether an under-five or day-player. That all comes with the territory. You can't think, "When am I going to get my big movie and be on Jay Leno?" Those are few and far between.

The only thing that's really different about Hollywood from New York is the amount of actors. It's just overpopulated with actors in L.A. But I heard someone say recently, "There's not a lot of competition out here, just a lot of people."

At auditions, you see a lot of faces and a lot of guys better-looking than you or taller than you, and you think, "They're gonna kick my ass." But really they are some of the worst actors or the most unprepared.

So whenever you're at an audition, don't ever get discouraged by somebody seemingly better—better-looking than you, more charactery, taller, or someone trying to psyche you out. Don't let that throw you. It doesn't mean squat.

The big thing is just the amount of people. There are probably six times as many actors out here for your part than in New York. But this is where you've got to be. With the economy affecting our business so much, they don't fly out to New York looking for actors as much anymore, because they know they have such an abundance of actors here. There's no need for the extra expense of money and time. Today, New York is basically theatre, soaps, and commercials. That's why I think actors are all flocking here to L.A.

Do you see any difference between New York agents and California agents?

In New York, if you have soap opera experience, they love that. That's a strong point. Here, they don't care about your soap work. It doesn't mean squat.

Also, at first, you don't want to be represented by too big of an agency that you'll get lost in. You want someone who's going to be a hard worker. I have five years of soap experience on three different soaps, and out here it didn't mean anything. I was shocked. I thought it would be no problem to get an agent. In New York, I got any agent I wanted basically. Out here, they want episodic work. They want nighttime series experience and film.

Interview with Veanne Cox, Actress

Can you tell me a little about your background and your studies?

I spent ten years in New York. The first two and a half were spent never saying "no." I never said "no" to anything. I said "yes" to everything. I did more Off-Off-Off-Broadway shows in dingy little no-budget, no-money productions. I was rehearsing at one in the morning. Rehearsing another show in the afternoon, and performing another one at nighttime. And it was a great training ground. Basically I went to the School of Hard Knocks. Actually, I went to the school of Doing-Is-Learning. Sitting at home saying I wanted to be an actress is not the way I did it. I went out there and I did it over and over and over again.

And then I finally got my Equity card by having balls—no fear—by sneaking into an Equity audition for the musical *Smile*. It was at the end of the day. They came out and said, "We're not seeing anybody else. I'll take your pictures and resumes." There were still ten girls in front of me. And while the woman was taking the pictures and resumes from all the other girls, I snuck in the door behind her, closed the door, went in, and said, "You have to see me. I'll sing sixteen bars, I'll sing eight bars. I'll sing one note." And they said, "Okay." They were all getting packed up to go, but they thought, well, nothing is going to stop this girl. So I did it. I had five callbacks, and I then made it on Broadway!

So you can't be afraid, because if you don't try, you won't ever know. And that was my philosophy, and I got a lot of jobs being fearless like that.

How did you support yourself when you first started out?

Well, I paid the bills by being a foot model. I was a size six, and in *Back Stage*, there was a little ad saying "Five/Six Shoe Models Needed for Shoe Shows." And that's how I got into it. I went to a modeling agency and they said, "You've got the perfect foot, we'll send you out on this." (After twelve years as a ballerina, I don't know how it happened!) So I did foot modeling, but basically I really committed to acting.

I lived very cheaply, without a lot of extravagance. Actually, no extravagance. And I committed myself to my art, and I basically suffered for it.

My ten years in New York were full and wonderful, and great, and I've been in L.A. for two years now. And I had a name in New York. People knew who I was in New York, and when I came out to L.A. nobody knew who I was. There were maybe a handful of people who might have seen one of the shows I did in New York. So I basically started from scratch all over again.

Basically I don't ever say "no." I don't know if that's the best philosophy, but I do know that work breeds work. And when you're working, the energy that you have and the confidence and the exposure is great. You never know who is going to see you, and you never know when that person will come around again. It also keeps your muscles up.

What are some of the things that help to keep you in-tune as an actor?

Well, I can highly recommend a couple of things. Studying. I believe in keeping your instrument in-tune, even when you're not working. Voice classes, acting classes, Shakespeare, everything. I don't have an accredited diploma, but I deserve about ten of them with the amount of studying that I've done!

Also, yoga is a wonderful mind, body, spirit connecting experience. Doing something physical or exercising is a great habit for any artistic person, because I think it clears out the blocks and everything else. Eating right is really important too because all of this running around can really take its toll on you.

I also do a morning diary. That's been a real wonderful thing.

Also, try to have friends who are creative and energetic towards their own artistic advancement. Getting together with them, and not being afraid to say something like, "hey, let's read a play" is important. Even playing charades is an incredibly creative artistic experience. It exercises a muscle that is totally applicable for whenever you walk into an audition.

Also, watching television is very important if you're going to try to get on television. Because having a knowledge of what's on there and the genres, and what you *can* do, is very important. You need to get a sense of the trends.

Let's say you know someone moving out here. What advice would you give them. How should they set their goals?

There are a lot of people in this business. So first of all, you have to want to do it more than anything else. You have to be willing to sacrifice. You have to be willing to struggle and commit, and dedicate yourself to it. If there is any chance that you want to do anything else, then do it. The competition out here is fiercely fierce.

I would tell them to be prepared to take risks. Like I said before, don't ever say "no." Go with your instincts. If your instinct says to go up to someone and say "Hi, I'm so and so, here's a picture and resume. I want to work for you," then do it. You've got nothing to lose and everything to gain.

Getting out there and being seen is incredibly important, which means working and doing plays. Getting on stage is important. People will come and see your work. It's much better than going into their office and saying "I'm really good!" Unless you're exquisitely beautiful and you have a great instrument, it's not going to be as good as someone coming to see your work.

Also, you have to have a knowledge of how much money you're going to need. You should have another job as a back-up at any given time to pay bills. Be prepared for long periods of time between jobs. There's a lot of work out there, but there are a lot of people trying to get it.

My biggest piece of advice would be don't be afraid to do something different. You have to just go for it. Do something wildly creative or commit to something wildly creative. Be different. You have to strike something extra-normal, something extraordinary. You have to believe that there is something inside of you, and use it and let it flow. There are just too many people not to do that.

What can you say about pictures and resumes?

It's important to have a picture where you look the best you can. If you're not stunningly beautiful, you need a picture that shows everything that you possibly have to offer, that really shows who you are. It needs to be 3-D, even though it's a two-dimensional picture. And if you are attractive, you need to make it as beautiful as you possibly can be, while still looking like you. In Hollywood, there is an attraction to aesthetics, which is beauty. It's never going to hurt to look the best you can possibly look. Your picture is very important because that's what's going to get you in the door.

When I first went to New York, I lied on my resume. When I say I lied, I mean that I stretched the truth. I put down things that I had done in my acting class, plays and stuff like that. I'm not advocating it, but if you've got nothing and you want to be an actor, you can't hand somebody a blank piece of paper! You never know what the right thing to do is.

If you stretch the truth and someone calls you on the table, you have to be prepared to say "You know what, I worked on that play in my acting class really hard, and I did a great job, and it was wonderful. I needed to put something on my resume." You have to be honest. You just have to be prepared if you lie. And if the person is a real jerk about it, say "Hey, you got me!"

Interview with Brad Greenquist, Actor

When you were first starting out in the business, what are some of the common obstacles you faced? In your opinion, what obstacles do most new actors in the business face?

Well, complete anonymity is one. You come to a place (in my case New York before Los Angeles) and you don't know anybody in the business. You may not have many friends, which is difficult too. And to succeed you have to let people know who you are.

That first year, I tried to just get settled into the city and become self-sustaining. I learned my way around. It was a step-by-step process of getting settled and getting into a good acting class. I eventually started taking acting classes, which got me out of the college thing and into the real world.

The acting class which I was in eventually led to putting up a one-person production, which in turn led to my agent. I had courted the agent for a year. After having seen my one-person show, he signed me. Soon I started booking jobs. I wasn't expecting any sort of quick success, but actually in a way, that's what happened. (If you can call two years of anonymity a quick success.)

During that first year I had new headshots taken. After another year, I got another set of headshots made. My own personality had changed a great deal in one year, having come from Virginia to New York, which has a way of slamming you around. You grow up very fast! I had changed a great deal as a person in that time, and that was reflected in the second set of pictures. The first pictures were just "average guy" pictures. I look at them now, and I see a hayseed from Virginia! But with the second set, I took some chances with the way I presented myself. I knew how I wanted to present myself. I knew the kinds of actors whose footsteps I felt I could realistically follow in.

Defining who you are and what you can play, rather than thinking you can play everything is important too. You have to figure out what roles you're going to be marketable in. This is a real problem with a lot of actors, a very valid problem of defining what kind of roles are going to be most suited to you. It takes asking a lot of people—people you know as well as people who don't.

Playing any and every role isn't going to happen unless you are a star. When you're starting out, it's better to have a niche. A certain type of role that you could get known for. I had stumbled on it, basically. The roles I found myself getting were invariably bad guys.

Very often in colleges and universities, they still teach the theatre repertory system, where you are hired for several seasons in theatre and you play everything. With television and film, you've got to find your niche that's going to get you in the door—something that identifies you with a type of role. A lot of actors resent this, but it's just the way it is. Once you've got your foot in the door, then you can try and expand your realm, or (more likely) your agent will try and expand your realm.

It's hard to define what roles you can play because most actors are fairly regular people. It's hard to know exactly where you fit in. It takes years to figure that out and it's really difficult, but it's something you have to do. Often it's figured out for you. In my case, I was fortunate in that the roles I started getting were generally bad guys and other extreme roles. After the fact, I found out that I was quite comfortable playing them and that I enjoyed playing them. But at the beginning I never would have imagined it. Not at all.

So that's what the first year was all about, basically. I've known many actors who in their first year, were just so anxious and impatient and wanted everything to happen all at once. It rarely does, though occasionally that happens. Impatience is good, but you also need persistence.

What are the important things to remember along the way, as you pursue acting?

I think one important thing that is highly underrated among actors and other artists is to find some form of financial stability. You need to find a job that can pay your bills that also doesn't crush you. It should be something you can enjoy that also brings in enough money to sustain you. You're not going to live high off of survival jobs, but you need money for expenses like pictures, resumes, mailings, food, rent, and all that stuff.

My first survival job was as a theatre usher and I was fired after one day! It was an awful job. I had to sit and take tickets, and I couldn't talk to anybody. It was terribly boring. As it happened, I was scheduled to work on a night when Olivier's *King Lear* was on television, and this was before VCRs were in vogue, or at least before I could afford one. I told my supervisor that I had a conflict that night, so she fired me! Thank God!

Good friends are very important too, both actors with whom you can talk about the business as well as people who are not in the business who can give you a sense of reality about the whole thing. They'll help you realize that not only actors can be downtrodden at times. The things that happen with actors—unemployment, competition, etc.—are not isolated to the acting profession. They are everywhere. Actors are just very vocal about it.

Keeping a good sense of self-confidence about yourself is also important, and that can be done through acting classes. Some teachers like to rip people down, and a lot of actors like being ripped down, but I think it's a waste of energy. It's important to find a good teacher, someone you trust, and someone who encourages you. You have to shop around. Every teacher has a different style. It's a very personal thing.

Let's say someone you know is coming out to L.A. to start an acting career and they don't know anything about the business or the way Hollywood works. Based on your observations, what would you tell them about the way Hollywood works?

My image of Hollywood (and Los Angeles, in general) is that the industry works behind closed doors. Every door has a big bright smile on it and everybody is very happy. Very few people say "Get lost!" They'll say, "Oh, nice to meet you," and then they don't remember your name.

It's a huge network of who-knows-who. This can be very difficult to get into. Some people have success at doing the party thing—meeting people and schmoozing up to them, which is great if you have that ability. There's going to come a time when you'll have to schmooze, as with any business. It's something to be learned.

Another important quality about Los Angeles is that it's an industry, an entertainment industry, unlike New York. That's a big difference I've found between New York and Los Angeles. In New York, you always have the feeling that you are pursuing something as an artist and that the quality of your art is something important, something to be proud of. In Los Angeles, however, it's an industry. The actor is basically a cog in a machine. As an actor, you are at the low end of the totem pole and you don't have much power, unless you're a star. So you've got to learn to behave like a businessperson. If some art creeps into your work, great, but that seems secondary somehow. That's what you do once you have the job and you're on the set.

You've got to learn how to write letters, how to call people, how to keep up relations, how to advertise yourself, and how to make a lot of noise. It doesn't really matter what kind of noise you make, just some kind of noise. Get people to notice you, because there are thousands and thousands of actors out here. You've got to develop a business mind-set. I think actors tend to be more on the artistic side, and often don't want to deal with that stuff.

And in high school or college, there's usually not even one class that talks about the business side of the acting profession. . . .

Where I went to school, nobody knew how to teach any of that. You just have to jump in and figure your way through it. A lot of it depends on luck too. Sometimes you're unlucky, sometimes you're lucky. Actors often beat themselves up because they feel they are not doing enough, or they're not good enough, when it often just comes down to pure luck.

Sometimes it comes down to, "This actor is with this agency, that actor is with that agency, and we owe that agency a favor." Sometimes it comes down to what they had for breakfast. There's nothing you can do about those things.

One person may say, "That was a terrible audition," and another person may say, "That was a great audition!" It's all very subjective. So you have to satisfy yourself. Don't try to move the auditors, move yourself. Because there is no way you can know what they want. You can guess at what's necessary from the scene and the script. But you don't know what they want, unless they tell you. If they do, you make an adjustment. Otherwise you have to make yourself happy. They'll know what they want when they see it. Sometimes it's you and sometimes it's not.

What helps to keep your creative juices flowing?

I think acting classes help. Putting together your own show is good too. If you do that, then be sure to get a director. Don't imagine that you're Woody Allen. Get a director.

Also, with audition preparation, it's good to have somebody you trust that can read through the scene with you and help you work on it. It could be another actor, a teacher, a director, or somebody who has nothing to do with the business but has a good sense of what's necessary. It doesn't have to be an actor. Actually, I've found that when I work on a scene with another actor, they'll generally tell me to act more, and that's exactly what you don't want to do.

If you have the urge to do something creative, it's going to come out somehow. You can't keep it locked up.

What can you say about demo tapes?

Here in Los Angeles it's important to have a good tape of scenes. The only problem is: you can only get one by working. In New York, it's not as important to have a tape. But in Los Angeles, it seems to be necessary to have a tape.

I would discourage anybody from filming an acting class scene or a theatre piece unless you have a very good photographer. What happens is that, though your acting might be brilliant, if the lighting, photography, and editing aren't excellent, it's not going to impress anybody. And the point of the tape is to impress people and entertain people. You are going to want to put together a tape that people will enjoy watching, not something boring or painful. You want it to be entertaining, like an eight-minute TV show or movie preview! You want to leave them wanting to see more.

Put on little clips in an order that is entertaining. But don't put on something that you've taped yourself with a little video camera. It will hurt more than help. You've got to put yourself in the mind-set of these people who are hiring you—casting directors, directors, producers. They don't know you, and so you don't want to present yourself as some cheap product. You want to present yourself professionally. After all, this is your career, your profession.

Whatever you do, whether it's getting pictures or resumes, auditioning, putting up your own show, performing a scene before cameras, always present yourself professionally. Strive for a certain level of quality.

A lot of actors will opt for cheap pictures because they may not have the money for good pictures. I think it's better to wait until you can afford really good pictures. I've known many actors who every year get a new picture done, the cheapest thing possible, and every year it's a lousy picture. Whereas if they had just waited a while and saved up some money, then hired a good photographer, they probably would get much better pictures.

The same quality and professionalism goes for resumes, the letters you write, and how you conduct yourself, whether on the phone or in person. If you put up your own show, make sure you have enough money to do it in a professional manner. Don't throw things together, because it only reflects badly on you. It looks like you're a used-car salesman, and you want to behave as if you are selling a Mercedes. You are the Mercedes. I think it's very important that you have a sense of quality about everything. A lot of actors seem to throw things together at the last minute. That's no good. It reflects badly on them.

Of course, it means that there is a financial consideration, which means that you've got to save up the money. If you put up your own show, don't do it unless you have money to advertise it. And advertise it well. Don't just scribble out some flyer, like so many showcase productions do. Why would anyone want to go see a show represented by a less-than-professional flyer? Get a little money together and have somebody help you design something that's really nice. It doesn't have to be tremendously expensive, but it takes a lot of thought, consideration, and asking for a lot of advice.

What about taking risks?

There's a lot of talk in acting classes about taking risks, and of course that's part of your job as an actor. In the craft of acting as well as in business, you do have to take risks. However, a lot of actors really go overboard with this, and behave totally inappropriately in certain situations. Of course, you hear anecdotes of people who are now stars, who say, "When I was starting out, I did this and this outrageous thing." A lot of people emulate these anecdotes, but generally they don't work. There's a level of appropriateness.

Take risks, but within a certain context. If you're doing a Shakespeare play, you're not going to start in a style of Sam Shepard. Take risks, but don't make yourself look really foolish.

In Conclusion

I hope this book serves as a useful and inspiring companion during your first year in Hollywood. If you apply all of the preceding information and advice, you will definitely have a head start over other newcomers in town. So focus, work smart, be dedicated, and have fun with everything you do!

I believe that everyone who has ever pursued an artistic dream is a personal success, regardless of how far they got. This is because beginning such a path requires courage—courage to journey into an unknown future, leaving behind a path of relative security. And that courage, unwavering through a winding road, is a remarkable energy that expands and transforms your life forever.

So I wish you great personal success on your journey. I also wish you great worldly success. May you create everything you've ever dreamed of!

SAG-Franchised Talent Agencies

Below is a list of all SAG-franchised agencies in the Los Angeles area, as of January 1996. Included for each agency is the type of representation it offers, its relative size, its address, and telephone number. With regard to size, I've used "small," "medium," and "large" to describe them. "Small" means it is run by typically one to five agents. "Medium" means there is a larger group of agents that collectively represents at least a few hundred clients or more. "Large" means one with at least fifteen or twenty agents representing hundreds of clients, if not over a thousand.

Before sending pictures and resumes to any of these agencies, it is smart to call and check whether or not they still exist, and if they do, whether or not they are accepting submissions. (During an average year, twenty or more agencies can go out of business! Like actors, agencies face tough competition, too!) You'll save a lot on postage. Also verify with them that their address is still the same, as some agencies relocate often. Additionally, find out to whom you should direct your submission.

Realize that if you are a newcomer with very few credits, your best chances of landing representation are with smaller agencies. Many of them seem to be more open to new talent. Understand also that an agency's size isn't necessarily indicative of how good it is. In fact, some small agencies are highly respected and influential. It really boils down to finding an agent who is interested in you and who also has some respect in the industry.

Medium-sized agencies and large agencies tend to represent more established talent and stars. For example, three of the largest agencies—William Morris, CAA, and ICM, only represent star-level talent. Thus, if you are new and aren't a proven money-maker, they aren't going to want you. However, many medium-sized agencies do have openings for a few new clients, so they might be worth a try.

Okay, here's the list:

Above the Line Agency
(Mostly Literary/Small)
9200 Sunset Blvd., Ste. 401
Los Angeles, CA 90069
(310) 859-6115

Abrams Artists & Associates
(Full Service/Medium)
9200 Sunset Blvd., Ste. 625
Los Angeles, CA 90069
(310) 859-0625

Abrams-Rubaloff & Lawrence
(Commercial/Medium)
8075 West Third St., Ste. 303
Los Angeles, CA 90048
(213) 935-1700

Acme Talent & Literary
(Full Service/Small)
6310 San Vicente Blvd., Ste. 520
Los Angeles, CA 90048
(213) 954-2263

AFH Talent Agency
(Full Service/Small)
5724 W. 3rd Street, Ste. 509
Los Angeles, CA 90036
(213) 932-6042

The Agency
(Full Service/Medium)
1800 Avenue of the Stars, Ste. 400
Los Angeles, CA 90067
(310) 551-3000

Agency for Performing Arts
(Full Service-Adults/Medium)
9000 Sunset Blvd., Ste. 1200
Los Angeles, CA 90069
(310) 273-0744

Aimee Entertainment
(Theatrical/Small)
15000 Ventura Blvd., Ste. 340
Sherman Oaks, CA 91403
(818) 783-9115

Allen Talent Agency
(Full Service/Small)
11755 Wilshire Blvd., Ste. 1750
Los Angeles, CA 90025
(310) 474-7524

Bonni Allen Talent Inc.
(Theatrical/Small)
260 S. Beverly Dr.
Beverly Hills, CA 90212
(310) 247-1865

Alliance Talent Inc.
(Full Service/Small)
8949 Sunset Blvd., Ste. 202
West Hollywood, CA 90069
(310) 858-1090

Carlos Alvarado Agency
(Full Service/Small)
8455 Beverly Blvd., Ste. 406
Los Angeles, CA 90048
(213) 655-7978

Ambrosio/Mortimer
(Theatrical-Adults/Small)
9150 Wilshire Blvd., Ste. 175
Beverly Hills, CA 90212
(310) 274-4274

Amsel, Eisenstadt, & Frazier
(Theatrical/Small)
6310 San Vicente Blvd., Ste. 401
Los Angeles, CA 90048
(213) 939-1188

Angel City Talent
(Full Service/Small)
1680 Vine St., Ste. 716
Los Angeles, CA 90028
(213) 463-1680

Chris Apodaca Agency
(Full Service/Small)
2049 Century Park East, Ste. 1200
Los Angeles, CA 90067
(310) 284-3484

Apodaca/Munro Agency
(Full Service/Small)
13801 Ventura Blvd.
Sherman Oaks, CA 91423
(818) 380-2700

Irvin Arthur Associates Ltd.
(Full Service/Medium)
9363 Wilshire Blvd., Ste. 212
Beverly Hills, CA 90210
(310) 278-5934

Artist Management Agency
(Full Service/Small)
4340 Campus Dr., Ste. 210
Newport Beach, CA 92660
(714) 261-7557

Artist Network
(Theatrical/Small)
8438 Melrose Place
Los Angeles, CA 90069
(213) 651-4244

Artists Agency
(Full Service/Medium)
10000 Santa Monica Blvd., Ste. 305
Los Angeles, CA 90067
(310) 277-7779

Artists Group, Ltd.
(Full Service/Medium)
10100 Santa Monica Blvd.,
Ste. 2409
Los Angeles, CA 90067
(310) 552-1100

A.S.A.
(Full Service/Small)
4430 Fountain Ave., Ste. A
Hollywood, CA 90029
(213) 662-9787

Atkins & Associates
(Theatrical/Small)
303 S. Crescent Heights
Los Angeles, CA 90048
(213) 658-1025

Badgley & Conner
(Theatrical/Small)
9229 Sunset Blvd., Ste. 311
Los Angeles, CA 90069
(310) 278-9313

Baier-Kleinman International
(Theatrical-Adults/Small)
3575 Cahuenga Blvd. West,
Ste. 500
Los Angeles, CA 90068
(818) 761-1001

Baldwin Talent, Inc.
(Full Service/Small)
500 Sepulveda Blvd., 4th Floor
Los Angeles, CA 90049
(310) 472-7919

Bobby Ball Talent Agency
(Full Service/Medium)
8075 West Third St., Ste. 550
Los Angeles, CA 90048
(213) 964-7300

BAMM Talent Agency
(Commercial-Adults/Small)
8609 Sherwood Dr.
W. Hollywood, CA 90069
(310) 652-6252

Bauman, Hiller & Associates
(Theatrical/Small)
5757 Wilshire Blvd., Penthouse 5
Los Angeles, CA 90036
(213) 857-6666

Sara Bennett Agency
(Full Service/Small)
6404 Hollywood Blvd., Ste. 316
Hollywood, CA 90028
(213) 965-9666

The Benson Agency
(Theatrical-Adults/Small)
8360 Melrose Ave., Ste. 203
Los Angeles, CA 90069
(213) 653-0500

Marian Berzon Talent Agency
(Full Service/Small)
336 East 17th St.
Costa Mesa, CA 92627
(714) 631-5936

The Bigley Agency
(Full Service/Medium)
6442 Coldwater Canyon Ave.,
Ste. 211
N. Hollywood, CA 91606
(818) 761-9971

Yvette Bikoff Agency, Ltd.
(Full Service/Small)
8721 Santa Monica Blvd., Ste. 21
Los Angeles, CA 90069
(213) 655-6123

Bonnie Black Talent Agency
(Full Service-Adults/Small)
4405 Riverside Dr., Ste. 305
Burbank, CA 91505
(818) 840-1299

The Blake Agency
(Theatrical-Adults/Small)
415 N. Camden Dr., Ste. 121
Beverly Hills, CA 90210
(310) 246-0241

J. Michael Bloom
(Theatrical/Small)
9255 Sunset Blvd., 7th Floor
Los Angeles, CA 90069
(310) 275-6800

B.O.P.-LA Talent Agency
(Full Service/Small)
1467 N. Tamarind Ave.
Hollywood, CA 90028
(213) 466-8667

Nicole Bordeaux Talent Agency
(Commercial-Adults/Small)
616 N. Robertson Blvd.,
2nd Floor
West Hollywood, CA 90069
(310) 289-2550

Borinstein Oreck Bogart
(Theatrical-Adults/Small)
8271 Melrose Ave., Ste. 110
Los Angeles, CA 90046
(213) 658-7500

Brand Model and Talent
(Full Service/Small)
17941 Skypark Circle, Ste. F
Irvine, CA 92714
(714) 251-0555

Paul Brandon & Associates
(Theatrical-Adults/Small)
1033 N. Carol Dr., Ste. T-6
Los Angeles, CA 90069
(310) 273-6173

Bresler, Kelly, & Associates
(Theatrical-Adults/Small)
15760 Ventura Blvd., Ste. 1730
Encino, CA 91436
(818) 905-1155

Brustein Company
(Theatrical-Adults/Small)
12233 W. Olympic Blvd., Ste. 110
Los Angeles, CA 90064
(310) 571-3500

Don Buchwald & Associates Inc.
(Theatrical/Medium)
9229 Sunset Blvd.
West Hollywood, CA 90069
(310) 278-3600

Burkett Talent Agency
(Full Service/Small)
12 Hughes, Ste. D-100
Irvine, CA 92718
(714) 830-6300

Iris Burton Agency
(Full Service-Youth/Small)
8916 Ashcroft
Los Angeles, CA 90049
(310) 288-0121

Cactus Talent Agency
(Theatrical/Small)
13601 Ventura Blvd., Ste. 112
Sherman Oaks, CA 91423
(818) 986-7432

Camden ITG
(Theatrical/Small)
822 S. Robertson Blvd., Ste. 200
Los Angeles, CA 90035
(310) 289-2700

Barbara Cameron & Associates
(Full Service-Youth/Small)
8369 Sausalito Ave., Ste. A
West Hills, CA 91304
(818) 888-6107

Capital Artists
(Theatrical/Small)
8383 Wilshire Blvd., Ste. 954
Beverly Hills, CA 90211
(310) 658-8118

Career Artists International
(Full Service/Small)
11030 Ventura Blvd., Ste. 3
Studio City, CA 91604
(818) 980-1315

William Carroll Agency
(Full Service/Small)
139 N. San Fernando Road, Ste. A
Burbank, CA 91502
(818) 848-9948

Castle-Hill Talent Agency
(Full Service-Small)
1101 S. Orlando Ave.
Los Angeles, CA 90035
(213) 653-3535

Cavaleri & Associates
(Full Service/Small)
405 Riverside Dr., Ste. 200
Burbank, CA 91506
(818) 955-9300

Century Artists, Ltd.
(Theatrical-Adults/Small)
9744 Wilshire Blvd., Ste. 308
Beverly Hills, CA 90212
(310) 273-4366

The Chasin Agency
(Theatrical-Adults/Small)
8899 Beverly Blvd., Ste. 716
Los Angeles, CA 90048
(310) 278-7505

Chateau Billings Talent Agency
(Full Service/Small)
5657 Wilshire Blvd., Ste. 340
Los Angeles, CA 90036
(213) 965-5432

Jack Chutuk & Associates
(Theatrical-Adults/Small)
2121 Ave. of the Stars, Ste. 700
Los Angeles, CA 90067
(310) 552-1773

Cinema West Talent Agency
(Full Service-Small)
2609 Wyoming Avenue
Burbank, CA 91505
(818) 845-3816

Circle Talent Associates
(Full Service/Small)
433 N. Camden Dr., Ste. 400
Beverly Hills, CA 90212
(310) 285-1585

W. Randolph Clark Company
(Full Service/Small)
2431 Hyperion Ave.
Hollywood, CA 90027
(213) 953-4960

C' La Vie Model and Talent Agency
(Full Service-Adults/Small)
7507 Sunset Blvd., Ste. 201
Los Angeles, CA 90046
(213) 969-0541

Colleen Cler Modeling
(Full Service-Youth/Small)
120 S. Victory Blvd., Ste. 206
Burbank, CA 91502
(818) 841-7943

CL Inc. [Cassell-Levy]
(Commercial/Small)
843 N. Sycamore Ave.
Hollywood, CA 90038
(213) 461-3971

CNA
(Full Service-Adults/Medium)
1801 Ave. of the Stars, Ste. 1250
Los Angeles, CA 90067
(310) 556-4343

C.N.T.V. Talent & Literary Agency
(Full Service/Small)
1680 N. Vine, Ste. 1105
Los Angeles, CA 90028
(213) 463-5677

Coast to Coast Talent Group, Inc.
(Full Service/Medium)
4942 Vineland Ave., Ste. 200
N. Hollywood, CA 91601
(818) 762-6278

Colours Model & Talent Mgt.
(Full Service/Small)
8344½ W. 3rd St.
Los Angeles, CA 90048
(213) 658-7072

Commercials Unlimited Inc.
(Full Service/Medium)
9601 Wilshire Blvd., Ste. 620
Beverly Hills, CA 90210
(310) 888-8788

Contemporary Artists, Ltd.
(Full Service/Small)
1427 Third St. Promenade, Ste. 205
Santa Monica, CA 90401
(310) 395-1800

The Coppage Company
(Theatrical-Adults/Small)
11501 Chandler Blvd.
N. Hollywood, CA 91601
(818) 980-1106

Coralie Jr. Theatrical Agency
(Full Service/Small)
4789 Vineland Ave., Ste. 100
N. Hollywood, CA 91602
(818) 766-9501

The Cosden Agency
(Theatrical/Small)
3518 West Cahuenga Blvd.,
Ste. 216
Los Angeles, CA 90068
(818) 874-7200

The Craig Agency
(Full Service-Adults/Small)
8485 Melrose Place, Ste. E
Los Angeles, CA 90069
(213) 655-0236

Creative Artists Agency
(Full Service/Large)
9830 Wilshire Blvd.
Beverly Hills, CA 90212-1825
(310) 288-4545

Susan Crow & Associates
(Full Service/Small)
1010 Hammond St., Ste. 102
West Hollywood, CA 90069
(310) 859-9784

Lil Cumber Attractions
(Full Service/Small)
6363 Sunset Blvd., Ste. 807
Los Angeles, CA 90028
(213) 469-1919

Cunningham, Escott & Dipene
(Full Service/Medium)
10635 Santa Monica Blvd., Ste. 130
Los Angeles, CA 90025
(310) 475-2111

Dade/Schultz Associates
(Theatrical/Small)
11846 Ventura Blvd., Ste. 101
Studio City, CA 91604
(818) 760-3100

Mary Webb Davis Talent Agency
(Full Service-Adults/Small)
515 N. La Cienega Blvd.
Los Angeles, CA 90048
(310) 652-6850

The Devroe Agency
(Variety Acts-Adults/Small)
3224 Glendale Blvd., Ste. 400
Los Angeles, CA 90039
(213) 962-3040

d.H, Talent Agency
(Full Service/Small)
1800 N. Highland Ave., Ste. 300
Hollywood, CA 90028
(213) 962-6643

Durkin Artists
(Full Service/Small)
127 Broadway, Ste. 210
Santa Monica, CA 90401
(310) 458-5377

Dytman & Schwartz Talent Agency
(Mostly Literary/Small)
9200 Sunset Blvd., Ste. 809
Hollywood, CA 90069
(310) 274-8844

DZA Talent Agency
(Full Service/Small)
8981 Sunset Blvd., Ste. 204
Los Angeles, CA 90069
(310) 274-8025

Efendi, The Agency
(Full Service/Small)
1923½ Westwood Blvd., Ste. 3
Los Angeles, CA 90025
(310) 441-2822

Elite Model Management
(Full Service-Adults/Small)
345 N. Maple Dr., Ste. 397
Beverly Hills, CA 90210
(310) 274-9395

Ellis Talent Group
(Theatrical-Adults/Small)
6025 Sepulveda Blvd., Ste. 201
Van Nuys, CA 91411
(818) 997-7447

Epstein-Wyckoff & Assoc. Inc.
(Theatrical/Small)
280 S. Beverly Dr., Ste. 400
Beverly Hills, CA 90212
(310) 278-7222

Estephan Talent Agency
(Mostly Literary/Small)
6018 Greenmeadow Rd.
Lakewood, CA 90713
(310) 421-8048

Eileen Farrell/Cathy Coulter
Talent Agency
(Full Service/Small)
P.O. Box 15189
N. Hollywood, CA 91615
(818) 765-0400

Favored Artists Agency
(Theatrical-Adults/Small)
122 S. Robertson Blvd., Ste. 202
Los Angeles, CA 90048
(310) 247-1040

Ferrar-Maziroff Associates
(Commercial-Adults/Small)
8430 Santa Monica Blvd., Ste. 220
Los Angeles, CA 90069
(213) 654-2601

Liana Fields Talent Agency
(Full Service/Small)
3325 Wilshire Blvd., Ste. 749
Los Angeles, CA 90010
(213) 292-8550

Film Artists Associates
(Full Service/Small)
7080 Hollywood Blvd., Ste. 1118
Hollywood, CA 90028
(213) 463-1010

First Artists Agency
(Theatrical/Small)
10000 Riverside Dr., Ste. 10
Toluca Lake, CA 91602
(818) 509-9292

Flick East & West Talents, Inc.
(Full Service-Adults/Small)
9057 Nemo St., Ste. A
West Hollywood, CA 90069
(310) 271-9111

FPA, Talent Agency
(Theatrical-Adults/Small)
12701 Moorpark, Ste. 205
Studio City, CA 91604-4531
(818) 508-6691

Barry Freed Company
(Theatrical-Adults/Small)
2029 Central Park East, Ste. 600
Los Angeles, CA 90067
(310) 277-1260

Alice Fries Agency
(Theatrical/Small)
6381 Hollywood Blvd., Ste. 600
Los Angeles, CA 90028
(213) 464-6491

Future Agency
(Full Service/Small)
8929 S. Sepulveda Blvd., Ste. 314
Los Angeles, CA 90045
(310) 338-9602

Gage Group, Inc.
(Theatrical-Adults/Medium)
9255 Sunset Blvd., Ste. 515
Los Angeles, CA 90069
(310) 859-8777

Helen Garrett Talent Agency
(Full Service/Small)
6525 Sunset Blvd., 5th Floor
Hollywood, CA 90028
(213) 871-8707

Dale Garrick International Talent
(Full Service/Small)
8831 Sunset Blvd., Ste. 402
Los Angeles, CA 90069
(310) 657-2661

The Geddes Agency
(Theatrical-Adults/Small)
1201 Green Acre Ave.
West Hollywood, CA 90046
(213) 878-1155

Laya Gelff Associates
(Theatrical-Adults/Small)
16133 Ventura Blvd., Ste. 700
Encino, CA 91436
(818) 713-2610

Paul Gerard Talent Agency
   (Theatrical-Adults/Small)
11712 Moorpark St., Ste. 112
Studio City, CA 91604
(818) 769-7015

Don Gerler Agency
   (Full Service/Small)
3349 Cahuenga Blvd. West, Ste. 1
Los Angeles, CA 90068
(213) 850-7386

The Gersh Agency
   (Full Service/Large)
232 N. Canon Dr.
Beverly Hills, CA 90210
(310) 274-6611

David Gershenson Talent Agency
   (Theatrical/Small)
11757 San Vicente Blvd., Ste. 2
Los Angeles, CA 90049
(310) 207-1345

Gold/Marshak & Associates
   (Full Service/Medium)
3500 West Olive Ave., Ste. 1400
Burbank, CA 91505
(818) 972-4300

Goldey Company, Inc.
   (Theatrical/Small)
Robertson Plaza
116 N. Robertson Blvd.
Los Angeles, CA 90048
(310) 657-3277

Michele Gordon & Associates
   (Full Service-Adults/Small)
260 S. Beverly Dr., Ste. 308
Beverly Hills, CA 90212
(310) 246-9930

Haegstrom Office, Talent Agency
   (Theatrical-Adult/Small)
6404 Wilshire Blvd., Ste. 1100
Los Angeles, CA 90048
(213) 658-9111

Buzz Halliday & Associates
   (Full Service/Small)
8899 Beverly Blvd., Ste. 620
Los Angeles, CA 90048
(310) 275-6028

Halpern & Associates
   (Theatrical-Adults/Small)
12304 Santa Monica Blvd., Ste. 104
Los Angeles, CA 90025
(310) 571-4488

Mitchell J. Hamilburg Agency
   (Mostly Literary/Small)
292 S. La Cienega, Ste. 312
Beverly Hills, CA 90211
(310) 657-1501

Vaughn D. Hart & Associates
   (Theatrical-Adults/Small)
8899 Beverly Blvd., Ste. 815
Los Angeles, CA 90048
(310) 273-7887

Headline Artists Agency
   (Full Service/Small)
16400 Ventura Blvd., Ste. 324
Encino, CA 91436
(818) 986-1730

Beverly Hecht Agency
   (Full Service/Small)
12001 Ventura Blvd., Ste. 320
Studio City, CA 91604
(818) 505-1192

Henderson/Hogan Agency
   (Theatrical-Adults/Small)
247 S. Beverly Dr.
Beverly Hills, CA 90212
(310) 274-7815

Hervey/Grimes Talent Agency
   (Full Service/Small)
12444 Ventura Blvd., Ste. 103
Studio City, CA 91604
(818) 981-0891

House of Representatives Talent
   Agency
   (Theatrical-Adults/Small)
9911 Pico Boulevard, Ste. 1060
Los Angeles, CA 90035
(310) 772-0772

Howard Talent West
   (Full Service-Adults/Small)
11712 Moorpark St., Ste. 205B
Studio City, CA 91604
(818) 766-5300

Martin Hurwitz & Associates
   (Theatrical-Adults/Small)
427 N. Canon Dr., Ste. 215
Beverly Hills, CA 90210
(310) 274-0240

HWA Talent Representatives
   (Theatrical/Small)
1964 Westwood Blvd., Ste. 400
Los Angeles, CA 90025
(310) 466-1313

I.F.A. Talent Agency
   (Theatrical/Small)
8730 Sunset Blvd., Ste. 490
Los Angeles, CA 90069
(310) 659-5522

Innovative Artists Talent &
   Literary Agency
   (Theatrical/Medium)
1999 Ave. of the Stars, Ste. 2850
Los Angeles, CA 90067
(310) 553-5200

International Creative Mgt.
   (Full Service/Large)
8942 Wilshire Blvd.
Beverly Hills, CA 90211
(310) 550-4000

IT Model Management
   (Full Service/Small)
526 N. Larchmont Blvd.
Los Angeles, CA 90004
(213) 962-9564

Jackman & Taussig
   (Full Service/Small)
1815 Butler Ave., Ste. 120
Los Angeles, CA 90025
(310) 478-6641

George Jay Agency
   (Commercial/Small)
6269 Selma Ave., Ste. 615
Hollywood, CA 90028
(213) 466-6665

Thomas Jennings & Associates
   (Theatrical/Small)
28035 Dorothy Dr., Ste. 210A
Agoura, CA 91301
(818) 879-1260

The Kaplan-Stahler Agency
(Theatrical-Adults/Small)
8383 Wilshire Blvd., Ste. 923
Beverly Hills, CA 90211
(213) 653-4483

Karg/Weissenbach & Associates
(Theatrical-Adults/Small)
329 N. Wetherly Dr., Ste. 101
Beverly Hills, CA 90211
(310) 205-0435

Kazarian-Spencer & Associates
(Full Service/Medium)
11365 Ventura Blvd., Ste. 100
Studio City, CA 91604
(818) 769-9111

Kelman/Arletta
(Full Service/Small)
7813 Sunset Blvd.
Hollywood, CA 90046
(213) 851-8822

Sharon Kemp Talent Agency
(Theatrical/Small)
9812 Vidor Drive
Los Angeles, CA 90035
(310) 552-0011

William Kerwin Agency
(Full Service-Adults/Small)
1605 N. Cahuenga Blvd., Ste. 202
Hollywood, CA 90028
(213) 469-5155

Tyler Kjar Agency
(Full Service/Small)
10653 Riverside Dr.
Toluca Lake, CA 91602
(818) 760-0321

Eric Klass Agency
(Theatrical/Small)
144 S. Beverly Dr., Ste. 405
Beverly Hills, CA 90212
(310) 274-9169

Paul Kohner, Inc.
(Full Service/Medium)
9300 Wilshire Blvd., Ste. 555
Beverly Hills, CA 90212
(310) 550-1060

Victor Kruglov & Associates
(Full Service/Small)
7060 Hollywood Blvd., Ste. 1220
Hollywood, CA 90028
(213) 957-9000

L.A. Artists
(Theatrical-Adults/Small)
606 Wilshire Blvd., Ste. 416
Santa Monica, CA 90401
(310) 395-9589

L.A. Talent & L.A. Models
(Full Service/Medium)
8335 Sunset Blvd., 2nd Floor
Los Angeles, CA 90069
(213) 656-3722

Lauren Laine Talent Agency
(Full Service/Small)
1370 N. Brea Blvd., Ste. 2000
Fullerton, CA 92635
(714) 441-1140

Stacey Lane Talent Agency
(Full Service/Small)
13455 Ventura Blvd., Ste. 240
Sherman Oaks, CA 91423
(818) 501-2668

The Lawrence Agency
(Theatrical/Small)
3575 Cahuenga Blvd. West,
Ste. 125-3
Hollywood, CA 90068
(213) 851-7711

Guy Lee & Associates
(Full Service/Small)
8961 Sunset Blvd. Ste. V
Los Angeles, CA 90069
(310) 888-8737

Lenhoff/Robinson Talent &
Literary Agency
(Theatrical/Small)
1728 S. La Cienega Blvd.
Los Angeles, CA 90035
(310) 558-4700

The Levin Agency
(Full Service/Small)
8484 Wilshire Blvd., Ste. 745
Beverly Hills, CA 90211
(213) 653-7073

Levy, Robin & Associates
(Full Service/Small)
9701 Wilshire Blvd., Ste. 1200
Beverly Hills, CA 90212
(310) 278-8748)

Terry Lichtman Co.
(Theatrical-Adults/Small)
4439 Wortser Ave.
Studio City, CA 91604
(818) 783-3003

Robert Light Agency
(Full Service-Adults/Small)
6404 Wilshire Blvd., Ste. 900
Los Angeles, CA 90048
(213) 651-1777

Ken Lindner & Associates
(Theatrical-Adults/Small)
2049 Century Park East, Ste. 2750
Los Angeles, CA 90067
(310) 277-9223

Lovell & Associates
(Theatrical/Small)
1350 N. Highland Ave.
Hollywood, CA 90028
(213) 462-1672

Lund Agency/Industry Artists
Agency
(Full Service/Small)
10000 Riverside Dr., Ste. 4
Toluca Lake, CA 91602
(818) 508-1688

Lynne & Reilly Agency
(Full Service/Small)
6735 Forest Lawn Dr., Ste. 313
Los Angeles, CA 90068
(213) 850-1984

LW 1, Inc.
(Commercials/Small)
8383 Wilshire Blvd., Ste. 649
Beverly Hills, CA 90211
(213) 653-5700

Mademoiselle Talent Agency
(Full Service/Small)
8693 Wilshire Blvd., Ste. 200
Beverly Hills, CA 90211
(310) 289-8005

Major Clients Agency
(Theatrical-Adults/Medium)
345 N. Maple Dr., Ste. 395
Beverly Hills, CA 90210
(310) 205-5000

Alese Marshall Model &
Commercial Agency
(Full Service/Small)
23900 Hawthorne Blvd., Ste. 100
Torrance, CA 90505
(310) 378-1223

The Martel Agency
(Full Service-Adults/Small)
1680 N. Vine St., Ste. 203
Hollywood, CA 90028
(213) 461-5943

Maxine's Talent Agency
(Full Service-Adults/Small)
4830 Encino Ave.
Encino, CA 91316
(818) 986-2946

Media Artists Group
(Full Service/Medium)
8383 Wilshire Blvd., Ste. 954
Beverly Hills, CA 90211
(213) 658-5050

Metropolitan Talent Agency
(Theatrical-Adults/Medium)
4526 Wilshire Blvd.
Los Angeles, CA 90010
(213) 857-4500

MGA/Mary Grady Agency
(Full Service/Small)
4444 Lankershim Blvd., Ste. 207
N. Hollywood, CA 91602
(818) 766-4414

Miramar Talent Agency
(Full Service-Adults/Small)
7400 Beverly Blvd., Ste. 200
Los Angeles, CA 90036
(213) 934-0700

Patty Mitchell Agency
(Full Service-Youth/Small)
4605 Lankershim Blvd., Ste. 201
N. Hollywood, CA 91602
(818) 508-6181

Moore Artists Talent Agency
(Theatrical/Small)
1551 S. Robertson Blvd.
Los Angeles, CA 90035
(310) 286-3150

William Morris Agency
(Full Service/Large)
151 El Camino Dr.
Beverly Hills, CA 90212
(310) 274-7451

H. David Moss & Associates
(Theatrical-Adults/Small)
733 North Seward St., Penthouse
Los Angeles, CA 90038
(213) 465-1234

Mary Murphy Agency
(Full Service-Adults/Small)
6014 Greenbush Ave.
Van Nuys, CA 91401
(818) 989-6076

Susan Nathe & Associates/CPC
(Commercials-Adults/Small)
8281 Melrose Ave., Ste. 200
Los Angeles, CA 90046
(213) 653-7573

Omnipop Inc.
(Full Service-Adults/Small)
10700 Ventura Blvd., 2nd Floor
Studio City, CA 91604
(818) 980-9267

Orange Grove Group, Inc.
(Theatrical/Small)
12178 Ventura Blvd., Ste. 205
Studio City, CA 91604
(818) 762-7498

Cindy Osbrink Talent Agency
(Full Service/Small)
4605 Lankershim Blvd., Ste. 401
N. Hollywood, CA 91602
(818) 760-2488

Dorothy Day Otis & Associates
(Full Service/Small)
373 S. Robertson
Beverly Hills, CA 90211
(310) 652-8855

Pakula-King & Associates
(Theatrical/Small)
9229 Sunset Blvd., Ste. 315
Los Angeles CA 90069
(310) 281-4868

Paradigm Talent & Literary Agency
(Theatrical/Large)
10100 Santa Monica Blvd.,
Ste. 2500
Los Angeles, CA 90067
(310) 277-4400

Paragon Talent Agency
(Full Service/Small)
8439 Sunset Blvd., Ste. 301
Los Angeles CA 90069
(213) 654-4554

The Partos Company
(Theatrical/Small)
6363 Wilshire Blvd., Ste. 227
Los Angeles, CA 90048
(213) 876-5500

Players Talent Agency
(Full Service/Small)
8770 Shoreham Dr., Ste. 2
West Hollywood, CA 90069
(310) 289-8777

Premiere Artists Agency
(Theatrical/Medium)
8899 Beverly Blvd., Ste. 510
Los Angeles, CA 90048
(310) 271-1414

Prima EastWest Model Mgt., Inc.
(Full Service/Medium)
933 N. La Brea Ave.
Los Angeles, CA 90038
(213) 882-6900

Privilege Talent Agency
(Full Service-Adults/Small)
8170 Beverly Blvd., Ste. 204
Los Angeles, CA 90048
(213) 658-8781

Progressive Artists
(Theatrical-Adults/Small)
400 S. Beverly Dr., Ste. 216
Beverly Hills, CA 90212
(310) 553-8561

Pro-Sport and Entertainment
  (Full Service-Adults/Small)
1990 S. Bundy Dr., Ste. 700
Los Angeles, CA 90025
(310) 207-0228

Gordon Rael Company
  (Full Service-Adults/Small)
9255 Sunset Blvd., Ste. 727
Los Angeles, CA 90069
(213) 285-9552

Renaissance Talent & Literary
  Agency
  (Theatrical-Adults/Medium)
8523 Sunset Blvd.
Los Angeles, CA 90069
(310) 289-3636

Stephanie Rogers & Assoc.
  (Mostly Directors, Writers,
  Producers/Small)
3575 Cahuenga Blvd. West,
  Ste. 249
Los Angeles, CA 90068
(213) 851-5155

Cindy Romano Modeling &
  Talent Agency
  (Full Service/Small)
P.O. Box 1951
Palm Springs, CA 92263
(619) 323-3333

Gilla Roos Ltd.
  (Full Service-Adults/Small)
9744 Wilshire Blvd., Ste. 203
Beverly Hills, CA 90212
(310) 274-9356

Marion Rosenberg
  (Theatrical-Adults/Small)
8428 Melrose Place, Ste. B
Los Angeles, CA 90069
(213) 653-7383

The Samantha Group
  (Commercials/Small)
1126 Hollywood Way, Ste. 203-A
Burbank, CA 91505
(818) 953-4801

The Sanders Agency
  (Full Service/Small)
8831 Sunset Blvd., Ste. 304
Los Angeles, CA 90069
(310) 652-1119

The Sarnoff Company, Inc.
  (Theatrical-Adults/Small)
3900 W. Alameda
Burbank, CA 91505
(818) 972-1779

The Savage Agency
  (Full Service/Small)
6212 Banner Ave.
Los Angeles, CA 90038
(213) 461-8316

Jack Scagnetti Talent Agency
  (Full Service-Adults/Small)
5118 Vineland Ave., Ste. 102
N. Hollywood, CA 91601
(818) 762-3871

The Irv Schechter Company
  (Full Service/Medium)
9300 Wilshire Blvd., Ste. 410
Beverly Hills, CA 90212
(310) 278-8070

Schiowitz/Clay Inc.
  (Theatrical-Adults/Medium)
1680 N. Vine St., Ste. 614
Los Angeles, CA 90028
(213) 463-7300

Sandie Schnarr Talent
  (Voice-Over/Small)
8281 Melrose Ave., Ste. 200
Los Angeles, CA 90046
(213) 653-9479

Judy Schoen & Associates
  (Theatrical-Adults/Small)
606 N. Larchmont Blvd., Ste. 309
Los Angeles, CA 90004
(213) 962-1950

Don Schwartz Associates
  (Full Service/Small)
6922 Hollywood Blvd., Ste. 508
Hollywood, CA 90028
(213) 464-4366

Screen Artists Agency/Model
  Team Los Angeles
  (Full Service/Small)
12435 Oxnard St.
N. Hollywood, CA 91606
(818) 755-0026

Screen Children's Talent Agency
  (Full Service-Youth/Small)
4000 Riverside Dr., Ste. A
Burbank, CA 91505
(818) 846-4300

SDB Partners, Inc.
  (Theatrical-Adults/Small)
1801 Ave. of the Stars, Ste. 902
Los Angeles, CA 90067
(310) 785-0060

Selected Artists Agency
  (Full Service-Adults/Small)
3900 W. Alameda Ave., Ste. 1700
Burbank, CA 91505
(818) 972-1747

David Shapira & Associates Inc.
  (Full Service-Adults/Medium)
15301 Ventura Blvd., Ste. 345
Sherman Oaks, CA 91403
(818) 906-0322

Shapiro-Lichtman
  (Theatrical-Adults/Medium)
8827 Beverly Blvd.
Los Angeles, CA 90048
(310) 859-8877

Showbiz Entertainment
  (Full Service/Small)
6922 Hollywood Blvd., Ste. 207
Hollywood, CA 90028
(213) 469-9931

Dorothy Shreve Agency
  (Full Service/Small)
2665 N. Palm Canyon Dr.
Palm Springs, CA 92262
(619) 327-5855

The Shumaker Talent Agency
  (Full Service/Small)
6533 Hollywood Blvd., Ste. 301
Hollywood, CA 90028
(213) 464-0745

Jerome Siegel Associates
(Theatrical/Small)
7551 Sunset Blvd., Ste. 203
Los Angeles, CA 90046
(213) 850-1275

Sierra Talent Agency
(Full Service-Adults/Small)
14542 Ventura Blvd., Ste. 207
Sherman Oaks, CA 91403
(818) 907-9645

Silver Massetti & Associates/
West Ltd.
(Theatrical-Adults/Small)
8730 Sunset Blvd., Ste. 480
Los Angeles, CA 90069
(310) 289-0909

Richard Sindell & Associates
(Theatrical-Adults/Small)
8271 Melrose Ave., Ste. 202
Los Angeles, CA 90046
(213) 653-5051

Sirens Model Management
(Commercial-Adult/Small)
6404 Wilshire Blvd., Ste. 720
Los Angeles, CA 90028
(213) 782-0310

Michael Slessinger & Associates
(Theatrical-Adults/Small)
8730 Sunset Blvd., Ste. 270
Los Angeles, CA 90069
(310) 657-7113

Susan Smith & Associates
(Theatrical/Medium)
121 N. San Vicente Blvd.
Beverly Hills, CA 90211
(213) 852-4777

Camille Sorice Talent Agency
(Full Service/Small)
16661 Ventura Blvd., Ste. 400-E
Encino, CA 91436
(818) 995-1775

Special Artists Agency
(Commercial/Medium)
345 North Maple Dr., Ste. 302
Beverly Hills, CA 90210
(310) 859-9688

Star Talent Agency
(Full Service/Small)
4555 1/2 Mariota Ave.
Toluca Lake, CA 91602
(818) 509-1931

Starwil Talent Agency
(Full Service/Small)
6253 Hollywood Blvd., Ste. 730
Hollywood, CA 90028
(213) 874-1239

Charles H. Stern Agency
(Mostly Voice-Overs/Small)
11766 Wilshire Blvd., Ste. 760
Los Angeles, CA 90025
(310) 479-1788

Steven R. Stevens Talent Agency
(Theatrical/Small)
3518 Cahuenga Blvd. West,
Ste. 301
Los Angeles, CA 90068
(213) 850-5761

Stone Manners Agency
(Theatrical-Adults/Small)
8091 Selma Ave.
Los Angeles, CA 90046
(213) 654-7575

Sutton, Barth & Vennari Inc.
(Commercial/Medium)
145 S. Fairfax Ave., Ste. 310
Los Angeles, CA 90036
(213) 938-6000

Talent Group, Inc.
(Commercial/Medium)
6300 Wilshire Blvd., Ste. 2110
Los Angeles, CA 90048
(213) 852-9559

Talon Theatrical Agency
(Full Service/Small)
567 South Lake
Pasadena, CA 91101
(818) 577-1998

Tannen & Associates
(Full Service/Medium)
1800 N. Vine St., Ste. 305
Los Angeles, CA 90028
(213) 466-6191

Thomas Talent Agency
(Full Service/Small)
124 S. Lasky Dr., 1st Floor
Beverly Hills, CA 90212
(310) 247-2727

Arlene Thornton & Associates
(Commercials, Voice-Overs/
Medium)
12001 Ventura Place, Ste. 201
Studio City, CA 91604
(818) 760-6688

Tisherman Agency, Inc.
(Voice-Overs/Small)
6767 Forest Lawn Dr., Ste. 101
Los Angeles, CA 90068
(213) 850-6767

A Total Acting Experience
(Full Service/Small)
20501 Ventura Blvd., Ste. 112
Woodland Hills, CA 91364
(818) 340-9249

The Turtle Agency
(Mostly Literary/Small)
12456 Ventura Blvd., Ste. 1
Studio City, CA 91604
(818) 506-6898

Twentieth Century Artists
(Full Service/Medium)
15315 Magnolia Blvd., Ste. 429
Sherman Oaks, CA 91403
(818) 788-5516

Umoja Talent Agency
(Full Service-Small)
2069 W. Slauson Ave.
Los Angeles, CA 90047
(213) 290-6612

United Talent Agency, Inc.
(Full Service-Adults/Large)
9560 Wilshire Blvd., 5th Floor
Beverly Hills, CA 90212
(310) 273-6700

Erika Wain Agency
(Theatrical-Adults/Small)
1418 N. Highland Ave., Ste. 102
Los Angeles, CA 90028
(213) 460-4224

Wallis Agency
   (Voice-Over/Small)
1126 Hollywood Way, Ste. 203-A
Burbank, CA 91505
(818) 953-4848

Sandra Watt & Associates
   (Full Service-Adults/Small)
7551 Melrose Ave., Ste. 5
Los Angeles, CA 90046
(213) 851-1021

Ann Waugh Talent Agency
   (Full Service/Small)
4731 Laurel Canyon Blvd., Ste. 5
N. Hollywood, CA 91607
(818) 980-0141

Ruth Webb Enterprises
   (Theatrical/Small)
13834 Magnolia Blvd.
Sherman Oaks, CA 91423
(213) 874-1700

The Whitaker Agency
   (Full Service-Adults/Small)
4924 Vineland Ave.
N. Hollywood, CA 91601
(818) 766-4441

Shirley Wilson & Associates
   (Full Service/Small)
5410 Wilshire Blvd., Ste. 227
Los Angeles, CA 90036
(213) 857-6977

World Class Sports
   (Full Service-Adults/Small)
880 Apollo St., Ste. 337
El Segundo, CA 90245
(310) 535-9120

World Wide Acts
   (Full Service-Adults/Small)
7226 Leota Lane
Canoga Park, CA 91304
(818) 387-2443

Carter Wright Talent Agency
   (Full Service/Small)
6513 Hollywood Blvd., Ste. 210
Hollywood, CA 90028
(213) 469-0944

Writers and Artists Agency
   (Full Service-Adults/Medium)
924 Westwood Blvd., Ste. 900
Los Angeles, CA 90024
(310) 824-6300

Stella Zadeh & Associates
   (Theatrical-Adults/Small)
11759 Iowa Ave.
Los Angeles, CA 90025
(310) 207-4114

Zealous Artists
   (Full Service/Small)
139 S. Beverly Dr., Ste. 222
Beverly Hills, CA 90212
(310) 281-3533

Soap Opera Addresses

asting directors for soap operas often consider new or relatively new actors, so you should send your picture to each. Often they need very specific physical types, usually very beautiful people, rather than just experienced actors. (Plus some experienced actors would rather work in film because it pays much more and is considered more prestigious.)

Along with your picture, attach a brief note explaining that you'd like to be considered for principal work, U/5's (Under Five's—parts with five lines or less) and/or extra work. Also, it's nice to briefly introduce yourself. A nice paragraph will do. Letters more than a page long usually don't get read.

Hopefully you'll get a call sometime within a few weeks.

The Bold & The Beautiful
All Casting Submissions to:
Christy Dooley
c/o CBS
7800 Beverly Blvd. #3371
Los Angeles, CA 90036
(No phone calls. Please include AFTRA membership number, if you have one, on your picture and resume.)

Days of Our Lives
Principal Casting Submissions to:
Fran Bascom
3400 Riverside Dr., Ste. 765
Burbank, CA 91505
(818) 972-8339

Extras Casting and Under-Fives to:
Linda Poindexter
3400 Riverside Dr., Ste. 767
Burbank, CA 91505
(818) 972-0973
(Casting Call-In Number is (818) 972-0971. Call it once a week to leave your availability, once your picture is on file.)

General Hospital
Principal Casting:
Mark Teschner
ABC Prospect
4151 Prospect Ave., Stage 54
Los Angeles, CA 90027
(310) 557-5542

Extras Casting and U/5's (Under Five Lines):
Lisa Snedeker (same address as above)
Casting Call-In Number is (310) 520-CAST. Call this to leave your availability, if you have already worked the show before.

The Young and the Restless
Principal Casting and U/5's (Under Five Lines):
Jill W. Newton
c/o CBS
7800 Beverly Blvd., #3305
Los Angeles, CA 90036
No Phone Calls.
Extras Casting:
Gail Camacho (same address as above)
(Include your AFTRA membership number, if you have one, on your picture and resume.)

SAG MOTION PICTURE / TELEVISION
AGENCY CONTRACT

THIS AGREEMENT, made and entered into at _____, by and

between _____, a talent agent, hereinafter called the "Agent", and

_____, _____,
   (please print or type)   (social security number)

hereinafter called the "Actor".

WITNESSETH:

(1) The Actor engages the Agent as his agent for the following fields as defined in Screen Actors Guild Codified Agency Regulations, Rule 16(g) and the Agent accepts such engagement:

[Mark appropriate space(s)]

☐ Theatrical Motion Pictures   ☐ Television Motion Pictures

If television motion pictures are included herein for purposes of representation and if during the term of this agency contract, the Actor enters into a series or term employment contract for services in television motion pictures, under which he agrees also to render services in program commercials or spots, this agency contract shall include representation of the Actor in connection with his employment in said commercials, and representation of the Actor in said commercials shall not be deemed included in any separate agency contract which the Actor may have entered into covering commercials.

This contract is limited to motion pictures in the above-designated field(s) and to contracts of the Actor as an actor in such motion pictures, and any reference herein to contracts or employment whereby Actor renders his services refers to contracts or employment in such motion pictures unless otherwise specifically stated.

(2) The term of this contract shall be for a period of _____, commencing

_____, 19____.

(3) (a) The Actor agrees to pay to the Agent as commissions a sum equal to _____ percent of all moneys or other consideration received by the Actor, directly or indirectly, under contracts of employment (or in connection with his employment under said employment contracts) entered into during the term specified in Paragraph (2) or in existence when this agency contract is entered into except to such extent as the Actor may be obligated to pay commissions on such existing employment contract to another agent. Commissions shall be payable when and as such moneys or other consideration are received by the Actor, or by anyone else for or on the Actor's behalf. Commission payments are subject to the limitations of Rule 16(g).

(b) Commissions on compensation paid to Actors for domestic reruns, theatrical exhibition, foreign exhibition or supplementary market exhibition of television motion pictures are subject to the provisions of Rule 16(g).

(c) Commissions on commercials included herein under paragraph (l) above shall be subject to the rules governing commercials provided by Rule 16(g).

(d) No commissions shall be payable on any of the following:

(i) Separate amounts paid to Actor not as compensation but for travel or living expenses incurred by Actor;

(ii) Separate amounts paid to Actor not as compensation but as reimbursement for necessary expenditures actually incurred by Actor in connection with Actor's employment, such as for damage to or loss of wardrobe, special hairdress, etc.;

(iii) Amounts paid to Actor as penalties for violations by Producer of any of the provisions of the SAG collective bargaining contracts, such as meal period violations, rest period violations, penalties or interest on delinquent payments;

(iv) Sums payable to Actors for the release on free television or for supplemental market exhibition of theatrical motion pictures produced after January 31, 1960, under the provisions of the applicable collection bargaining agreement providing for such payment; however, if an Actor's individual theatrical motion picture employment contract provides for compensation in the event the motion picture made for theatrical exhibition is exhibited over free television or in supplemental market exhibition, in excess of the minimum compensation payable under the applicable collective bargaining agreement in effect at the time the employment contract was executed, commissions shall be payable on such compensation.

(v) Sums payable to Actors for foreign telecasting on free television of television motion pictures and commercials under the provisions of the applicable collective bargaining agreements; however, if an individual Actor's contract provides for compensation in excess of minimum under the applicable collective bargaining agreements in effect at the time of employment, commissions shall be payable on such sums.

(vi) On any employment contract which is in violation of SAG collective bargaining agreements. For example, employment contracts providing for "free days", "free rehearsal", "free looping", "a break in consecutive employment", etc., shall not be commissionable. This paragraph is not subject to SAG waiver.

(vii) On any employment contract for television motion pictures which provide for any prepayment or buyout of domestic or foreign residuals or theatrical release, or supplemental market fees, other than those permitted by the appropriate SAG collective bargaining agreement, unless such provisions of individual employment contracts are expressly approved by SAG.

(e) Any moneys or other consideration received by the Actor, or by anyone for or on his behalf, in connection with any termination of any contract of the Actor by virtue of which the Agent would otherwise be entitled to receive commission, or in connection with the settlement of any such contract, or any litigation arising out of any such contract, shall also be moneys in connection with which the Agent is entitled to the aforesaid percentage; provided, however, that in such event the Actor shall be entitled to deduct attorney's fees, expenses and court costs before computing the amount upon which the Agent is entitled to his percentage. The Actor shall also be entitled to deduct reasonable legal expenses in connection with the collection of moneys or other consideration due the Actor arising out of an employment contract in motion pictures before computing the amount upon which the Agent is entitled to his percentage.

(f) The aforesaid percentage shall be payable by the Actor to the Agent during the term of this contract and thereafter only where specifically provided herein and in the Regulations.

(g) The Agent shall be entitled to the aforesaid percentage after the expiration of the term specified in Paragraph (2) for so long a period thereafter as the Actor continues to receive moneys or other consideration under or upon employment contracts entered into by the Actor during the term specified in Paragraph (2) hereof, including moneys or other consideration received by the Actor under the extended term of any such employment contract, resulting from the exercise of an option or options under such an employment contract, extending the term of such employment contact, whether such options be exercised prior to or after the expiration of the term specified in Paragraph (2), subject, however, to the applicable limitations set forth in the Regulations.

(h) If during the period the Agent is entitled to commissions a contract of employment of the Actor be terminated before the expiration of the term thereof, as said term has been extended by the exercise of options therein contained, by joint action of the Actor and employer, or by the action of either of them, other than on account of Act of God, illness, or the like, and the Actor enters into a new contract of employment with said employer within a period of sixty (60) days, such new contract shall be deemed to be in substitution of the contract terminated as aforesaid, subject, however, to the applicable limitations set forth in the Regulations. No contract entered into after said sixty (60) day period shall be deemed to be in substitution of the contract terminated as aforesaid. Contracts of substitution have the same effect as contracts for which they were substituted; provided, however, any increase or additional salary, bonus or other compensation payable to the actor thereunder over and above the amounts payable under the contract of employment which was terminated shall be deemed an adjustment and, unless the Agent shall have a valid agency contract in effect at the time of such adjustment, the Agent shall not be entitled to any commissions on any such additional or increased amounts. In no event may a contract of substitution with an employer extend the period of time during which the Agent is entitled to commission beyond the period that the Agent would have been entitled to commission had no substitution taken place. A change in form of an employer for the purpose of evading this provision or a change in the corporate form of an employer resulting from reorganization or the like shall not preclude the application of these provisions.

(i) So long as the Agent receives commissions from the Actor, the Agent shall be obliged to service the Actor and perform the obligations of this agency contract with respect to the services of the Actor on which such commissions are based, unless the Agent is relieved therefrom under express provisions of the Regulations.

(j) The Agent has no right to receive money unless the Actor receives the same, or unless the same is received for or on his behalf, and then only in the above percentage when and as received. Money paid pursuant to legal process to the Actor's creditors, or by virtue of assignment or direction of the Actor, and deductions from the Actor's compensation made pursuant to law in the nature of a collection or tax at the source, such as Social Security, Old Age Pension taxes, State Disability taxes or income taxes shall be treated as compensation received for or on the Actor's behalf.

(4) Should the Agent, during the term specified in Paragraph (2), negotiate a contract of employment for the Actor and secure for the Actor a bona fide offer of employment, which offer is communicated by the Agent to the Actor in reasonable detail and in writing or by other corroborative

action, which offer the Actor declines, and if, within sixty (60) days after the date upon which the Agent gives such information to the Actor, the Actor accepts said offer of employment on substantially the same terms, then the Actor shall be required to pay commissions to the Agent upon such contract of employment. If an agent engaged under a prior agency contract is entitled to collect commissions under the foregoing circumstances, the Agent with whom this contract is executed waives his commission to the extent that the prior agent is entitled to collect the same.

(5) (a) The Agent may represent other persons who render services in motion pictures, or in other branches of the entertainment industry.

(b) Unless and until prohibited by the Actor, the Agent may make known the fact that he is the sole and exclusive representative of the Actor in the motion picture fields covered hereby. However, it is expressly understood that even though the Agent has not breached the contract the Actor may at any time with or without discharging the Agent, and regardless of whether he has legal grounds for discharge of the Agent, by written notice to the Agent prohibit him from rendering further services for the Actor or from holding himself out as the Actor's Agent, and such action shall not give Agent any rights or remedies against Actor, the Agent's rights under this paragraph continuing only as long as Actor consents thereto but this does not apply to the Agent's right to commissions. In the event of any such written notice to the Agent the 91-day period set forth in Paragraph (6) of this agency contract is suspended and extended by the period of time that the Agent is prohibited from rendering services for the Actor.

(6) (a) If this is an initial agency contract and if actor fails to be employed and receive, or be entitled to receive, compensation for ten (10) days' employment in the initial 151 days of the contract, provided further that if ao bona fide offer of employment is received by the Actor within any consecutive period of 120 days during the initial 151 day period, or if during any other period of 91 days immediately preceding the giving of the notice of termination hereinafter mentioned in this paragraph, the Actor fails to be employed and receive, or be entitled to receive compensation for ten (10) days' employment, whether such employment is from fields under SAG's jurisdiction or any other branch of the entertainment industry in which the Agent may be authorized by written contract to represent the Actor, then either the Actor or Agent may terminate the engagement of the Agent hereunder by written notice to the other party, subject to the qualifications hereinafter in this paragraph set forth. Each day the Actor renders services or may be required to render services in motion pictures shall count as one (1) day's employment. For the purpose of determining what is a day's employment in other fields of the entertainment industry the following rules shall govern:

(i) Each separate original radio broadcast (including rehearsal time), whether live or recorded, and each transcribed program shall be considered a day's employment.

(ii) Each separate live television broadcast shall be considered a minimum of two (2) days' employment. However, each day spent in rehearsal over the minimum of two (2) days inclusive of the day of telecast, shall be considered an additional one-half (1/2) day's employment.

(iii) A rebroadcast, whether recorded or live, or by an off the line recording, or by a prior recording, or time spent in rehearsal for any employment in the radio broadcasting or radio transcription industry shall not be considered such employment. A retelecast of a live television program and a rerun of television motion picture entertainment film or commercial shall likewise not be considered such employment.

(iv) Each master phonograph record recorded by the Actor shall be one (1) day's employment.

(v) In all other branches of the entertainment industry, except as set forth above, each day the Actor renders services or may be required to render services for compensation shall count as one (1) day's employment.

(b) The 91 day period which is the basis of termination shall be extended by the amount of employment the Actor would have received from calls for his services in any other branch of the entertainment industry in which the Actor is a recognized performer and at or near the Actor's usual places of employment at a salary and from an employer commensurate with the Actor's prestige, which calls are actually received by the Agent and reported to the Actor in writing or by other corroborative action, when the Actor is in such a locality (away from his usual places of employment) that he cannot return in response to such a call, or when the Actor is unable to respond to such a call by reason of physical or mental incapacity or any other reason beyond his control, or by reason of another engagement in a field in which the Actor is not represented by the Agent; provided, however, that if the Actor is rendering services in another engagement in a field in which the Agent is authorized to represent the Actor, then the time spent in such engagement shall not be added to the 91 day period. Regardless of whether or not the Agent is authorized to represent the Actor on the legitimate stage, if the Actor accepts an engagement on the legitimate stage under a run of the play contract, the 91 day period which is the basis of termination shall be extended by the length of such run of the play contract including rehearsals. The 91 day period which is the basis of termination shall also be extended for any period of time during which the Actor has declared himself to be unavailable and has so notified the Agent in writing or by other corroborative action or has confirmed in writing or by other corroborative action a communication from the Agent to such effect.

(c) In the event that the Agent has given the Actor notice in writing or by other corroborative action, of a bona fide offer of employment as an actor in any branch of the entertainment industry in which the Actor is a recognized performer at or near his usual place of employment at a salary and from an employer commensurate with the Actor's prestige (and there is in fact such an offer), which notice sets forth in detail the terms of the proposed employment and the Actor refuses or fails within a reasonable time after receipt of such notice to accept such proffered employment, then the period of guaranteed employment in said offer shall be deemed as time worked by the Actor in computing time worked with reference to the right of the Actor to terminate under the provisions of this paragraph.

(d) The Actor may not exercise the right of termination if at the time he attempts to do so:

The Actor is under a contract or contracts for the rendition of his services in the entertainment industry in any or all fields in which the Agent is authorized by written contract to represent the Actor, which contract or contracts in the aggregate guarantee the Actor:

(i) compensation for such services of Seventy Thousand ($70,000.00) Dollars or more, or

(ii) Fifty (50) or more days' employment,

during the 91 days in question plus the succeeding 273 days after said 91 day period.

(e) Saturdays, Sundays and holidays are included in counting days elapsed during the 91 and 273 day periods provided.

(f) No termination hereunder shall deprive the Agent of the right to receive commission or compensation on moneys earned or received by the Actor prior to the date of termination, or earned or received by the Actor after the date of termination of the Agent's engagement, on contracts for the Actor's services entered into by the Actor prior to the effective date of any such termination.

(g) Periods of lay-off, leave of absence, or any periods during which the Actor is not performing and is prohibited from rendering services for others in the motion picture field under and during the term of any motion picture employment contract shall not be deemed periods of unemployment hereunder. The "term of any motion picture employment contract" as used in this subparagraph shall not include any unexercised options.

(h) Where the Actor does not actually render his services for which he has been employed but nevertheless is compensated therefor, the same shall be considered as employment hereunder. This shall not apply to employment on live television shows, which employment is computed according to the formula set forth in subparagraph (a) (ii) hereof.

(i) If, at any time during the term of the agency contract, the production of motion pictures in general (as distinguished from production at one or more studios) should be suspended, thereupon the 91-day period herein mentioned shall be extended by the period of such suspension.

(j) If the Actor is under an employment contract which provides that any part of the Actor's guaranteed compensation shall be deferred or if said compensation is spread over a period prior or subsequent to the time of the actual performance of Actor's services under said employment contract, then for the purpose of determining the Actor's right to terminate under the provisions of subparagraph (d) hereof, the guaranteed compensation shall be deemed to have been paid to the actor during the period of the actual performance of Actor's services under said employment contract.

(k) Anything herein to the contrary notwithstanding, if the Agent submits to the Actor a bona fide offer of employment in writing or by other corroborative action, as defined in Paragraph (6) subparagraph (c), after the right of termination has accrued under Paragraph (6) but the Actor has not yet terminated the agency contract, and if the Actor thereafter terminates the agency contract pursuant to Paragraph (6) and thereafter accepts the offer within sixty (60) days of the date of submission of the offer to the Actor by the Agent, the Actor shall pay the Agent commission on the compensation received by the Actor pursuant to such offer.

(l) Other than in cases of initial agency contracts subject to the 151 day clause provided by the first paragraph of this paragraph (6), the right of termination provided by the 91 day termination provisions of this Paragraph (6), the Actor shall also have the right of termination beginning with the 82nd day of the 91-day period whenever it becomes apparent that the Agent will be unable to procure the required employment pursuant to this Paragraph (6) during such 91-day period. In considering whether it has become so apparent, the possibility that after the Actor exercises the right of termination, the Agent might preclude exercise of the right by compliance with subparagraphs (b), (c) or (d) hereof, shall be disregarded. To illustrate: If the Actor has had no employment for 82 days, Actor may terminate on the 82nd day, since only 9 days remain, and Agent cannot obtain 10 days' employment for the Actor in such period. If Actor received one day's employment in 83 days, Actor may terminate on the 83rd day, since only 8 days remain, and Agent cannot obtain 10 days' employment for Actor in such period.

(m) Employment at SAG minimum shall be deemed "employment" and/or "work" for purposes of this Paragraph (6).

(7) Rule 16(g) of the Screen Actors Guild, Inc. which contains regulations governing the relations of its members to talent agents is hereby referred to and by this reference hereby incorporated herein and made a part of this contract. The provisions of said Rule are herein sometimes referred to as the

"Regulations" and the Screen Actors Guild, Inc. is herein sometimes referred to as "SAG".

(8) The Agent agrees that during the term of this contract the following person only shall have the responsibility of personally supervising the Actor's business, and of servicing and being available to the Actor. The name of the person shall be inserted in the Actor's own handwriting. *(This italicized provision is a note from SAG to the Actor, and is not a part of the contract. If the Actor is executing this contract in reliance on the fact that a particular person is connected with the Agent, the Actor should insert only such person's name in the space following. If the Actor is not executing this contract in reliance on such fact, then the Actor shall insert one name).*

_____

The Agent upon request of the Actor and on reasonable notice shall assign such person to conduct negotiations for the Actor at such city or its environs and such person shall do so; it being understood that sub-agents employed by the Agent who are not named herein may handle agency matters for the Actor or may aid the above named person in handling agency matters for the Actor. In the event the person above named shall cease to be active in the affairs of the Agent by reason of death, disability, retirement or any other reason, the Actor shall have the right to terminate this contract upon written notice to the Agent. The rights of the parties in such case are governed by Sections XI and XII of the Regulations.

(9) The Agent agrees to maintain telephone service and an office open during all reasonable business hours (emergencies such as sudden illness or death excepted) within the city of _____, or its environs, throughout the term of this agreement and that some representative of the Agent will be present at such office during such business hours. This contract is void unless the blank in this paragraph is filled in with the name of a city at which the Agent does maintain an office to render services to actors.

(10) If the Actor is employed under a series or term contract the Actor shall have the right to terminate this contract during the 30-day period immediately following any annual anniversary date of the series or term contract then in effect by giving the Agent 30-days' written notice of his intention to so terminate this contract. Exercise of this termination right shall not affect the Actor's commissions obligation hereunder.

(11) Any controversy under this contract, or under any contract executed in renewal or extension hereof or in substitution hereof or alleged to have been so executed, or as to the existence, execution or validity hereof or thereof, or the right of either party to avoid this or any such contract or alleged contract on any grounds, or the construction, performance, nonperformance, operation, breach, continuance or termination of this or any such contract, shall be submitted to arbitration in accordance with the arbitration provisions in the Regulations regardless of whether either party has terminated or purported to terminate this or any such contract or alleged contract. Under this contract the Agent undertakes to endeavor to secure employment for the Actor. This provision is inserted in this contract pursuant to a rule of the SAG, a bona fide labor union, which Rule regulates the relations of its members to talent agents. Reasonable written notice shall be given to the Labor Commissioner of the State of California of the time and place of any arbitration hearing hereunder. The Labor Commissioner of the State of California, or his authorized representative, has the right to attend all arbitration hearings. The clauses relating to the Labor Commissioner of the State of California shall not be applicable to cases not falling under the provisions of Section 1700.45 of the Labor Code of the State of California.

(12) Both parties hereto state and agree that they are bound by the Regulations and by all of the modifications heretofore or hereafter made thereto pursuant to the Basic Contract and by all waivers granted by SAG pursuant to said Basic Contract or to the Regulations.

(13) (a) Anything herein to the contrary notwithstanding, if the Regulations should be held invalid, all references thereto in this contract shall be eliminated; all limitations of the Regulations on any of the provisions of this contract shall be released, and the portions of this contract including, but not limited to Paragraphs (8) and (11) which depend upon reference to the Regulations shall be deleted, and the provisions of this contract otherwise shall remain valid and enforceable.

(b) Likewise, if any portion of the Regulations should be held invalid, such holding shall not affect the validity of remaining portions of the Regulations or of this contract; and if the portion of the Regulations so held invalid should be a portion specifically referred to in this contract, then such reference shall be eliminated herefrom in the same manner and with like force and effect as herein provided in the event the Regulations are held invalid; and the provisions of this contract otherwise shall remain valid and enforceable.

Whether or not the Agent is the Actor's agent at the time this contract is executed, it is understood that in executing this contact each party has independent access to the Regulations and has relied exclusively upon his own knowledge thereof.

IN WITNESS WHEREOF, the parties hereto have executed this agreement the _____

day of _____, 19_____.

_____
Actor

_____
Agent

By:_____
(Parties please sign in ink)

This talent agent is licensed by the Labor Commissioner of the State of California.
This talent agent is franchised by the Screen Actors Guild, Inc.
The form of this contract has been approved by the State Labor Commissioner of the State of California on January 11, 1991.
This form of contract has been approved by the Screen Actors Guild, Inc.
(The foregoing references to California may be deleted or appropriate substitutions made in other states.)

**THE ARTIST MAY NOT WAIVE ANY PROVISION OF THIS CONTRACT
WITHOUT THE WRITTEN CONSENT OF SCREEN ACTORS GUILD, INC.**

SCREEN ACTORS GUILD

DAILY CONTRACT
(DAY PLAYER)
FOR THEATRICAL MOTION PICTURES

Company_____   Date_____

Date Employment Starts_____   Actor Name_____

Production Title_____   Address_____

Production Number_____   Telephone No. (____)_____

Role_____   Social Security No._____

Daily Rate $_____   Date of Birth_____

Weekly Conversion Rate $_____   Legal Resident of (State)_____

Citizen of U.S._____Yes _____No

Wardrobe supplied by Actor _____Yes _____No

Complete for "Drop-And-Pick-Up" Deals ONLY:

Firm recall date on _____ or

on or after* _____

("On or after" recall only applies to pick-up as Weekly
Player.)

As ☐ Day Player   ☐ Weekly Player

*Means date specified or within 24 hours thereafter

If so, number of outfits _____ @ $ _____

(formal) _____ @ $ _____

Date of Actor's next engagement_____

The employment is subject to all of the provisions and conditions applicable to the employment of DAY PLAYERS contained
or provided for in the Producer-Screen Actors Guild Codified Basic Agreement of 1986 as the same may be supplemented
and/or amended.

The Player (does) (does not) hereby authorize the Producer to deduct from the compensation hereinabove specified an
amount equal to _____ per cent of each installment of compensation due the Player
hereunder, and to pay the amount of so deducted to the Motion Picture and Televison Relief Fund of America, Inc.

Special Provisions:

PRODUCER_____ PLAYER_____

BY_____

Production time reports are available on the set at the end of each day.
Such reports shall be signed or initialed by the Player.

Attached hereto for your use is Declaration Regarding Income Tax Withholding.

NOTICE TO ACTOR: IT IS IMPORTANT THAT YOU RETAIN A COPY OF THIS CONTRACT FOR YOUR PERMANENT
RECORDS.

28

THE ARTIST MAY NOT WAIVE ANY PROVISION OF THIS CONTRACT WITHOUT THE WRITTEN CONSENT OF SCREEN ACTORS GUILD, INC.

SCREEN ACTORS GUILD
MINIMUM FREE LANCE CONTRACT
FOR THEATRICAL MOTION PICTURES

Continuous Employment—Weekly Basis—Weekly Salary
One Week Minimum Employment

THIS AGREEEMENT, made this _____ day of _____, 19____, between_____
_____, hereafter called "Producer", and
_____, hereafter called "Player".

WITNESSETH:

1. PHOTOPLAY, ROLE, SALARY AND GUARANTEE. Producer hereby engages Player to render services as such in the role of _____, in a photoplay, the working title of which is now _____, at the salary of $_____ per "studio week" (Schedule B Players must receive an additional overtime payment of four (4) hours at straight time rate for each overnight location Saturday). Player accepts such engagement upon the terms herein specified. Producer guarantees that it will furnish Player not less than_____week's employment (if this blank is not filled in, the guarantee shall be one week). Player shall be paid pro rata for each additional day beyond guarantee until dismissal.

2. TERM: The term of employment hereunder shall begin on

on _____

on or about* _____
and shall continue thereafter until the completion of the photography and recordation of said role.

3. BASIC CONTRACT. All provisions of the collective bargaining agreement between Screen Actors Guild, Inc. and Producer, relating to theatrical motion pictures, which are applicable to the employment of the Player hereunder, shall be deemed incorporated herein.

4. PLAYER'S ADDRESS. All notices which the Producer is required or may desire to give to the Player may be given either by mailing the same addressed to the Player at _____,
or such notice may be given to the Player personally, either orally or in writing.

5. PLAYER'S TELEPHONE. The Player must keep the Producer's casting office or the assistant director of said photoplay advised as to where the Player may be reached by telephone without unreasonable delay. The current telephone number of the Player is _____

6. MOTION PICTURE AND TELEVISION RELIEF FUND. The Player (does) (does not) hereby authorize the Producer to deduct from the compensation hereinabove specified an amount equal to _____ per cent of each installment of compensation due the Player hereunder, and to pay the amount so deducted to the Motion Picture and Television Relief Fund of America, Inc.

7. FURNISHING OF WARDROBE. The (Producer) (Player) agrees to furnish all modern wardrobe and wearing apparel reasonably necessary for the portrayal of said role; it being agreed, however, that should so-called "character" or "period" costumes be required, the Producer shall supply the same. When Player furnishes any wardrobe, Player shall receive the cleaning allowance and reimbursement, if any, specified in the basic contract.

Number of outfits furnished by Player _____ @ $_____
(formal) _____ @ $_____

8. ARBITRATION OF DISPUTES. Should any dispute or controversy arise between the parties hereto with reference to this contract, or the employment herein provided for, such dispute or controversy shall be settled and determined by conciliation and arbitration in accordance with the conciliation and arbitration provisions of the collective bargaining agreement between the Producer and Screen Actors Guild relating to theatrical motion pictures, and such provisions are hereby referred to and by such reference incorporated herein and made a part of this Agreement with the same effect as though the same were set forth herein in detail.

9. NEXT STARTING DATE. The starting date of Player's next engagement is_____.

10. The Player may not waive any provision of this contract without the written consent of Screen Actors Guild, Inc.

11. Producer makes the material representation that either it is presently a signatory to the Screen Actors Guild collective bargaining agreement covering the employment contracted for herein, or that the above-referred-to photoplay is covered by such collective bargaining agreement under the Independent Production provisions of the General Provisions of the Producer-Screen Actors Guild Codified Basic Agreement of 1983 as the same may be supplmented and/or amended.

IN WITNESS WHEREOF, the parties have executed this agreement on the day and year first above written.

PRODUCER _____ PLAYER _____

BY _____ Social Security No. _____

*The "on or about" clause may only be used when the contract is delivered to the Player at least seven days before the starting date. See Codified Basic Agreement of 1983, Schedule B, Schedule C, otherwise a specific starting date must be stated.

Production time reports are available on the set at the end of each day, which reports shall be signed or initialed by the Player.

Attached hereto for your use are the following: (1) Declaration Regarding Income Tax Withholding ("Part Year Employment Method of Withholding") and (2) Declaration Regarding Income Tax Withholding. You may utilize the applicable form by delivering same to Producer. Only one of such forms may be used.

NOTICE TO ACTOR: IT IS IMPORTANT THAT YOU RETAIN A COPY OF THIS CONTRACT FOR YOUR PERMA-NENT RECORDS.

APPENDIX D
Sample Sign-In Sheet

THIS IS A NEW SIGN-IN SHEET. PLEASE FILL OUT CAREFULLY AND COMPLETELY; USE "YES" OR "NO" TO ANSWER QUESTIONS; PRINT LEGIBLY.

SCREEN ACTORS GUILD THEATRICAL & TELEVISION SIGN-IN SHEET

PRODUCER: _____

PROD'N. CO: _____

PROD'N. OFFICE PHONE: _____

CASTING REP: _____

CASTING REP. PHONE: _____

PROJECT TITLE/EPISODE: _____

CASTING REP: Fill in TIME SEEN for each actor. Sign completed form. Attach copy of appointment list. Send to SAG: Attn. Casting Dir. Relations Committee. Forms are due weekly.

AUDITION DATE: _____

SIGNATURE OF CASTING DIRECTOR _____

NAME	SOCIAL SECURITY	ROLE	AGENT	PROVIDED? PARK	PROVIDED? SCRIPT	ARRIVAL TIME	APPT. TIME	TIME SEEN Cast. Rep.	TIME OUT	WERE YOU TAPED?	WISH TAPE ERASED?*	ACTOR INITIALS**

*If you request, audition tape will be erased upon completion of casting.   **Indicates times are accurate, answers complete. If you have questions and/or complaints, call SAG Cast. Dir. Relations Comm. (213) 549-6427.

APPENDIX E
Game Shows

If you have some free time, you might consider trying out for one of the many game shows taped in Los Angeles. Not only could you have a lot of fun, but you might also win some money and/or lavish prizes. (I know of a guy from my college who won $100,000 on "Jeopardy"!)

To become a participant on a show, you typically have to pass several rounds of interviews, from which the best players are selected. It gets to be pretty competitive with written tests and mock game-playing.

Listed below are the programs and their respective contact:

American Gladiators
Four Point Entertainment
3575 Cahuenga Blvd., West,
    Ste. 600
Los Angeles, CA 90068
(213) 850-1600

Gladiators 2000
Four Point Entertainment
3575 Cahuenga Blvd., West,
    Ste. 600
Los Angeles, CA 90068
(213) 850-1600

Jeopardy
Quadra Productions
10202 Washington Blvd.
Culver City, CA 90230
(310) 280-8855
(tapes at Sony Studios)

The Price Is Right
Jonathan Goodson Partners, LLC.
5750 Wilshire Blvd., Ste. 475
Los Angeles, CA 90036
(213) 965-6500
(tapes at CBS-Television City)

Trivial Pursuit
Martindale Hillier Productions
1330 S. Glendale Avenue
Glendale, CA 91205
(818) 502-5550
*(tapes at Oakridge TV Studios-
Glendale)*

Wheel of Fortune
Quadra Productions, Inc.
3400 Riverside Drive, 2nd Floor
Burbank, CA 91505
(310) 280-6859
*(tapes at Sony Pictures
Entertainment)*

Games Shows on
Basic Cable:

Family Challenge
Woody Fraser Enterprises, Inc.
2220 Colorado Ave.
Santa Monica, CA 91504
(818) 502-4800
(tapes at Glendale Studios)

Free for All
Fun House Productions
1040 N. Las Palmas
Hollywood, CA 90038
(213) 960-2599
(tapes at KTLA)

Quick Silver
Fun House Productions
1040 N. Las Palmas
Hollywood, CA 90038
(213) 960-2599
(tapes at KTLA)

Wild Animal Games
Woody Fraser Enterprises, Inc.
2220 Colorado Ave.
Santa Monica, CA 91504
(818) 502-4800
(tapes at Glendale Studios)

APPENDIX F
Studio Addresses

ABC-Prospect
4151 Prospect Ave.
Hollywood, CA 90027
(310) 557-7777

CBS/MTM Studios
4024 Radford Ave.
Studio City, CA 91604
(818) 760-5000

CBS Television City
7800 Beverly Blvd.
Los Angeles, CA 90036
(213) 852-2345

Chandler Studios
11401 Chandler Blvd.
N. Hollywood, CA 91601
(818) 763-3650

Cole Avenue
1006 N. Cole Ave.
Los Angeles, CA 90038
(213) 463-1600

The Complex
2323 Cornith
West Los Angeles, CA 90064
(310) 477-1938

Culver Studios
9336 W. Washington Blvd.
Culver City, CA 90230
(310) 836-5537

Disney Studios
500 S. Buena Vista St.
Burbank, CA 91521
(818) 560-5151

Empire Studios
1845 Empire Ave.
Burbank, CA 91504
(818) 840-1400

Fox Television Center
5746 Sunset Blvd.
Hollywood, CA 90028
(213) 856-1000

Hollywood Center Studios
1040 N. Las Palmas
Los Angeles, CA 90038
(213) 469-5000

KCAL TV
5515 Melrose Ave.
Los Angeles, CA 90038
(213) 467-5459

KCBS - Local CBS
6121 Sunset Blvd.
Hollywood, CA 90028
(213) 460-3000

KCOP
915 N. La Brea
Los Angeles, CA 90038
(213) 851-1000

KTLA
5842 Sunset Blvd., Bldg. #1
Hollywood, CA 90028
(213) 460-5500

NBC-Burbank
3000 W. Alameda Ave.
Burbank, CA 91523
(818) 840-4444

NBC-Hollywood, Sunset-Gower
   Studios
1420 N. Beachwood Ave.
Hollywood, CA 90028
(818) 840-7500

Oakridge TV Studios
1239 Glendale Ave.
Glendale, CA 91205
(818) 502-5300

Paramount Pictures
5555 Melrose Ave.
Los Angeles, CA 90038
(213) 956-5000

Post Group Studios
6335 Homewood Ave.
Hollywood, CA 90028
(213) 462-2300

Production Group
1330 N. Vine St.
Hollywood, CA 90028
(213) 469-8111

Raleigh Studios
650 N. Bronson Ave.
Los Angeles, CA 90004
(213) 466-3111

Ren-Mar Studios
846 N. Cahuenga Blvd.
Hollywood, CA 90038
(213) 463-0808

Sony Pictures
10202 W. Washington Blvd.
Culver City, CA 90232
(310) 280-8000

Sunset-Gower Studios
1438 N. Gower St.
Hollywood, CA 90028
(213) 467-1001

T.A.V. Studios
1541 Vine St.
Hollywood, CA 90028
(213) 466-2141

20th Century Fox
10201 W. Pico Blvd.
Los Angeles, CA 90067
(310) 277-2211

Universal Studios
100 Universal City Plaza
Universal City, CA 91608
(818) 777-1000

Valley Production Center
6633 Van Nuys Blvd.
Van Nuys, CA 91401
(818) 988-6601

Warner Hollywood Studios
1041 N. Formosa
Hollywood, CA 90046
(213) 850-2500

Warner Bros. Studios
4000 Warner Blvd.
Burbank, CA 91522
(818) 954-6000

Glossary of Terms for the Actor

action: a director's cue to begin filming.

A.D.: an assistant director. While a hierarchy of A.D.s exists (i.e., first assistant director, second assistant director, second second assistant director), their duties generally include helping to set up shots, coordinating and writing call sheets, and directing and corralling extras.

AFTRA: the American Federation of Television & Radio Artists, which governs programs that are shot on video tape (not film). These include sitcoms and soap operas, as well as voice-overs for radio and television.

agent: an individual representing actors. They submit actors for parts, negotiate contracts, and support and guide their careers.

atmosphere: another term for "extras" or "background artists."

audition: when you try out for a role in a production.

back to one: going back to your starting, or first, positions when a scene is being shot take after take.

background: another term for extras or atmosphere.

bit part: a small part, usually consisting of a few lines.

boom: the overhead microphone used to record actors' voices.

bump: a pay adjustment or increase for performing a special activity in a scene (pertains to extras).

callback: when you're called in to audition for a part a second, third, or fourth time.

call sheet: the daily sheet for a production that lists all the scenes to be shot that day as well as actor and crew arrival times.

call time: the time you are supposed to report to the set.

calling service: for extras, a company that helps to book them on extra jobs.

camera right: when looking into the camera, your left.

camera left: when looking into the camera, your right.

casting director: the person who is hired to find the most appropriate actors for each role in a production.

continuity: the concept that all shots in a scene should match in terms of props, dialogue, and extras.

craft service: the food table on a set, or refers to the person(s) who handle the food.

crew: everyone on the set who is contributing to the production, in addition to the cast.

CU: a close-up shot.

cut: the director's cue to stop filming.

day-player: someone who is hired at SAG scale (minimum) for the day.

D.P.: Director of Photography. The person in charge of designing and lighting the shot. They have tremendous influence on the overall style of the film.

first team: the actual cast members who are being used in a given scene.

golden time: refers to overtime paid after working sixteen hours straight, equal to one's daily rate every hour.

grip: someone who handles, carries, moves, and stores lighting, electrical, and other equipment on the set.

headshot: an eight-by-ten photograph of an actor.

holding area: place where extras are kept on a set or location.

honey wagon: the trailer on a set that has mini-bathrooms.

(on) location: place other than a studio lot where filming is done.

looping: when actors re-record their voices after filming has been completed, usually to replace or repair unclear dialogue.

marks: exact locations of an actor's feet on the floor during sequences of a shot.

meal penalty: a small payment actors receive when not being served a full meal after every six hours of continuous work.

must join: a non-union actor who must join SAG because they have already worked union once before under the Taft-Hartley law.

omnies: sounds or exclamations extras make as a group.

P.A.: a production assistant. A coordinator on a set, who usually gophers and manages the extras.

pantomime: being silent, yet appearing to talk.

photo double: an actor, usually an extra, used in place of a principal actor who is either unavailable or only seen partially. Never any speaking lines.

pick-up shot: small parts of a scene that are re-shot, usually because all angles were not captured satisfactorily during the first shooting.

P.O.V.: the point of view that is filmed, usually referring to that of one of the actors.

principal player: an actor with lines, paid at least SAG scale.

print: director's cue that the shot was good enough to "print" or use.

reel or tape: an actor's video compilation tape of his or her best work.

residuals: payments an actor receives each time a commercial or program airs.

rolling: cameras have been turned on and film is rolling.

rush call: when actors, usually extras, are rushed to a set on a moment's notice.

SAG: the Screen Actors Guild, a union which protects actor's rights and guarantees certain wages.

SAG-eligible: an non-union actor who is eligible to join SAG by being cast in a principal role, being a member of an affiliated union and having had a principal role under that union's jurisdiction, or performing three days of union extra work. Also known as a "must join."

SAG-franchised: status of an agent or agency that has signed papers with SAG and agrees to operate within SAG guidelines.

scale: minimum SAG daily wage for principal actors.

second team: group of stand-ins who replace principals before each shot on a set.

sides: partial script pages used for an audition.

silent bit: when an actor or extra performs a noticeable or required action in a scene (no lines).

slate: at an audition, stating your name and sometimes your agency for the camera.

speed: exclamation that indicates the film and the audio tape are running simultaneously at the correct speed.

stand-in: person who stands in place for a principal actor when shots are being set up. Usually similar in height, weight, and appearance.

strike: remove something from a set, or tear it down.

Taft-Hartley Law: law that allows non-union actors to work under a union contract for their first role. After that, they must join the union.

U/5 (Under Five): five lines or less, on AFTRA shows. This category has a specific pay-rate, less than day-player.

upgrade: a pay-rate increase, usually from "extra" status to "principal" status.

voice-over: when an actor has lines but is not seen, often for a radio or T.V. commercial.

wrapped: finished, done for the day.

Index

Allworth Books

Allworth Press publishes quality books to help individuals and small businesses. Titles include:

Writing Scripts Hollywood Will Love by Katherine Atwell Herbert
(softcover, 6 × 9, 160 pages, $12.95)

The Performing Arts Business Encyclopedia by Leonard DuBoff
(softcover, 6 × 9, 320 pages, $19.95)

Booking and Tour Management for the Performing Arts
by Rena Shagan (softcover, 6 × 9, 256 pages, $19.95)

Stage Fright: Health Hazards in the Theater by Monona Rossol
(softcover, 6 × 9, 144 pages, $16.95)

The Business of Multimedia by Nina Schuyler
(softcover, 6 × 9, 240 pages, $19.95)

Arts and the Internet by V. A. Shiva
(softcover, 6 × 9, 208 pages, $18.95)

The Internet Research Guide by Timothy K. Maloy
(softcover, 6 × 9, 208 pages, $18.95)

Legal Guide for the Visual Artist, Third Edition by Tad Crawford
(softcover, 8½ × 11, 256 pages, $19.95)

Business and Legal Forms for Authors and Self-Publishers
by Tad Crawford. (softcover, 8⅞ × 11, 176 pages, $15.95)

The Secret Life of Money by Tad Crawford
(softcover, 6 × 9, 290 pages, $16.95)

The Money Mirror by Annette Lieberman and Vicki Lindner
(softcover, 6 × 9, 256 pages, $14.95)

Immigration Questions and Answers by Carl R. Baldwin
(softcover, 6 × 9, 176 pages, $12.95)

Please write to request our free catalog. If you wish to order a book, send your check or money order to Allworth Press, 10 East 23rd Street, Suite 400, New York, NY 10010. Include $5 for shipping and handling for the first book ordered and $1 for each additional book. Ten dollars plus $1 for each additional book if ordering from Canada. New York State residents must add sales tax.

If you wish to see our catalog on the World Wide Web, you can find us at Millennium Production's Art and Technology Web site:
http://www.arts-online.com/allworth/home.html
or at **http://www.interport.net/~allworth**